The Deaconess Heritage

Ruth W. Rasche

One Hundred Years of Caring, Healing and Teaching

The Deaconess Foundation
St. Louis, Missouri

Copyright © 1994 by The Deaconess Foundation

Library of Congress Catalog Card Number 94-67873

ISBN 0-9642849-0-1

Includes Index.

Photography by William L. Mathews
Designed by Paul E. Woolverton

Front cover: Deaconess Emblem in Deaconess Chapel Window
Back cover: Deaconess Hospital, center, with Deaconess Medical Office Center, left, and
Deaconess College of Nursing, right, 1989.

Printed in the United States of America

The Deaconess Foundation
6150 Oakland Avenue
St. Louis, Missouri 63139

One Hundred Years of Caring, Healing and Teaching

Contents

FOREWORD

In this book Ruth Rasche traces the Deaconess hundred-year history and puts it into perspective as part of God's eternal covenant with us. She tells us that Deaconess is not "of itself" but rather reflects how a faithful and very human group of people seek to live in response to their vision of that love that constrains us. The agenda which she describes therefore is not merely the evolving plan which characterizes the life and development of any organization or institution.

Deaconess has listened to the incessant call to faithful service. Educate the caregivers; practice the art and science of medicine; surround the physicians with the best technology and technicians; practice good stewardship (frequently translated as frugality); in all, be open to the Spirit and go and do as the Spirit leads.

This story is not without its heartaches and its tears, but it is mostly about triumphs. It moves from an 1890s program oriented primarily to serve the needs of German immigrants (who largely comprised both the caregivers and the cared-for) to an international, interracial, and intercultural expression of *diakonia*, loving, compassionate service and education for the love of God.

Ruth has had to struggle with how best to present this vibrant story, which is not precisely linear. It is a rich collage of subthemes, taking us from the beginning of prayerfully meeting personal needs in a frankly parochial manner, to increasing outreach: the Indian subcontinent; Central and South America; the cities and towns of this land...and from cholera and infectious disease, to alcoholism, mental illness, sleeping and eating disorders, sexual medicine, "spare parts medicine" and more.

As a child, wife, and mother of the manse, Ruth is herself a product of the tradition that this narrative reflects in words and pictures. She alludes to the conflicts and reports a few, but she is light on the failures and modestly proud of the successes. This is because the triumphs of faithfulness are the kernels of the real story. She does not detail each item in the Deaconess history but records the triumphant way in which ordinary people, convicted and captured by an extraordinary faith, proceed to make a profound difference.

One of the subthemes, "outpatient care," is played again and again in concert with a variety of services and programs. Note how from the beginning, the first edifice of Deaconess Hospital was built only to support the need for housing patients who could not stay at home. Deaconess Sisters were involved in "home care" long before the federal government discovered it. Indigent outpatient clinics and the Deaconess mental health clinic on Oakland Avenue were pacesetters. Today the largest part of the Deaconess Health System's annual revenue comes from other than inpatient sources.

Education is another recurring subtheme. In today's vernacular it is sometimes referred to as "empowerment." The Life that God would give us in abundance requires light or enlightenment. Deaconess knows or senses this, and you can catch this theme as it shines through these pages.

"Tradition with Vision" is one of the expressions that attempts to capture the essence of Deaconess. Rooted in historic events of our faith and in our cultural heritage, bound as we are to the constraints of our own times and places and circumstances, products of our prejudices and biases...in short, tossed into the milieu as we are, there is yet above us and in us and under us "A God Who Acts in History," as G. Ernest Wright entitled his monograph many years ago.

Ruth captures in a great way the acts of God and the reactions of the people in this book which traces a particular organization through a particular time but is in itself a story with a timeless quality.

RICHARD P. ELLERBRAKE

ACKNOWLEDGEMENTS

This is a story about health care and health education during the 100 years beginning in 1889. It was commissioned to celebrate the centennial of Deaconess Hospital, a large church-related, teaching hospital in St. Louis, Missouri.

Deaconess has a rich heritage of devoted service, marked by professional skills, academic excellence, and a spiritual dimension which cares for the whole person. In many ways it mirrors the history of medicine in this century of great scientific discoveries, medical miracles and social changes never before known.

When Deaconess was established in 1889, most illnesses were treated at home, and hospital admissions were few. The average lifespan in America however was then less than forty years. Since that time the lifespan of Americans has almost doubled. Nuclear medicine, keyhole surgery, and organ transplants have become routine.

The history of Deaconess Hospital records these and many other amazing achievements. But this story is primarily about people and how the wonders of healing take place when devoted service is given in order to provide compassionate, professional health care and education of the highest quality. Devoted service, known since Biblical times as *diakonia*, gives Deaconess Hospital its name and its mission.

The Deaconess Sisters provide some of the unique characteristics of this story, and I am most grateful to UNITED CHURCH PRESS for granting me permission to use material which was first published in Chapter 7, "The Deaconess Sisters: Pioneer Professional Women," *Hidden Histories in the United Church of Christ, Volume I.*

Many of the Deaconess Sisters have shared their individual stories and career experiences with me, and they have recorded oral tapes for the Deaconess Archives. Executive Deaconess Frieda Ziegler provided records from the St.

Louis Deaconess Sisterhood files, and Sister Velma Kampschmidt organized historical documents, publications and pictures for the Archives. Sister Elizabeth Lotz expertly translated numerous early records and reports from German script into English. I am deeply indebted to each of them and to my great-aunt, Sister Adele Hosto of Lincoln, Illinois, and to my aunt, Sister Clara Weltge of St.Louis, who enlightened me long ago with the many possibilities of ministry for women. Their legacy of obedience, willingness and faithfulness helped me realize that while history begins with the syllable "his," heritage begins with "her," suggesting its inclusiveness.

I am also very grateful to Media Specialist William Mathews of Deaconess Media Services who expertly prepared the photographs for publication. Unless otherwise designated, all photos are from the Deaconess Archives. Some are recent gifts from the personal collections of Marian Schneider Clayton, Arlie Groenemann, Robert D. Haack, Karla Niehaus Izo, Marie Van Gels Keller, Irma Schlottach Scott, Elizabeth Schmidt, Homer Schmitz, Loretta Schoenberg, Jerry Shriver and Elizabeth Ziercher. The Missouri Historical Society granted permission for the use of several rare photographs from its collection. Lynne Boyle of the Deaconess Print Shop created the graphic emblems and symbols which appear throughout the book. Biographical information was provided by Robert D. Haack, Carolyn Keck, Helen Osterhage, Marie Schafale, Alpha Daries Scheer, Loretta Schoenberg and the St. Louis Medical Society Library.

Members of the Deaconess Hospital staff provided copies of records and information needed for research. President Emeritus Richard P. Ellerbrake graciously read the original script, made many valuable suggestions, and wrote the Foreword. Dr. M. Robert Hill, Chief of Medicine and Director of Medical Education; President Elizabeth Krekorian of the College of Nursing; Executive Chaplain Ernest W. Luehrman; and Director of Volunteer Services Jeanette Weber read the chapters related to their particular areas of responsibility and gave helpful advice. My husband, President Emeritus Carl C. Rasche, served as chief professional consultant. His patience, thirty-four-year experience in healthcare administration and his generosity in allowing me unlimited use of his computer made this volume possible. I am deeply grateful to him and to all who have assisted me.

The complexity of the modern healthcare institutional environment suggested a topical rather than a chronological approach. Each chapter is therefore complete in and of itself while at the same time part of a larger story. As a result, some events are described more than once but each time from a different perspective.

Every effort has been made to tell this story as accurately and true to the facts as possible. It is by no means the whole story. There were interesting and provocative incidents which could not be included because they could not be appropriately documented. Only primary sources and verified information have been used. Endnotes give the complete sources.

The Deaconess approach to health care and health education is a rich heritage of caring, healing and teaching which honors the past, enriches the present, and enlightens the future.

Chapter One

THE EVANGELICAL DEACONESS SOCIETY
"Caring, Healing and Teaching"

1-1. The Evangelical Deaconess Society Seal.

On Monday evening, March 18, 1889, seventy people braved blustery winds and heavy rain to attend a meeting at St. Peter's Evangelical Church, then located at Fourteenth and Carr Streets in St. Louis, Missouri. Though they came from many directions on foot, by horse and buggy or by streetcar, these people came with one purpose—to consider the establishment of deaconess work to care for the sick and the poor.

The impetus for this meeting had begun one year earlier on March 5, 1888, when the Rev. Henry H. Walser of St. Luke's Evangelical Church was summoned to give Holy Communion to a critically ill parishioner. He found the sick woman being cared for in her home by a Roman Catholic Sister of Mercy who had been called by the doctor. Though the pastor respected very highly the care being given, he was distressed that his church did not provide such service for its own sick members. As a result, he took the matter to the next monthly meeting of the St. Louis Evangelical Pastors' Association and asked, "Why can't we train the young women of our churches to care for the poor and the sick as do the Deaconess Sisters of Germany?"[1]

That question created considerable discussion in Evangelical churches throughout the St. Louis area. Primarily of German heritage, the members of these churches were well acquainted with deaconess work in Europe. There were more than 8,000 Deaconess Sisters serving in sixty-five locations worldwide by the late 1880s, most of them in Germany where they were well known for their compassionate care of the poor and the sick regardless of nationality or creed.

This was not the first time, however, that deaconess work had been considered in St. Louis. A generation earlier in 1857, when the Good Samaritan Hospital was established by Pastor Louis Nollau and members of St. Peter's Church, the services of Deaconess Sisters had been sought. But that earlier hope for help did not materialize. In 1872, nine Episcopal Deaconess Sisters of the Good Shepherd came to St. Luke's Hospital in St. Louis to provide internal management of that institution, but those deaconesses all returned to their motherhouse in Baltimore before 1889. In the meantime, the needs of the poor and the sick had become much greater and more urgent.[2]

St. Louis in 1889

Like other large cities in the United States at that time, St. Louis had grown very rapidly with the arrival of many new immigrants from Europe. More than 5.5 million came to America in the 1880s alone, twice as many as in the preceding decade. Of these, 1.4 million were from Germany and most of them had settled in the cities of the Middle West. Quite a few of the newcomers were educated and some were affluent, but many were poor.

St. Louis had a population of more than 450,000 in 1889 and it was then the fourth largest city in the United States. Shoe, stove and furniture factories made it an industrial center offering many opportunities for employment. A good public school system, two universities, a renowned botanical garden, an outstanding symphony orchestra and a variety of theaters and entertainment facilities made it a cultural center in the new world as well. Twenty-nine railroad lines coming into the city provided excellent transportation. But there was another side to the picture. St. Louis also suffered from poor sanitation, poor social services and blighted housing. Many residents lived in overcrowded conditions conducive to accidents, epidemics and disease.[3]

There were more than thirty so-called hospitals in St. Louis at that time. Some were small, church-related facilities already hard-pressed to care for their own constituents, and others were centers for the treatment of specific illnesses or contagious diseases such as tuberculosis. City Hospital, opened in 1846, was theoretically available to anyone, but German immigrants were said to have felt unwelcome there because of their language barrier. Worse yet, reliable reports as late as 1884 described the patient care offered there as inadequate and miserable.

> The wards were unspeakably filthy. Ladies in long dresses with trains, trailed through the wards issuing orders to the women employed to look after the patients. One saw bed bugs crawling along the baseboards, and on the walls behind the beds. Roaches and rats scurried about the wards and pantries. Medicines were left beside the beds to be self-administered, whether for internal or external use. If some poor unfortunate swallowed an external medicine with disastrous results—well, it was too bad, an accident—nothing could be done about it.[4]

Given these circumstances, it is not surprising that the members of the St. Louis Evangelical Pastors' Association found many of their parishioners asking, "Why can't we train the young women of our churches as Deaconess Sisters to care for

1-2. St. Peter's Evangelical Church, 14th and Carr Streets, St. Louis, Missouri, where the Deaconess Society was organized in 1889.

3

the poor and the sick?" So much interest was aroused that a committee was appointed, more discussions were held, and the meeting at St. Peter's Church on March 18, 1889, was scheduled to consider creating an appropriate organization for establishing deaconess work.

St. Peter's Church was a good location for this meeting. One of the largest and most influential of the more than 100 Evangelical churches in the St. Louis area at that time, it had among its members some of the prominent leaders of the community and it was well known for its philanthropy. In addition, it was centrally located and accessible by streetcar, important considerations in that day of limited public transportation.[5]

The Charter Members

Preparations for the organizational meeting were thorough and well planned. The host pastor, Rev. John F. Klick, and other church leaders spoke with enthusiasm and were persuasive. When brought to a vote, the decision to organize an "Evangelischer Diakonissen-Verein von St. Louis, Mo." (The Evangelical Deaconess Society of St. Louis, Mo.) was unanimous! Seventy people—sixty men and ten women—all signed their names as willing to become charter members of the new organization.

1-3. Mrs. Henry Tibbe, who travelled fifty miles from her home in Washington, Missouri, to become a charter member of the Deaconess Society in St. Louis.

1-4. Parochial School Teacher J. A. Schmiemeier, a charter member of the Deaconess Society.

Among the signatures of the charter members were those of many German Evangelical leaders of that day. Included were Pastors John Baltzer, H. F. Deters, Carl F. Fritsch, Jacob P. Irion, John F. Klick, John M. Knopf and Henry H. Walser; Parochial School Teachers J. A. Schmiemeier and G. H. Stocksieck; Dr. H. Summa; business leaders Mr. Frank Astroth, Mr. Fred S. Bolte, Mr. W. E. Hess, Mr. G. Mueller, Mr. F. W. Peters, and Mr. F. H. Peters; and prominent church women including Mrs. Katherine Haack, Mrs. Pauline Bontjes, Mrs. Emma Pauley, Mrs. Dorothea Zipf, and Mrs. Henry Tibbe, the latter having travelled fifty miles from Washington, Missouri, to attend this meeting.[6]

The First Board of Directors

In the weeks following March 18, more meetings were held and the number of Deaconess Society members increased. Articles of Association were introduced on April 24 and accepted. Though official incorporation under Missouri state law did not come until 1891, a board of directors was elected immediately. It consisted of "4 ministers, 4 laymen and 4 ladies," as stipulated in The Articles of Association, which also stated that:

> The ministers must be members of denominations founded on Scripture, and who have received their ordination of such denominations.

> The laymen [and ladies] must also be regular members of like denominations.

After that time, requirements for election to the board included at least one year's membership in the Deaconess Society.

The first board of directors organized itself by electing the following officers: Rev. John F. Klick, president; Rev. Henry H. Walser, vice-president; Rev. Carl F. Fritsch, secretary; Mr. A. G. Toennies, financial secretary; and Mr. W. E. Hess, treasurer. The other members of the board in 1889 were: Rev. Jacob P. Irion, Mr. W. E. Stocksieck, Mr. Fred S. Bolte, Mrs. Dorothea Zipf, Mrs. L. Wiegand, Mrs. Pauline Bontjes and Mrs. J. M. Knopf.[7]

It was not a requirement in the Articles of Association that the president and vice president of the board of directors had to be ministers, but this became an unwritten precedent.

The Articles of Association

The Articles of Association of The Evangelical Deaconess Society of St. Louis are remarkable in a number of ways and they were, in their day, amazingly ahead of their time.

The term of office for members of the board of directors was limited to four years. This was a breakthrough. Most institutions of that day had self-perpetuating boards whose members held their positions for life, but the Articles of Association of the Evangelical Deaconess Society stipulated that annually the term of office of three directors would terminate. One was to be a minister, one a layman and one a woman. They could be re-elected for a second term after which they had to be out of office at least one year before becoming eligible for board membership again. This provision, designed to bring new talent and lead-

1-5. First Officers, Evangelical Deaconess Society, 1889.

6

ership to the board of directors on a regular and continuing basis, proved to be a valuable asset.[8]

The election of four "ladies" as members of the board of directors of the Deaconess Society was another breakthrough. In most organizations at that time women seldom had voice, much less vote, and they usually sat on one side of a public meeting room while the men sat on the other. Moreover, a woman's membership was ordinarily held in her husband's name, giving him the privilege to vote and speak for her and the whole family.

Whether a stroke of genius or simply a matter of practical consideration, the decision to include women as one-third of the board of directors of the Deaconess Society proved to be far-sighted and fortunate in many ways. Women of the Evangelical churches throughout the St. Louis area mobilized for action and rallied to the deaconess cause. Mrs. Mebus, a benevolent widow of St. Peter's Church, donated a house and lot at Fourteenth Street and Clark Avenue to be used as the first Deaconess Home and Hospital. When this property proved to be unsuitable for such a purpose, it was rented and the proceeds used to rent an eleven-room residence at 2119 Eugenia Street near Union Station. The one objection to this house, however, was that it was for sale and in that event would have to be vacated. In order to prevent this possibility, board member Mrs. Dorothea Zipf bought that house and donated it for use by the Deaconess Society for as long as desired.

The "Ladies and Young Ladies Aid Societies" of the Evangelical churches from all parts of the metropolitan area then helped to prepare the eleven-room house for occupancy. While it was being renovated, cleaned, and furnished, they spread the news about its purpose.[9]

The Purpose of the Deaconess Society

The two-fold purpose of the Deaconess Society was clearly stated in the Articles of Association, Article II:

> 1. To nurse the sick and to exercise care for the poor and aged by deaconesses, i.e. theoretically and practically trained Christian nurses.
>
> 2. To found and support a deaconess home where deaconesses shall be educated and trained, and from which they shall be sent as

7

nurses, and where sick and aged under circumstances, provided by bylaws, may be admitted and receive attendance.

Having declared this purpose, and having acquired a location for carrying it out, the members of the Deaconess Society were then confronted with the need to find Deaconess Sisters to give leadership to the work. In this regard they were again most fortunate.

The First Evangelical Deaconess Sisters

One of the charter members of the Deaconess Society, Mrs. Katherine Haack, was the widow of Evangelical Pastor Jacob Haack and she was a nurse trained in deaconess methods. A year earlier she and her adopted daughter, Miss Lydia Daries, had completed a course in nursing at St. Luke's Hospital in St. Louis where instructions were given by Sisters of the Good Shepherd, deaconesses of

the Episcopal Church from Baltimore who had since returned to that city. Mrs. Haack was asked to become the first Evangelical Deaconess Sister in St. Louis, and her daughter, Lydia Daries, agreed to become a deaconess with her.

The board of directors and its various committees then held many meetings in which the house regulations and arrangements for the Deaconess Sisters were carefully worked out.

On Sunday, August 18, 1889, Mrs. Katherine Haack and Miss Lydia Daries were consecrated as the first Deaconess Sisters of the Evangelical Church in

1-6. Sister Katherine Haack, first consecrated Evangelical Deaconess Sister and Sister Superior, 1889.

1-7. Sister Lydia Daries, first Deaconess Sister recruited and consecrated to work with Sister Katherine Haack.

America, and Sister Katherine was appointed sister superior. The special Consecration Service was held at St. Peter's Church, where the two deaconesses were members. Pastors Klick, Irion and Walser officiated.[10]

Dedication of the First Deaconess Home

On the same day, following the consecration of Sisters Katherine and Lydia, the new Evangelical Deaconess Home at 2119 Eugenia Street was dedicated and the record says,

Everybody connected with the work was glad and grateful to God that the beginning had been made, although it was very small, and all were cheerful and enthusiastic in the spirit of Christian faith and love.[11]

During the following week, Sister Katherine and Sister Lydia moved into the Deaconess Home and began preparations for their work. Wearing a distinctive deaconess garb similar to that of the Deaconesses Sisters in Europe, they were soon recognized wherever they went throughout the community.

What's in the Name?

The sign on the front of the house at 2119 Eugenia Street read "Evang. Diakonissenhaus" (Evang. Deaconess Home). Though it was soon to become a hospital, it was first called a "home" and for good reason. Most people who became sick in those days were accustomed to being cared for at home. Hospitals were considered places of last resort to be avoided if at all possible.[12]

As the name implied, the Evangelical Deaconess Home was, first of all, the home of the Deaconess Sisters. That gave it immediate acceptance and credibility as a

1-8. First Deaconess Home and Hospital, 2119 Eugenia Street, St. Louis, Missouri, near Union Station, 1889.

place of comfort and care. From this home the deaconesses went out into the community to nurse the sick in their own homes when possible. But patients could be brought into the Deaconess Home when care might best be given there, making it a hospital. Years later when the word "Hospital" was officially added to the name, this homelike atmosphere was still emphasized:

> Because our hospital is not so very large ...it is a quiet more home-like place. We take particular pains in serving good, wholesome, well-cooked meals, to keep everything about the hospital very clean, to give all patients and doctors careful personal attention, and assure our patrons, both doctors and patients, every comfort at our command at the most reasonable rates.[13]

The location of the first Evangelical Deaconess Home and Hospital in a quiet, residential neighborhood was another subtle message conveying the importance of the "homelike" atmosphere.

"Evangelical" in the name on the front of the Deaconess Home declared it to be church related, again a suggestion that it could be trusted. Though not owned and operated by The Evangelical Church, it was operated "under the auspices of

1-9. The Deaconess Hospital Neighborhood in St. Louis, 16th and Locust Streets, with horse-drawn streetcar, 1889. (Missouri Historical Society Photograph and Print Collection, used with permission.)

the Evangelical Deaconess Society of St. Louis, Mo., which was organized by the pastors and members of the German Evangelical Church."[14]

"Evangelical" came from "evangel" which means "good news," in this case the good news of the Christian faith. As a denominational name, "Evangelical" originated in Germany where the Evangelical Church of the Union was established in the early 1800s to bring together congregations of Lutheran and Reformed background. Many German immigrants in St. Louis in 1889, even those not members of the church, knew of this Evangelical heritage which placed a strong emphasis not only on personal piety but also on compassionate care for those in need.[15]

"Evang. Diakonissenhaus" as written on the front of the home on Eugenia Street was a sign of comfort and hope for many who saw it, and word soon spread throughout the city about the help for the sick offered by the Deaconess Sisters who lived and worked there.

Membership Privileges and Duties

Membership in the Deaconess Society was not limited to people belonging to Evangelical churches. The Articles of Association stated that,

> Every Protestant Christian whose belief is in conformity with the creed of the apostles and who agrees to fulfill the regulations of this association is welcome as a member.

There was one further condition for membership. An application had to be proposed in writing by someone already a member of the Society and then had to be approved by a majority of the board of directors.
The duties of membership were:

> a. To attend the meetings of the association as regularly as possible.

> b. To be active for the growth and promulgation of the association.

> c. To pay in advance an annual fee of at least two dollars.[16]

A membership fee of two dollars per year may seem to have been a rather small and unrealistic financial base for a voluntary organization proposing to give free care to the sick and the poor, much less maintain a home and livelihood for the

Deaconess Sisters. Actually, in 1889 two dollars was the equivalent of one full day's pay for most working people, quite a substantial annual fee for the privilege of Deaconess Society membership.[17]

Although 260 people each paid $2 as members by the end of 1889, that was hardly enough income to pay all of the bills. The clue to success lay in the words "at least" in the requirements for membership. The annual fee of "at least two dollars" was a very strong suggestion that much more was expected. It is evident from the Society's first financial records that many of the members took this suggestion seriously. They not only gave many additional gifts of money and goods but also accepted the duty "to be active for the growth and promulgation of the association." By the end of the first short fiscal year (May through December) a total income of $1,406 had been received. This left no room for luxury, but the necessities could be provided.[18]

Is There a Doctor in the House?

The necessity for having "a doctor in the house" was met when Dr. Henry Summa, a charter member of the Deaconess Society, and Dr. A. F. Bock, a prominent St. Louis physician and surgeon, offered their services in the treatment of patients at the new Evangelical Deaconess Home. Both had excellent medical credentials and, as members of the Evangelical Church, they were well acquainted with deaconess work.

1-10. Dr. A. F. Bock,

On September 23, 1889, Dr. Summa and Dr. Bock agreed in a joint meeting with the board of directors to alternate monthly as house physicians, and Dr. Bock took charge the first month.

The first two members of the Deaconess Medical Staff were joined almost immediately by two of their colleagues, Dr. A. E. Ewing and Dr. John Green Sr., also highly qualified and respected members of the St. Louis medical profession.[19]

The appointment of these founding members of the Deaconess Medical Staff in 1889 set a high standard of professional excellence in the medical care to be offered at Deaconess Hospital, and it was one of the most important decisions ever made by the board of directors of the Deaconess Society.

Who's In Charge?

With Deaconess Sisters living in the Deaconess Home and with highly capable doctors ready to treat patients there, the next question was, "Who's in charge?"

The Articles of Association of the Deaconess Society left no doubt about who had the ultimate authority and responsibility for the activities of the Society or for the deaconess work being established. Article IV, entitled, "Management," provided that "The management of this association shall be by a board of directors consisting of 12 persons...."

In order to facilitate the everyday management of the Deaconess Home, however, the board of directors was empowered and instructed, among its many duties, "to elect of its members a so-called home committee which shall especially oversee and manage all matters pertaining to the Deaconess Home."[20]

Management by committee no doubt had its drawbacks, but it also brought with it a combination of leadership skills which provided a strong administrative support system for the Deaconess Sisters. In that organizational structure, Sister Katherine Haack, the sister superior, clearly had responsibility for day-to-day management. Fortunately, she had served as a supervisor at St. Luke's Hospital after completing her nurse's training there. This experience enabled her to provide the administrative skills necessary for the efficient, everyday functioning of the Deaconess Home and Hospital with the help of the other embers of the home committee.[21]

Sharing the Good News

Membership in the Deaconess Society grew steadily during the first year and deaconess work in St. Louis appeared to have a very good beginning. Members of the board of directors felt the need, however, to share, in true Evangelical fashion, the good news of this new undertaking and the opportunities it offered for others to become involved.

Beginning in September 1889, articles about deaconess work began to appear in the denominational monthly paper, *Der Friedensbote* (Messenger of Peace). The first one was written by board member Pastor Jacob P. Irion, and the second by Pastor Carl F. Fritsch.[22]

The primary thrust of these promotional pieces was the need for more recruits in the Deaconess Sisterhood. As the number of patients in the Deaconess Home increased, the call for deaconesses became more urgent. Sisters Katherine and Lydia needed help!

The School for Deaconesses

In 1890 two young women, Sophie Brunner and Charlotte Wellpot, heard the call for help and applied for entrance to deaconess training. They were the first students in the School for Deaconesses in St. Louis.

When three more probationers applied for admission and were accepted for deaconess training in 1891, the future of the School for Deaconesses in St. Louis looked very promising. At the same time, so many patients were applying for admission to the eleven-room Deaconess Home and Hospital on Eugenia Street that it was soon crowded to capacity. That brought the Deaconess Society to the decision to authorize a search for a new, permanent location.[23]

1-11. The First Evangelical Deaconess Sisters, Sister Superior Katherine Haack (front center) and Sister Lydia Daries (right), with the first two Deaconess Probationers, Sophie Brunner and Charlotte Wellpot, 1890.

15

An Answer to Prayer

In less than two years, the founders of "The Evangelical Deaconess Society of St. Louis, Mo." had organized themselves and adopted Articles of Association, established a Deaconess Sisterhood, opened a Deaconess Home which quickly became Deaconess Hospital, appointed a first-rate medical staff, began a School for Deaconesses, and had so many patients applying for admission that larger facilities were urgently needed.

To many, it was an impressive beginning, characterized by deep commitment and hard work. To many others, it was an answer to prayer. One account says:

> It was a small beginning connected with many hardships and difficulties, but God heard and answered the many prayers of the workers and friends, and blessed their efforts wonderfully.[24]

Those efforts provided the foundation for Deaconess Hospital's ministry of caring, healing and teaching, a ministry which has continued in St. Louis and beyond for 100 years.

Chapter Two

THE DEACONESS SISTERS
"Pioneer Professional Women"

The Deaconess Sisters gave Deaconess Hospital its name, its first management model, first nursing staff, and first teaching program. Their story in St. Louis began in 1889 with the consecration of Sister Katherine Haack and Sister Lydia Daries, but it is part of a heritage almost two thousand years old.

Deaconess Sisters are women consecrated to the full-time Christian ministry of caring, healing and teaching. Their lifestyle and work began in Biblical times among the first Christians, yet they are a part of the modern women's movement today. They are the pioneer professional women of the church.

2-1. The St. Louis Deaconess Sisterhood, 1891. Sister Superior Katherine Haack, front center, with Sisters Philippine Buehn, Lydia Daries, Louise Lix, Magdalene Gerhold, Charlotte Wellpot, and Sophie Brunner.

Deaconesses in the Early Church

Deaconess means messenger, servant or helper. It comes from the Greek diakonos, which implies helping or standing beside someone in a critical situation. The Apostle Paul first used it in the Bible in Romans 16:1-2 to describe Phoebe, a woman leader in the early Christian community:

> I commend to you our sister Phoebe, a deaconess of the church at Cenchreae, that you may receive her in the Lord as befits the saints, and help her in whatever she may require from you, for she has been a helper of many and of myself as well.

Paul's letters and other New Testament documents indicate that there were many women like Phoebe who served as leaders among the first Christians. Theological scholarship affirms that they not only gave loving service to the poor, the sick and the persecuted but were also teachers, preachers and missionaries. When the time for definite ecclesiastical organization came, the work of deaconesses had become a necessity to the church and they received a place in its ordered ministry. Highly respected and counted among the clergy, they were ordained to some of the functions of the Christian ministry. It is on this Biblical foundation that the ministry of deaconesses in all succeeding generations rests.[1]

For five centuries deaconess work grew and spread over the Christian world. In 300 A.D. the first charity hospital was established in Rome by Fabiola, a patrician woman of wealth who became a deaconess and opened her large home to care for the poor and the sick. Other Christian women of the Roman era became deaconesses and devoted themselves to giving care in the xenodochia, institutions of relief which have been described as forerunners of the modern hospital. Medical and nursing care was offered there to "the homeless, the stranger—in fact, to all who needed help."[2]

Though deaconesses were mentioned in church records and were active in Constantinople until the twelfth century, their work declined during the Dark Ages, when Christianity retreated to monasteries and convents, and it disappeared altogether in most of northern Europe after the Protestant Reformation.[3]

The Modern Revival of Deaconess Work

A young Evangelical pastor, Theodore Fliedner of Kaiserswerth, Germany, was responsible for the modern revival of deaconess work. He traveled across Europe in the 1830s and was appalled by the suffering of the sick, the poor, the aged and the outcasts of society which he saw in many places. Inspired by Mennonites in Holland who had organized the care of the sick in their homes, and by Elizabeth Fry, the English reformer who cared for released prisoners in England, Theodore Fliedner returned to Kaiserswerth and with the help of his wife, Frederike, opened the first Deaconess Home and Hospital in Europe in 1836.

2-2. Rev. Theodore Fliedner, leader of the modern revival of deaconess work in Kaiserswerth, Germany.

2-3. Mrs. Frederike Fliedner, co-leader of modern revival of deaconess work in Kaiserswerth, Germany.

The Fliedners invited the young, unmarried women of their small congregation to join them in this venture of faith. Gertrude Reichard, a doctor's daughter, responded and became the first recruited deaconess of modern times.

Despite strong opposition from the townsfolk who did not want a "pest house" in their midst, and the skepticism of others who scoffed at the undertaking or disapproved of any career for women outside the home, the Kaiserswerth sisterhood grew and became a model for deaconess work all over the world.[4]

The Kaiserswerth Model

The deep Christian commitment of the Fliedners, combined with their organizational ability, attracted not only those who wished to become deaconesses but others who came to Kaiserswerth simply to observe and study their methods.

Florence Nightingale, often called the founder of modern professional nursing, studied with the Fliedners on two occasions and she remained as a student in Kaiserswerth for three months in 1851. This was her only formal nurse's training before she began her famous work in the Crimean War and later established the first schools of nursing in England. She spoke of her experience with the Fliedners as the turning point in her life. Of the Deaconess Sisters at Kaiserswerth she said, "Never have I met with a higher love, a purer devotion than there."[5]

The Kaiserswerth model of deaconess work was adopted not only in Germany but in many other locations worldwide. By the turn of the century, there were 25,000 deaconesses serving in central Europe, the United States and in such distant places as Cairo, Egypt; St. Petersburg, Russia; Edinburgh, Scotland; Madras, India; and Hong Kong.

In the United States, the Lutheran, Episcopal and Methodist denominations were all engaged in deaconess work before 1889. A variety of organizational patterns were used, but the basic principles of the Kaiserswerth model predominated.

Knowing of these deaconess success stories, The Evangelical Deaconess Society of St. Louis, Mo. likewise adopted the Kaiserswerth model for its work.[6]

Requirements for Training and Consecration

Earnest Christian character, an "absolutely blameless reputation," and commitment to full-time Christian ministry

2-4. Florence Nightingale, student at Kaiserswerth whose only formal nurse's training was from the Deaconess Sisters.

were the first requirements for admission to deaconess training. Parental consent, good health, basic ability in reading, writing and arithmetic, and an age of eighteen to forty were additional admission qualifications. It was suggested further that a deaconess should have a cheerful disposition. Group living in the motherhouse, the adoption of a distinctive deaconess garb, completion of a thorough course of instruction, written and oral examinations, and practical experience in nursing care were all necessary before the deaconess probationer could be approved for consecration.

Sister Katherine Haack and Sister Lydia Daries met all of these requirements in 1889 except that of proper age, which was waived in Sister Katherine's case. She was forty-nine at the time of her consecration.[7]

Life in the Motherhouse

Group living in the motherhouse, a primary concept for the Fliedners as they organized deaconess work, proved to be a significant element of their success and was an initial step in the modern women's movement. Single young women could, with parental approval, leave the family circle and find security living and working in the company of like-minded women who were dedicated to a career in the ministry of caring, healing and teaching.

Nineteenth-century society generally did not approve of single young women living outside the family circle. And only those of wealthy families could hope for more than an elementary education. The deaconess, however, could get a good education and pursue a meaningful career free from family responsibilities and the constant burden of childbearing which accompanied most marriages. She was, in a relative sense, a liberated woman, a pioneer professional woman within the protective circle of the church.[8]

Because family ties in the nineteenth century were strong, the Fliedners wisely made parental consent one of the requirements for admission to deaconess training. But unlike the Roman Catholic sister who was often described as "married to the church" for life, the deaconess was free to leave her work and return to her family at any time if the need arose for her to care for aged parents.

Celibacy was a foregone conclusion, not because of church doctrine but as a matter of practical necessity. Few women in the 1800's could have managed the time-consuming duties of caring for a large family and also given themselves to the long workdays (usually twelve hours) of a Deaconess Sister.[9]

21

If a deaconess did wish to marry, she was free to leave the sisterhood at any time to do so, and many did. The General Conference of Deaconess Motherhouses, meeting in Kaiserswerth in 1891, reaffirmed this position:

> As a deaconess is free to remain single, so she retains the freedom at all times to enter wedlock in a lawful manner. Neither before nor after consecration need she promise to remain single, but she honestly declares that after mature examination before God and her conscience it is her deliberate and firm determination to be a deaconess and to remain single so long as it may please God.[10]

Deaconess Sisters who did not marry and remained in the profession for life were assured complete care in old age and in times of disability and illness. This was possible only within the motherhouse setting where the Deaconess Sisters served one another as well as others in need of help.

Lifetime care was a necessity because deaconesses received only a small stipend for personal use and no salary. They could not, therefore, accumulate significant personal savings. Their assurance of a lifetime support system was an early form of social security and it provided wonderfully liberating opportunities for the women who chose to become deaconesses. No worries about old age! In a society where, until recently, most women depended on the men of the family for financial security, deaconess work provided an attractive alternative.[11]

The sister superior, or executive deaconess, was in charge of the internal affairs of the sisterhood and in small institutions she also served as the manager. Appointed by the board of directors, she was usually assisted by democratically chosen committees.

Since the motherhouse functioned not only as a home and as a training school for the deaconesses but also much like a local church congregation, a pastor often served as the superintendent in large institutions. He conducted the worship services, provided the spiritual training for probationers and acted as the business manager and public relations director.

The practice of calling deaconesses by their baptismal names instead of their family names was another affirmation of the family character of the motherhouse in which they lived. The title "Sister" was a title of respect that was not only Biblically based but also descriptive of the deaconess lifestyle:

The name Sister, by which Christian custom addresses the deaconesses, beautifully expresses the communion of faith in which they stand....A simpler and more suitable name for the deaconess cannot be imagined. Together with the prescribed dress, this name wipes out all differences of birth and position.[12]

The Deaconess Garb

The prescribed dress or garb worn by the Deaconess Sisters identified them immediately wherever they went. At first, the Fliedners had suggested only simplicity of dress, but circumstances compelled them to prescribe a special garb because "it is well known that feminine nature is easily beguiled on this subject, for which reason a precise and minute rule is necessary."[13]

The garb had a number of advantages. It not only wiped out all differences in birth and position but it also symbolized the spiritual relationship of the Deaconess Sisters to one another. Of equal importance was the fact that:

> The deaconess garb is a constant reminder of the dignity of the calling; it is also a protection, for a deaconess may go out at any time of the day or night, in pursuit of her calling, and may appear anywhere, without molestation. Her dress is, so to say, her ticket of admission, her letter of recommendation.[14]

Although some Deaconess Sisters did not like wearing a garb that made them all look alike, most welcomed it. The simple, long, black dress, usually worn with a white collar for street wear and a white apron for work, was much easier to care for than the outfits with many petticoats, tucks and ruffles worn by most women during the nineteenth century. A small cap, tied on with a bow under the chin, covered most of the Deaconess Sister's hair, which was parted in the middle, pulled straight back, and secured in a neat bun.

Thus liberated from the drudgery of the flatiron and the influence of the Gibson girl image, which was held up as an ideal for women at the turn of the century, most deaconesses agreed that "The garb cuts off at once all luxury in attire and saves much money, time and thought which women think they must spend in order to keep their clothing in current fashion."[15]

As the garb was updated from time to time for greater comfort and efficiency, the deaconess pin became the primary means of identification for a Deaconess Sister.

The Deaconess Pin

The Fliedners had discouraged the wearing of gold crosses or any other ornamentation as "smacking of Romanism," but some Lutheran deaconesses wore a large silver cross. Many sisterhoods adopted a pin with a red cross on a white background, the international sign of relief for the suffering, and at first the deaconesses in St. Louis wore a pin of that design. In 1905 they adopted the distinctive deaconess pin used by sisterhoods belonging to the Protestant Deaconess Conference, an interdenominational organization of Deaconess Associations in the United States. This pin was based on the symbol of Kaiserswerth, a white dove carrying an olive branch and resting on a blue background.[16]

2-5. The Deaconess Pin, officially adopted in 1905.

The deaconess pin was presented to the Deaconess Sister at the time of her consecration. The white dove denotes purity of purpose. It is on a blue background, representing courage and faithfulness. The gold cross signifies commitment to Christ and His work, and a gold olive wreath symbolizes God's eternal and encompassing love.

Threefold Training

The most revolutionary contribution of the Fliedners in their Kaiserswerth model for deaconess work was in the area of training. They required it to be threefold: spiritual, intellectual and technical. This concept changed the entire image of nurses, who were not held in high regard in the early nineteenth century.

With the motherhouse as a training school, the Deaconess Sisters soon became proficient in all three aspects of their work. Training was systematic and thorough.[17] As a result, doctors could write orders and know that consistent, careful, compassionate care would be given in their absence by deaconess nurses. These methods were studied by many who came to Kaiserswerth, including

24

Florence Nightingale who wrote:

> The Sisters are, however, bound, of course, punctually to obey the
> directions of the medical man, and they are too well trained not to
> do so, with far more correctness than is found in other hospitals.
> The superintending sister of every ward is always present during
> the daily visits of the medical man. The apothecary is a sister, and
> she goes the round of the patients with him, noting down all his
> prescriptions and directions which she afterwards transcribes into
> a book.[18]

This was the beginning of structured nursing care, based on the creation of a
comprehensive medical record for each patient.

Other visitors to Kaiserswerth, such as Dr. Jane Bancroft, a prominent Methodist
educator from the United States, called attention to the spiritual training of the
Deaconess Sisters:

> [The deaconess] must follow strictly the doctor's orders in all mat-
> ters pertaining to diet, medicine and ventilation, and must inform
> him daily of the patient's state. She also assists the clergyman...in
> ministering to spiritual needs.[19]

The Significance of Consecration

The Consecration Service was a religious as well as an academic ceremony signifying the Deaconess Sister's official entry into professional life. Held in a public church service in the presence of an assembled congregation, it was similar
to the liturgical procedure used in the ordination of a pastor and included the
laying on of hands, an ordination prayer dating back to the fourth century, and
the sacrament of Holy Communion.

As part of her consecration the Deaconess Sister promised obedience to the
Word of God and to the regulations of the church and the motherhouse, willingness to do any work required, and faithfulness in all things. This promise was
not considered a vow for life but a pledge in regard to a certain vocation. It was
believed in Protestant denominations that the one vow of a Christian is the baptismal vow and that no other special vow was justified. Nevertheless, the promise
given by a deaconess at the time of her consecration had tremendous implica-
tions.

Obedience to the word of God created a framework of commitment for service to the poor and the sick and provided the foundation for this ministry. Obedience to the regulations of the church included participation in worship and the sacrament of Holy Communion, the spiritual nurture necessary for a life of Christian service. Obedience to the rules of the motherhouse made it possible for a deaconess to live in community with other Deaconess Sisters and to carry out service in a harmonious and organized manner. In their preparatory studies deaconesses were cautioned, however, that "obedience...dare not be compulsory, but must be voluntary."[20]

Willingness to do any work that needed to be done was necessary if the deaconess was to endure the wretched situations often encountered in serving the sick and the poor. A positive, cheerful attitude could overcome a disagreeable and difficult assignment. The deaconess manual reminded deaconesses that "A willing mind and spirit make service easy" and that "whoever shows kindness to others, must do it cheerfully." (Romans 12:8)

Faithfulness enabled the deaconess to do justice to her work and duty in every respect. It showed itself in conscientiously using and applying all that was entrusted to her care and was her response to God's never-failing love and mercy toward her. The Deaconess Motto was a daily reminder and source of inspiration.[21]

Three Types of Deaconess Service

Prominent though it was, nursing was not the only type of service for which Deaconess Sisters were trained. Teaching and parish work were of equal importance, and missionary work combined all three.

Since the need for trained nurses was always great, most of the St. Louis deaconesses devoted themselves to a lifetime of nursing or to some phase of patient care. But many also became teachers, and others served as parish assistants and as missionaries at home and abroad. Every Deaconess Sister was, however, trained first as a nurse regardless of her subsequent responsibilities, "because in no other way can her physical and mental powers be so thoroughly disciplined as by nursing."[22]

Early Hardships and Success

Having been trained in the principles and methods of the Kaiserswerth model for deaconess work, Sisters Katherine Haack and Lydia Daries were well-prepared to care for the sick and the poor in St. Louis in 1889. Nonetheless, they were soon confronted with hardships.

Money was scarce. Financial records show that the Deaconess Society had a balance of only $461.63 in the treasury on August 18th when the Evangelical Deaconess Home on Eugenia Street was opened. Sister Katherine is reported to have told some of the younger deaconesses years later that she and Sister Lydia "moved in with 50 cents to stock their larder. They paid 15 cents for a soup bone and had 35 cents left to squander."[23]

Both Sister Katherine and Sister Lydia also experienced right from the start the necessity for willingness to do any work that needed to be done. While one responded to calls for nursing in patients' homes, the other maintained the Deaconess Home. In both instances this often meant cooking, cleaning, laundering, shopping, and keeping records as well as nursing.

In January 1891 two "maids" were employed to assist in maintaining the Home. Soon thereafter three additional probationers, Philippine Buehn, Louise Lix and Magdalene Gerhold, entered for deaconess training. Overcrowding then became a problem in the first eleven-room Deaconess Home and Hospital. But that was also a sign of success, and plans were soon made for larger facilities.[24]

A New Sisters' Home, 1893

By the time four more probationers arrived in 1892, property had been purchased at 4117 West Belle Place and a well-preserved vacant public school building at that location was being remodeled as a new Sisters' Home for fifteen Deaconess Sisters.

A new three-story hospital building, constructed adjacent to the Sisters' Home, provided accommodations for forty patients, and more deaconesses were needed to provide nursing care. By 1897 there were twenty in the sisterhood, but the number of patients in the hospital continued to increase so rapidly that construction was begun on an east wing addition. It was then that unforeseen difficulties developed.[25]

2-6. Deaconess Sisters' Home, 4117 West Belle Place, 1893.

Serious Trouble in the Sisterhood

Anticipating that the completion of the new addition would bring increased responsibilities for Sister Katherine, whose health had at times become fragile,

> ...the board of directors saw themselves forced to decide upon some changes. The need was recognized for a dedicated pastor to head the institution who would give full time to the work...The decision was made to relieve the Sister Superior of certain duties and let her be responsible for nursing care of patients and direction of the work for deaconesses. Her present status among the sisters was not to change but the leadership would be in the hands of another person.[26]

As a result of this decision, seven of the Deaconess Sisters resigned from the sisterhood in the Spring of 1897. At issue was the role of Sister Katherine Haack in the management of the institution.[27]

Sister Katherine Haack's Resignation, a "Backset"

When the board of directors proceeded with its plans, Sister Katherine resigned on December 1, 1897. She considered the appointment of a superintendent to be a demotion which she could not accept. In support of her action, six more Deaconess Sisters including her daughter, Sister Lydia Daries, also resigned and returned to private life. Only six remained in the sisterhood.[28]

This "serious trouble in the sisterhood," as it was described in some accounts, threatened to end deaconess work in St. Louis in 1897, but the official record says only that it "gave the whole work a backset for several years."[29]

Sister Magdalene Gerhold, Sister Superior, 1897

Following Sister Katherine Haack's resignation, Sister Magdalene Gerhold, who was on assignment as the nursing supervisor at the Emmaus Home in Marthasville, Missouri, was recalled to become the new sister superior in St. Louis.[30]

Though the record states that "dark days loomed ahead," Sister Magdalene proved herself equal to the challenge. The most experienced leader among the deaconesses remaining in the sisterhood, she managed to hold things together at the Deaconess Home and Hospital while a search was begun to fill the newly-created position of superinten-

2-7. Sister Superior Magdalene Gerhold, 1897

dent and pastor. When this proved to be more difficult than anticipated, Sister Magdalene finally suggested the Rev. Frederick P. Jens, who became superintendent on May 1, 1898.[31]

New Leadership and Revitalization

Sister Magdalene Gerhold and Superintendent Jens began immediately to rebuild the sisterhood, and under their leadership it grew again. Within a year they could report that,

> During the year one ordained sister and 9 young women entered

as probationers, so that there are at present 7 ordained and 11 probation deaconesses in our sisterhood. (Since then two more have entered, making 20 in all.)[32]

The sisterhood had not only survived a serious crisis but regained its previous numerical strength. Moreover, harmony was restored and construction of the new east wing to the hospital was completed.

2-8. Deaconess Sisters' Home and Hospital, 1899.

Deaconess Support Fund Established

One of the first innovations of the new administration was the establishment of a Deaconess Support Fund, created from gifts made to the deaconesses by grateful patients.

The Deaconess Sisters did not accept gifts for themselves, but quite a number of patients insisted on giving them something in appreciation for the services rendered. In 1899 the board of directors resolved "to create a fund with the income from such sources, from which the deaconesses are to be supported and cared for when sick or unable for service."[33]

The amount recorded by the financial secretary as receipts for the Deaconess Support Fund that first year was a modest $113. Once begun, however, the fund

2-9. A Deaconess Sister's Room.

grew slowly and steadily. During the next ten years the amount increased enough to encourage the Deaconess Society to pass a resolution:

> to keep a separate account of the Deaconess Support Fund, and to invest it at four per cent interest per annum. Five per cent of the surplus income shall be added to this fund annually.[34]

Under this arrangement, the fund eventually became a significant base of financial security for the Deaconess Sisters and continues to provide for them in retirement.

The Sisterhood and the "Progressive Era"

Few people were thinking very much about retirement at that time, however, because a new "progressive era" of growth and expansion was being felt across the land in the early 1900s. The City of St. Louis was preparing for the 1904 World's Fair and 20 million visitors were expected for that event.[35]

In a mood befitting the times, the Deaconess Sisters welcomed this great influx of visitors to the city as a unique opportunity to share their own story of growth and expansion with prospective deaconesses and supportive church groups. By 1904 there were thirty in the sisterhood and fifteen were living in rented quarters two blocks away from the hospital because the Sisters' Home could no longer provide enough accommodations.[36]

A 15th anniversary commemorative booklet, *A Short History of the Deaconess Calling and of Deaconess Institutions,* was circulated far and wide by the Deaconess Society in 1904. It included a list of requirements for admission to the School for Deaconesses and pictured many of the Deaconess Sisters of whom it was said, "Their work deserves high praise in the kingdom service."[37]

Their work soon received high praise not only in St. Louis but also in other Evangelical healthcare institutions across the land.

Leadership in Twenty-six Locations

Beginning with Sister Magdalene Gerhold's assignment to the Emmaus Home in Marthasville, as reported previously, Deaconess Sisters from the St. Louis Motherhouse were sent to new deaconess institutions in other cities to give professional leadership in management, teaching, and nursing supervision. Eventually they served in hospitals, schools, homes for the aged, homes for the developmentally disabled, children's homes, neighborhood houses, and church parishes in twenty-six different locations.[38]

Frequent contacts and fellowship between the St. Louis Deaconess Sisters and persons involved in deaconess work at other locations gradually created an institutional network which served as a clearinghouse for new ideas and financial support. This led to the establishment in 1909 of the Federation of Evangelical Deaconess Associations.[39]

An Updated Garb and New Benefits

As they travelled to and from meetings and assignments away from the Deaconess Home and Hospital in St. Louis, the Deaconess Sisters wore an updated version of their street garb beginning in 1909. The black hood tied on with a large white bow under the chin was replaced with an attractive, more comfortable, small black pillbox hat.

Changes were likewise made in their hospital work garb, which was worn with a small white cap on the back of the head similar to that worn by nurses in other healthcare institutions at that time. These changes came about "according to the wishes of a majority of the Sisters and by a majority vote of the board of directors."[40]

After their monthly stipend was increased in 1910, the Deaconess Sisters had more money for personal necessities. The record says:

> Formerly the consecrated Sister received $3 and the probationers $2.50 monthly, and all other expenses were paid by the Home. Beginning with January 1st, 1910, each consecrated deaconess is to receive $10, and each probationer $8 a month, and double that amount for their month of vacation. Out of this amount they are to pay for their clothing, personal expenses and vacation trips, but are provided and cared for otherwise during sickness and old age entirely by the motherhouse.[41]

Although a good pair of leather shoes could be purchased from the *1909 Sears Roebuck and Co. Consumers' Guide* for $1.89 plus 29 cents postage, the increased stipend provided the Deaconess Sisters with very little more than necessities.[42]

"The Farm" - Rx for Rest and Relaxation

A fringe benefit was added in 1911 when a small farm near Sappington in St. Louis County was purchased for the use of the Deaconess Sisters as a retreat from rigid institutional life and for rest and relaxation.

"The Farm," as it was fondly called, had a small farmhouse and several other buildings which provided comfortable quarters away from the hospital and the city for a day off, vacations, or for overnight and weekend visits.

For eighteen years "The Farm" was also the scene of birthday parties, picnics, retreats, and special board meetings. Produce grown there by the caretaker sometimes provided fresh fruit and vegetables for the hospital kitchen. But it was primarily an escape from the strict rigors of institutional life with which the

2-10. "The Farm."

Deaconess Sisters lived day in and day out. As such, it was also seen as a health measure contributing greatly to their well-being.[43]

State Board Examinations, 1913

Some of the deaconesses in St. Louis used "The Farm" as a quiet place for study and reflection while they prepared for consecration or for the State Board of Nursing Examinations which were given in Missouri for the first time in 1913.

Sister Sophie Hubeli was the first deaconess to pass the "state boards" and become a licensed registered deaconess nurse. Sister Anna Lenger was the first deaconess to become a registered nurse in both Missouri and Illinois.

All of the Deaconess Sisters were required to pass the "state boards" and they often made the highest grades.[44]

The 25th Anniversary

In March 1914, on the 25th anniversary of deaconess work in St. Louis, the Deaconess Sisters were pictured individually and featured prominently in a commemorative booklet which gave this summary of the sisterhood's growth and outreach:

> During the quarter century one hundred and forty-four young women were admitted to our Home, of which number forty-seven still belong to it, and fifteen are in the deaconess work in other institutions.[45]

34

The 25th anniversary year was only half over, however, when World War I broke out in Europe and wartime concerns became evident throughout the United States. Some German-speaking people, including some of the Deaconess Sisters, were careful not to speak German in public lest they be identified with the enemy. To emphasize their United States loyalty and to assist with the war effort, the deaconesses agreed to volunteer their services, if needed, when the American Red Cross issued a call for 5,000 nurses in June 1918.[46]

Denominational Recognition

Once the war was over, attention could be directed to some of the many social changes taking place at that time. Among these was the right of women to vote for the first time in national elections, a privilege brought about by ratification of the 19th Amendment to the U.S. Constitution in 1920.

The deaconesses had not participated actively in the women's suffrage rallies and public demonstrations, primarily because their long workdays left them with

2-11. Deaconess Street Garb adopted in 1921 and modeled by Sister Clara Weltge, (left), Sister Frieda Bergstrasser, (front), and Sister Martha Roglin, (right).

little time or energy for such pursuits. But as pioneer professional women, they were sympathetic and supportive of women's issues and they rejoiced in their new privilege to vote.

In keeping with the progressive spirit of the times, the Sisters adopted a new deaconess garb in 1921 which was quite different from any of those worn in the past. Very much like the fashionable outfits of many conservative, well-dressed women of that day, this new deaconess garb had a plain white shirtwaist, a long black skirt, a black jacket and a large black straw sailor hat for summer with one of black velvet for winter. It was strikingly attractive and up-to-date, yet distinctive when worn with the deaconess pin.[47]

Even the denominational leaders of the Evangelical Synod took notice of the Deaconess Sisters in a new way at that time. Whether it was the result of the new status of women with the right to vote or simply an idea whose time had come, the Deaconess Sisters were for the first time officially recognized in 1921 with denominational standing:

> In the Evangelical Synod of North America the female diaconate is successfully carried on since 1888. Deaconesses are now engaged in hospital nursing, parish work, city missions, homes for the aged, asylums for epileptics and feebleminded and private nursing in homes of the poor. The last General Conference of the Evangelical Synod of North America has recognized the Diaconate as a church office and given it denominational standing among the other organized branches of its activities.[48]

Although as individuals the Deaconess Sisters had always been members of the Evangelical Church and the sisterhood had functioned in most respects like a local Evangelical congregation, this denominational recognition was an important stamp of approval and pledge of support from the national church.

Leadership in Specialized Services

Meanwhile, by the early 1920s hospitals were becoming accepted as the primary places of healing and, as a result of many new scientific discoveries, Deaconess Sisters were trained to become specialists in charge of the X-ray room, the clinical laboratory, and the pharmacy.[49]

As described earlier, all deaconesses were trained first as nurses, but as early as 1901 it was recorded that the sisterhood had begun a division of responsibilities within the hospital to assist the superintendent with administrative duties. The "head sister," the "steward sister," and the "office sister" were mentioned that year as having divided among themselves the duties of admitting patients, attending to financial and business matters, buying for the hospital, and keeping the books.[50]

In 1928 the Staff of the School for Deaconesses reveals the extent of the spe-

2-12. Deaconess Sister Louise Lix working in the hospital office, 1901.

cialization in the sisterhood by that time. Included on this list are the names of the Deaconess Sisters who were serving as faculty members and also as hospital department heads:

Sr. Beata Schick, R.N . . . . .Instructor
Sr. Sophie Hubeli, R.N. . . . . .Supt. of Nursing
Sr. Hilda Mark, R.N. . . . . .Asst. Instructor
Sr. Clara Weltge, R.N. .Clinical Laboratory
Sr. Katherine Streib, R.N. . . . . .X-Ray and Physiotherapy
Sr. Hulda Echelmeier, R.N. . . . . .Operating Room Supervisor
Sr. Theresa Kettelhut, R.N. . . . . .Asst. Op. Room Supervisor
Sr. Olinda Fuhr, R.N. . . . . .Supt. of Maternity Division
Sr. Mary Feutz, R.N. Ph.G. . . . . .Pharmacist
Sr. Elizabeth Schaefer, R.N. . . . .[Med. Records] Historian
Sr. Bena Fuchs, R.N. . . . . .Dietician

Some of these Deaconess Sisters were pioneers in their field and among the first women to hold positions of leadership in their professional organizations. Sister Elizabeth Schaefer was a founding member of the Missouri Medical Records Association. Sister Clara Weltge served as president of the Missouri Clinical Laboratory Technologists. Sister Mary Feutz was one of two women who gradu-

2-13. Sister Elizabeth Schaefer, founding member of the Missouri Medical Records Association.

ated in a class of sixty-five men in 1921 from the St. Louis College of Pharmacy.[51]

This pattern of leadership continued as other Deaconess Sisters in succeeding years were elected to offices in their professional organizations. In 1949, Sister Hilda Muensterman served as vice-president of the Missouri State Nurses' Association and Sister Olivia Drusch was elected secretary. Sister Olivia also served as nurse coordinator between the Third District of the Missouri State Nurses' Association and the St. Louis branch of the National Polio Foundation. Sister Hulda Weise was elected in 1949 to the board of directors of the St. Louis League of Nursing and to the board of the Third District, Missouri State Nurses' Association.[52]

2-14. Sister Clara Weltge, president, Missouri Clinical Laboratory Technologists.

A New Home on Oakland Avenue

When expansion of facilities was no longer possible on West Belle Place, a beautiful new hospital building was constructed on Oakland Avenue and dedicated in 1930.

The Deaconess Sisters were assigned living quarters on the third and sixth floors of the new hospital. They had hoped for a new Sisters' Home at the new location, but building fund shortages during the Great Depression forced the postponement of that part of the construction program. Despite the inconvenience of temporary living arrangements, they rejoiced nonetheless in their spacious new workplace overlooking Forest Park. Sister Alvina Scheid spoke for all of the Sisters when she said,

> Thrilled with our new location and our large, beautiful new hospital, we as a Sisterhood, visualized the great possibilities of a greater work, yet never losing sight of the high principles on which our work was founded.[53]

Sister Magdalene Gerhold, Sister Superior Emeritus

Once the move from West Belle Place to Oakland Avenue was successfully completed, Sister Superior Magdalene Gerhold decided that the time had come for her to retire. Having given thirty-two years of strong leadership to the Deaconess Sisterhood and the hospital administration, she was granted a leave of absence and given less demanding duties.

Sister Alvina Scheid, Sister Superior, 1930

Sister Alvina Scheid was the newly appointed sister superior in 1930, to succeed Sister Magdalene Gerhold[54]

2-14b. Sister Superior Emeritus Magdalene Gerhold.

39

Sister Alvina came to her new position with fifteen years of experience in administration at The Good Samaritan Home for the Aged in St. Louis. Earlier she had served as a parish deaconess in Louisville, Kentucky, and as an instructor in the School for Deaconesses in St. Louis. Soft-spoken, gentle and unassuming, Sister Alvina was, at the same time, firm and persuasive. Her management style, so different from that of Sister Magdalene's vigorous, authoritative approach, brought a new era of growth to the sisterhood.[55]

The Sisterhood At Its Largest

2-15. Sister Superior Alvina Scheid, 1930.

In the new location on Oakland Avenue and under Sister Alvina's leadership, the St. Louis Sisterhood continued to grow steadily. It reached its largest size ever during the 1930s, numbering 144 in 1937. But growth proved to be a mixed blessing. Without a separate Sisters' Home, forty-four deaconesses still occupied living quarters on one floor of the hospital in 1937, and all of the other deaconesses and students were being housed in rented apartments in the neighborhood. This housing arrangement was not only expensive and inconvenient but also troublesome.

Serious problems soon developed within the sisterhood. Getting all of the Sisters together at one time for any purpose was almost impossible, and supervision of the probationers was increasingly difficult. Under these circumstances, some deaconesses expressed growing dissatisfaction with deaconess work as a special calling, and in 1937 ten of the Deaconess Sisters resigned.[56]

The Deaconess Study Committee

Confronted with these developments, the Deaconess Society voted in its annual meeting in November 1937 (1) to launch immediately a program to build a Sisters' Home and (2) to appoint from its membership a committee of five to study the whole policy and history of deaconess work and to bring recommendations to the Society. Appointed were: Rev. H. J. Damm, chairman; Rev. Theo. F. Stoerker, secretary; Mrs. F. A. Keck; Sister Marie Sprick; Sister Beata Schick; and Superintendent Jens.

At the annual meeting of the Deaconess Society one year later this committee reported that "The principal problems of most of the sisters seem to relate to remuneration, the meaning of the deaconess vow, the privilege to associate with the opposite sex, and the discipline and rules of the institution." Eight specific recommendations for solving some of these problems were presented in the report and there was a strong suggestion for opening a training school for nurses not wishing to become deaconesses.

The Study Committee was commended for its "thorough study and excellent analysis of the entire deaconess work" and was then given the responsibility to study the matter further and bring recommendations for "a proper integration of the deaconess work with the program of the Evangelical and Reformed Church." The president of the board of directors maintained in the 49th Annual Report of the Deaconess Society in 1938, however, that in his opinion, "Our greatest need is a sisters' home. The fact that we have been unable to provide a home for our deaconesses has involved us in serious difficulties."

Before further recommendations were made by the Study Committee, fourteen more Deaconess Sisters resigned from the sisterhood in 1939.[57]

50th Anniversary "Highlights"

Despite the continuing difficulties in the sisterhood, the Deaconess Society members directed their immediate attention in 1939 to a celebration being planned for the 50th anniversary of deaconess work in St. Louis.

An original pageant, "Highlights in the Ministry of Healing Through the Centuries", was written by Sister Beata Schick and members of the hospital staff for the occasion. Many of the deaconesses were in the cast of three hundred. Presented to an overflow audience at Kiel Auditorium on Sunday afternoon, March 26, 1939, this production was described as having "contributed much in placing the deaconess work into the very center of our interest and gratitude."[58]

The tremendous contribution made by the Deaconess Sisters during their fifty years of healing ministry in St. Louis was highlighted further in a 50th anniversary brochure, entitled "Fourteen Hundred Years", which stated,

> ...1400 years...14 centuries...42 generations...8 out of every 10 years since the birth of Christ....

> This span of years represents the total number of years' service of the Sisters now at Deaconess Hospital.[59]

2-16. Deaconess Sisters in 50th Anniversary Pageant.

2-17. The Deaconess Sisterhood, 50th Anniversary, 1939.

A New Sisters' Home, "For Greater Service"

Inspired by the enthusiastic response to the events of the 50th Anniversary Celebration, the Deaconess Society took bold action in December 1939 and voted "to launch a campaign to secure funds and pledges for the construction of a Sisters' Home at the earliest possible date."[60] The campaign, called an effort "For Greater Service," reemphasized the tremendous

2-18. The Sisters' Home, 1942.

contributions of the Deaconess Sisters and declared that an adequate and appropriate Sisters' Home was urgently needed if deaconess work was to continue in St. Louis. This appeal was well-timed and effective. Enough funds were raised to begin construction in 1940 of a new six-story building on property immediately west and adjacent to the hospital.

Dedication day, March 15, 1942, was a joyous celebration. Sister Alvina Scheid and Sister Magdalene Gerhold took part in the official ceremonies, and all of the deaconesses were present with many guests for the open house and luncheon which followed.[61]

After twelve years of living in temporary quarters, the Deaconess Sisters expressed great joy and gratitude as they moved into their new home, where they could all live together in comfortable accommodations adjacent to the hospital.

> The beauty and comfort of this our new home are far beyond our expectations...A hundred times as much. (Sister Mary Kramme) At last our dream came true, a place where we can be together and enjoy a home-like atmosphere, a place where we can have a room and take pride in dressing it up to suit our own desires. (Sister Frieda Ziegler)

As I look over our new home, the beautiful living room, the lovely library, the spacious recreation hall and all the other things that make it such a unique home, realizing that it belongs to the Deaconess Sisterhood, it makes me straighten my back just a little more and hold my head just a little higher. (Sister Velma Kampschmidt)[62]

The draperies and furnishings in the Sisters' Home were provided by the newly-organized Deaconess Women's Auxiliary, which had been nurtured into official organization a year earlier by Sister Alvina Scheid and the women members of the hospital board of directors.[63]

2-19. Sisters' Home Living Room.

Sister Olivia Drusch, Sister Superior, 1942

On June 18, 1942, Sister Olivia Drusch was appointed as the new sister superior to succeed Sister Alvina Scheid, who requested a leave of absence and less demanding duties because of frail health. Sister Olivia had completed advanced studies for a B.S. degree in Nursing Education at St. Louis University, and she was very much interested in strengthening the sisterhood. Her installation took place on July 7, 1942. Sister Hilda Muensterman was installed at the same time as director of the School for Deaconesses and director of nurses to succeed Sister Beata Schick, who died after a short illness in December, 1941.[64]

2-20. Sister Superior Olivia Drusch, (center), 1942. The Sisters' Council. (left to right): Sisters Frieda Ziegler, Marie Korte, Hilda Muensterman, Hulda Weise, Clara Weltge and Velma Kampschmidt.

The Sisters' Council

Under Sister Olivia Drusch's guidance, the Sisters' Council of five elected deaconesses began working diligently to represent the best interests of the sisterhood at every opportunity.

Addressing the growing problem of World War II personnel shortages and the difficulties of staffing nursing service departments of the hospital adequately with Deaconess Sisters, the Sisters' Council held a special meeting on September 11, 1942, and passed a resolution calling upon the board of directors of the Deaconess Society to open as soon as possible a training school for lay nurses to run concurrently with the School for Deaconesses. The Council, in taking this first formal action proposing a lay school of nursing, assured the board of directors that the Deaconess Sisters had given this matter a great deal of time and consideration. Moreover, the Council set forth in its report certain requirements and standards for the guidance of the board members in their planning for this new school.[65]

The establishment of the Deaconess School of Nursing for lay students in 1943 proved to be a landmark decision. The faculty was composed almost entirely of Deaconess Sisters. That placed the sisterhood in a strong position to provide the excellent training traditionally associated with the deaconesses for those who aspired to become professional lay nurses.[66]

The Deaconess Dolls Tell a Story

To preserve some of their heritage and to help tell their story to the new lay students in the School of Nursing, the Deaconess Sisters purchased a set of ten antique dolls in 1942.

2-21. The Deaconess Dolls in garbs designed and made by Sister Bena Fuchs, 1942.

Sister Bena Fuchs designed and created authentic garbs for the dolls like those worn by the Deaconess Sisters from 1889 to 1942. Displayed for the first time in an exhibit on Hospital Day 1943, the Deaconess Dolls continue to tell their story as part of the Heritage Display in the hospital front lobby.[67]

Deaconess Recruitment Discontinued in the 1950s

As classes in the School of Nursing grew larger and larger each year, the number of students enrolled in the School for Deaconesses became smaller. To offset this trend, the board of directors of the Deaconess Society decided in 1951 to appoint Sister Pauline Becker, who had graduated that year from Columbia University Teachers' College in New York with a B.S. degree in Nursing, to a newly-created position of Field Representative for Deaconess Work. Her assignment was to inform young women in the Evangelical and Reformed Church about deaconess work and to recruit them as deaconesses.

Endorsed by fifty delegates of the Conference of Evangelical and Reformed Deaconess Sisterhoods, which met in St. Louis in 1951 after more than twenty-five years of inactivity, Sister Pauline travelled across the land to churches, youth rallies, mission festivals and synod meetings. An able and enthusiastic speaker, she spoke and presented pictures to seventy-six different groups in one year

2-22. Sister Pauline Becker, (left) wearing Deaconess street garb of 1950, with Deaconess Sisters modeling earlier garbs: Elsie Jungerman (1926), Mary Kramme (1889), Gertrude Poth (1942), Velma Kampschmidt (1893), Elizabeth Lotz (1902), Frieda Hoffmeister (1908), Flora Pletz (1910), Ida Bieri (1921), Helen Schneider (1950) and Florentine Kramme, volunteer smock.

alone, and her message was well received.

After several years of intense recruiting and further committee consideration of the future for deaconess work, it became evident that although many prospective students were interested in nursing as a career, they were unwilling to commit themselves to consecration as Deaconess Sisters. Moreover, the seminaries of the church were beginning to admit women students for training in Christian education and in preparation for ordination as pastors and missionaries, thus diminishing the role of the parish deaconesses of former years.

Recruitment for deaconesses was therefore discontinued and The School for Deaconesses was phased out. Efforts were concentrated instead on offering high quality education in the School of Nursing, the School of X-Ray Technology, and other hospital training programs.[68]

Leadership in National and International Organizations

The Conference of Evangelical and Reformed Deaconess Sisterhoods continued to meet annually in St. Louis for fellowship and inspiration until 1960. Deaconess Sisters from the St. Louis Sisterhood gave strong leadership to these meetings and they also attended and gave leadership to national and interna-

47

tional deaconess organizations.

Sister Pauline Becker served as secretary of the executive committee of DOTA, the DIAKONIA OF THE AMERICAS, an ecumenical organization of Deaconess Sisters which was organized in 1968. At the same time, she and some of the other Deaconess Sisters from St. Louis attended biennial meetings of DIAKONIA, the World Federation of Sisterhoods and Diaconal Associations. This organization has more than 1600 members in some 50 member associations from Protestant denominations in 30 countries around the world.[69]

The St. Louis Sisterhood, a Unique UCC Congregation

Meanwhile, the Deaconess Sisterhood in St. Louis had for some time felt the need to strengthen its denominational relationship. As described earlier, the sisterhood had always functioned much like a local congregation and was recognized in 1921 as an organized branch of the Evangelical Synod, but the Deaconess Sisters became aware in 1951 that they no longer had legal standing in the denomination, which by then had become the Evangelical and Reformed Church.

Under the guidance of denominational officers and Administrator and Chaplain Carl C. Rasche, the Deaconess Sisterhood founded the Deaconess Evangelical and Reformed Church in 1952. Known as Deaconess Chapel, this new congregation's membership was limited to consecrated Deaconess Sisters. It is to this day a unique congregation, representative of the diversity that is possible within the structure of the denomination, now the United Church of Christ.[70]

Sister Frieda Ziegler, Executive Deaconess, 1954

Sister Frieda Ziegler was appointed sister superior in 1954 to succeed Sister Olivia Drusch, who became the director of the Deaconess School of Nursing and of nursing service.

At the time of her appointment, Sister Frieda was the chief pharmacist at Deaconess Hospital, a position she had held since her graduation from the St. Louis College of Pharmacy in 1944. Later earning a master of science degree in pharmacology, Sister Frieda continued to serve as chief pharmacist as well as the executive deaconess. The title, "executive deaconess," was adopted unanimously by the Deaconess Sisters in 1954 as more modern terminology for the sister

2-23. Sister Frieda Ziegler, Sister Superior - Executive Deaconess, 1954.

superior, and that change was approved by the hospital board of trustees. Sister Frieda's installation on March 1, 1954 was a particularly historic occasion in that three of her predecessors in that office, Sister Magdalene Gerhold, Sister Alvina Scheid and Sister Olivia Drusch, were all present and participated in the ceremony. Each has brought her own unique abilities to this leadership role, and together they have contributed a continuity of purpose and direction to the sisterhood.

Since 1889, when the Deaconess Sisterhood was first established in St. Louis, more than 500 young women have been educated in the School for Deaconesses and 197 have been consecrated in St. Louis alone to serve in the ministry of caring, healing and teaching.[71]

The Joys of Retirement

All of the deaconesses related to the United Church of Christ are now retired, but their heritage lives on. After her retirement as chief pharmacist in 1973, Sister Frieda Ziegler continued to serve as executive deaconess and to represent the Deaconess Sisters

2-24. Sisters Kate Nottrott and Naomi Pielemeier, volunteers in Gift Shop.

on the hospital administrative staff and board of trustees. In retirement, the deaconesses of the St. Louis Sisterhood live in the Sisters' Home, part of the Deaconess Health Services and College of Nursing complex. This living arrangement is made possible by the Sisters' Support Fund established in 1899, and it is a daily reminder for present-day nursing students and hospital employees alike of the great heritage of diakonia which precedes them. Some of the retired deaconesses serve as volunteers in the Deaconess Archives, Library, Park Place Gift Shop, Mail Room, Photo-Ident Service, Life-Dial Program, Volunteer Office, Deaconess Auxiliary, and in special projects from time to time. Their presence in these hospital-related activities continues to be an inspiration to others who work with them.

The Deaconess Legacy

Oral histories, recorded by many of the Deaconess Sisters for the Deaconess Archives in 1979, testify to the joys and satisfactions of their work as pioneer professional women during the past 100 years. Hardships, disappointments, overwork and emergency assignments to distant locations are part of some individual stories, but most of the deaconesses have declared in retrospect, "I would do it all over again."[72]

2-25. Sister Elizabeth Lotz and Executive Deaconess Frieda Ziegler representing the Deaconess Sisterhood at 100th Anniversary Recognition, UCC General Synod, Fort Worth, Texas, 1989, with Ruth W. Rasche, chair, UCC Historical Council.

Their ministry of loving service to others, given in a spirit of "obedience, willingness and faithfulness," has been felt at every level of the church's life and far beyond. Some historians have described them as the "forerunners of the ordination of women in Protestant denominations."[73]

Since 1889, the

Deaconess Sisters have been honored many times, both as individuals and as a sisterhood. A Centennial Commemorative, *The Deaconess Sisters: Pioneer Professional Women*, was published in 1989 to tell their story.

A "Resolution Honoring the 100th Anniversary of the Deaconess Sisterhood" was unanimously adopted, with a standing ovation, by the 750 delegates of the United Church of Christ General Synod Seventeen in 1989. This action "gratefully acknowledged the legacy of the Deaconess Sisters whose gifts and grace have abundantly enriched the life of the whole church."[74]

The Council for Health and Human Service Ministries of the United Church of Christ presented the Sisterhood with the "Hall of Fame Award" in 1972 and again in 1989, honoring them:

> For dedication to the ideas of Diakonia, for compassionate services
> to persons in need, for a particular awareness of the future role of
> health and healing in the ministry of the church, and for faithful-
> ness in responding to the love of our Lord Jesus Christ.[75]

2-26. St. Louis Deaconess Sisterhood, 1989. Front: Sisters Gertrude Poth, Executive Deaconess Frieda Ziegler, Elizabeth Lotz, Kate Nottrott. Back: Sisters Marie Lee, Elsie Jungerman, Flora Pletz, Bertha Grollmus, Velma Kampschmidt, Naomi Pielemeier and Mary Kramme. Not pictured were Sisters Marie Korte and Hulda Weise.

Chapter Three

THE MANAGEMENT
"Authority and Responsibility"

The founders of Deaconess Hospital in St. Louis had no textbooks on hospital organization and management in 1889. What they did have was a strong Christian commitment to care for the sick and the poor, knowledge about deaconess institutions in Europe where such care was given, and the services of two Deaconess Sisters who were consecrated to give leadership to the work.

Motivated by this combination of caring, commitment and consecration, the founders wrote and adopted Articles of Association which declared their purpose, gave clear-cut directives for authority and responsibility, and used a familiar model of organization to facilitate their work.

The Governing Board

The Articles of Association of The Evangelical Deaconess Society of St. Louis, Mo. made it very clear that the supreme authority and responsibility for all of its activities lay in a governing board.

> The management of this association shall be by a board of directors consisting of 12 persons who shall be elected by ballot at the annual meeting.[1]

Board meetings were held once a month, therefore considerable responsibility was delegated to the officers and the home committee.

> The board of directors shall elect from its members a lady, who with the sister superior of the Deaconess Home, and the president, recording secretary and treasurer, shall be a so-called home committee... It [the home committee] shall specially oversee and manage all matters pertaining to the Deaconess Home.[2]

The personal involvement of board members was an accepted management pattern in institutions of that day. Sometimes called the "Visiting Committee" or the

"Inspecting Committee," these board members were on the scene frequently and they took their responsibilities seriously as an expression of their Christian stewardship.

As the Deaconess Home and Hospital grew in size and complexity, more and more committees were appointed to carry out the board's functions. By 1935, when the first comprehensive textbook on hospital organization and management was written, the duties of the Deaconess governing board followed the generally accepted pattern of that day and could be described specifically as:

1. Responsibility for the selection of competent personnel;

2. Control of hospital funds;

3. Supervision of the physical plant.[3]

Since then, it has been observed by some experienced hospital executives that, "However they may be enumerated, board responsibilities all relate in one way or another to money, management, and medicine."[4]

Sister Katherine's Management with the Home Committee

Addressing the immediate necessity for competent management in the new Deaconess Home in 1889, the Evangelical Deaconess Society board of directors quickly appointed a home committee as instructed in the Articles of Association.

Management by committee is seldom easy, but in this case it seems to have worked. Sister Katherine Haack lived in the Deaconess Home as the sister superior and was the one member of the home committee most accessible for day-to-day management. She was therefore soon acknowledged as the person in charge.

Trained in deaconess methods and in nursing supervision, as mentioned earlier, Sister Katherine brought to her new position basic healthcare and management skills. She had also had many years of experience in the parsonage as a pastor's wife. The Deaconess Home and Hospital was at first very much like many large households of that era, and Sister Katherine managed it as such—under the watchful eyes of the other members of the home committee.

3-1. Sister Superior Katherine Haack, Deaconess Manager 1889-1897, in work garb.

Keeping records was one of Sister Katherine's daily duties, and she did this meticulously in two ledgers, one titled *Patient Admissions and Discharges* and another called *Household Income and Expenses.* Some of the entries for major expenses reveal not only the economy of the times but also the frugality practiced in the Deaconess Home. Typical are these monthly entries:

Gas Bill $4.65
Butcher 9.60
Groceries 20.75
6 Garbs for Sisters, $2 ea. 12.00

Flour was only 3 cents a pound, steak 12 cents a pound and coffee less than 20 cents a pound in 1889, but making ends meet was a constant challenge in the Deaconess Home.

Gifts Saved the Day

The generous gifts of Deaconess Society members helped to balance the budget. They brought everything from chicken soup to blankets and "cotton flannel night drawers" to help the Deaconess Sisters provide necessities, and Sister Katherine recorded those gifts as carefully as she handled money.

Evangelical church women's groups were the largest cash contributors to the new institution. Financial reports for 1889 record the following gifts, which were large sums of money in that day:

St. Peter's Women's Society - $75.00
St. Peter's Young Women's Society - .45.25
St. Paul's Women's Society - 100.00
Zion's Women's Society - 46.40
St. Luke's Women's Society - 55.05

54

To insure the accuracy of the records, the president of the board of directors kept a close check on finances and he audited the books regularly, signing his name at the end of each month's entries with the designation, "up to now exact."[5]

Early Success and Long-Range Planning

A total cash income of $1,406.03 during the first fiscal year was very encouraging to the members of the Deaconess Society. When the income for 1890 increased to $1,600.30, they began to do some long-range planning.

> The number of patients that applied for admission and for the services of deaconesses at private homes were so numerous that the Association at its annual meeting in January 1891 authorized its board of directors to look for a suitable location as a permanent home on which the necessary buildings could be erected.[6]

The First Lay Employees, 1891

In the meantime, the Deaconess Sisters were becoming so hard-pressed to keep up with the increasing work load that in January 1891, two "maids" were employed to assist them with housekeeping duties.

These first two lay employees at the Deaconess Home and Hospital were paid monthly wages of $14 and $9 respectively, plus room and board. This was in keeping with the prevailing wage scale for unskilled help in the 1890s. Many skilled workers at that time received only $2 for a twelve-hour work day. The Deaconess Sisters, meanwhile, received only room and board plus a small monthly stipend of a few dollars for personal necessities.[7]

Relocation on West Belle Place

In 1892 the board of directors found suitable property for a permanent location at 4117 West Belle Place and purchased it for $9,500. As mentioned earlier, a vacant public school building already on that property was remodeled as a Sisters' Home. Adjacent to it, a new three-story hospital building for forty patients was constructed at a cost of $22,000.

The day of dedication, January 15, 1893, was described as "a day of rejoicing and gratitude to God for all the friends of deaconess work."[8]

Publication of *The Evang. Diakonissenfreund*

In order to keep all of the friends of deaconess work informed about the progress of the hospital and the sisterhood, the Deaconess Society began a monthly publication in January 1893 entitled *Evang. Diakonissenfreund* (The Evangelical Deaconess Friend). The first issue explained:

> Since deaconess work is so new in the country and people are so unacquainted with its meaning and function, misjudgments and misunderstandings occurred about which enlightenment is necessary if interest among people should be awakened. That very purpose this paper shall serve.[9]

Printed in the German language, the *Diakonissenfreund* published articles which were written about deaconess work by members of the board of directors and by Sister Katherine Haack. Financial reports and the acknowledgments of gifts were also included, but the need for more deaconesses and more contributions was a recurring theme. The subscription price was 25 cents per year.

3-2. First page of *Diakonissenfreund*, with picture of new Deaconess Hospital, 1893.

The First "Large Donor"

At the new location, the patient census continued to grow, and plans for expansion were begun when a very generous gift of $9,000 was received in 1895 from a grateful patient, Mr. Henry Tibbe.

Mr. Tibbe was a prominent businessman from Washington, Missouri. His wife, as mentioned earlier, was a charter member of the Deaconess Society. He had previously given $800 for the first lot and building on West Belle Place and Mrs. Tibbe had given $100. He was therefore acknowledged as the largest donor to Deaconess Hospital for many years, a distinction he maintained until the 1930s.

With Mr. Tibbe's gift, the board of directors purchased the corner lot at Sarah and West Belle Place adjoining the hospital property, and construction was begun on a new three-story east wing estimated to cost $4,000.[10]

A Serious Management Crisis, 1897

In anticipation of the completion of this first new hospital addition, the members of the Deaconess Society concluded early in 1897 that more professional help was needed in the management of the rapidly growing institution. The board of directors was therefore instructed to seek the services of an Evangelical pastor to become superintendent and financial secretary. This decision was made with the intention of giving Sister Katherine Haack relief from administrative duties so that she could concentrate on the growing needs of leadership in patient care and the sisterhood. She concluded, however, that this action questioned her management ability, and most of the Deaconess Sisters agreed with her[11]

The Rev. Jacob Irion, a member of the board of directors, reported in the *Diakonissenfreund* that the board had tried to reach an agreement with the sister superior but that Sister Katherine had handed the books over in perfect condition and had, with other Deaconess Sisters, resigned and retreated into private life. This was, as described previously, a serious "backset" for deaconess work in St. Louis, but the foundations had been well established and were strong.[12]

Sister Katherine Haack's Management Legacy

Acknowledged as the first chief executive of Deaconess Hospital, Sister Katherine Haack was an able and dedicated leader. The extent of her management legacy is best described in a letter written to the board of directors on December 14, 1897, signed by all of the members of the Deaconess Medical Staff who said,

1. Under her most admirable management in the short space of nine years your institution has grown from nothing to be one of the most respected hospitals in the city; this too, with very limited means.

2. During this time every cent of the running expenses of the hospital has been paid by the earnings of the hospital itself.

3. The cleanliness of the hospital has been above criticism and beyond reproach, an imperative necessity to the success of a hospital.

4. The training of nurses who are capable and willing has been exceptionally fine, and all that could be desired.

5. In surgical and medical work no institution can boast of greater success.

6. The nurses trained under her have everywhere been received without question, and their work has been entirely satisfactory.

7. She has maintained the dignity of the institution.

8. She has been absolutely faithful in the trust.[13]

The Rev. Frederick P. Jens, Superintendent, 1898

In the management emergency which followed Sister Katherine's resignation, the board appointed Sister Magdalene Gerhold sister superior. As indicated earlier, she recommended the Rev. Frederick P. Jens for the new position of superintendent.

Rev. Jens was a highly regarded, thirty-two-year-old Evangelical pastor who had been one of Sister Magdalene's first patients in the hospital on Eugenia Street. He had already at that time expressed a strong interest in deaconess work.

When the board of directors contacted Rev. Jens early in 1898, he was serving a church in Kansas, and he responded that he could not leave that pastorate immediately. However, after several discussions with the search committee, he accepted the position of superintendent and pastor of the Deaconess Home and Hospital in St. Louis on agreement that he would begin May 1, 1898. His salary was $50 per month the first year, and he received $50 for moving expenses. In 1899, his salary was increased to $750 per year.[14]

3-3. Rev. Jens in First Superintendent's Office.

At the annual meeting of the Deaconess Society in 1899, President Walser of the board of directors reported the good news that:

> The past year, 1899, has been one of successful effort, rich bless-
> ings, and undisturbed harmony in our deaconess work, for which
> we are sincerely thankful to our heavenly Father. He has brought
> to our Home quite a number of able young women who entitle us
> to good hopes for efficient work in the future.[15]

The 15th Anniversary, A Celebration of Progress

Many people in the City of St. Louis were looking to the future with high hopes at that time. Preparations were underway for the 1904 World's Fair, which celebrated the centennial of the Louisiana Purchase and the great scientific and social progress of the previous century.[16]

The Deaconess Society, thankful for the progress which had been made in establishing deaconess work in St. Louis, also had much to celebrate. There were thirty Deaconess Sisters in the sisterhood by that time and so many patients in the hospital that ten lay employees were on the payroll. President Walser reported at the 15th Annual Meeting of the Society in 1904,

> In the past fifteen years the Lord has never permitted the want of the necessary means. Without any capital to begin with, the question never arose...what shall the workers eat, and wherewith shall they be clothed?.... Our deaconess home is not only free from debt but has a handsome surplus on hand.[17]

Part of that surplus was used in 1904 to publish a 15th anniversary commemorative booklet, *A Short History of the Deaconess Calling and of Deaconess Institutions.*

3-4. Deaconess Board of Directors, Fifteenth Anniversary, 1904. (Left to right front) Mrs. H. Welker, Mrs. F. L. Graubner, Pastor B. Pfeiffer, Pastor H. Walser, Pastor J. F. Klick, Mr. G. H. Wetterau, Miss Adele Hammacher; (back) Mr. F. A. Sudholt, Mr. W. H. Drese, Sister Superior Magdalene Gerhold, Mr. F. W. Helmkamp, Superintendent F. P. Jens, Pastor R. Pleger and Mrs. H. Stumborg.

It included articles designed not only to reach the members of Evangelical churches who had given their support but also to publicize deaconess work to some of the 20 million visitors expected to come to St. Louis that summer for the World's Fair. Also included in the booklet was the first published picture of the board of directors.[18]

Government Regulation in 1905

In 1905 the Deaconess Society was informed again at its annual meeting that "Our home and hospital is too small in every respect." Half of the Deaconess Sisters had to be housed in rented flats two blocks away from the hospital in order to make room for the large numbers of patients seeking admission to the hospital.

In response to this situation, the members of the Society authorized the board of directors to "build a new hospital on the grounds to meet the necessary requirements." The necessary "requirements" in this case referred to fireproof construction which had been demonstrated in the public buildings at the 1904 World's Fair a year earlier and had become mandatory in order to meet building codes in the City of St. Louis.[19]

First Fund-Raising Campaign, 1906

Estimates for constructing a new fireproof hospital building west of the existing Sisters' Home in 1905 came to about $77,000, a large amount of money in the early 1900s. But the Rev. J. F. Klick, serving again as the president of the Deaconess Society, was optimistic and he had some suggestions for raising the needed funds:

> If every member of the society donates on an average of $10 and if a collection is taken in all of our churches in the city and the surrounding territory, in addition to the nearly $10,000 which we now have on hand, we ought to be able to raise quite a large sum of money.[20]

Ten dollars was a big donation for most people to consider at that time. Yet, even though this was a relatively low-key campaign, enough funds were contributed so that the new hospital could be completed in 1906 at a cost of $106,000. The cost overrun was attributed to improvements in the plans during construction.

The next year, 1907, was described in the Deaconess Society's annual report as "the most prosperous year in the history of our Evangelical Deaconess Hospital and Home." And in 1908, there were enough contributions to purchase a residence next door to the hospital at a cost of $6,150 for the use of the superintendent, who had been living in rented quarters.[21]

Board Enlarged by Constitutional Amendment, 1909

Although the superintendent and the sister superior had always attended and participated in meetings of the board of directors, they did so only by invitation until 1909 when the Deaconess Society adopted the first amendment to its constitution enlarging the board of directors from twelve to fourteen members. The superintendent and sister superior were then included as ex-officio members.[22]

This was a strong vote of confidence for the administration of Superintendent Jens and Sister Superior Magdalene Gerhold. It was also a sign of the times. As "the amount of work done was greater than ever before," members of the board of directors had to depend increasingly on the superintendent for efficient hospital management. A job description, as such, had not yet been developed, but many board members were beginning to understand that the demands of the position were extraordinarily diverse and demanding. One authority in 1912 described it in this way and the Deaconess board seems to have agreed that,

> He [the superintendent] requires the strength of Samson, the meekness (at times) of Moses and the patience of Job. He ought to be a good beggar, a good business man, a physician, a bit of a lawyer, and have enough piety to admit him to the pulpit.[23]

In spite of such perceived requirements, there was no formal training program in hospital administration available at that time and successful superintendents, like Rev. Jens, learned on the job. They also learned from each other in institutional organizations such as the Protestant Deaconess Conference, an ecumenical deaconess association in the United States in which the Deaconess Society of St. Louis held membership and gave strong leadership.[24]

The Federation of Evangelical Deaconess Associations

Meanwhile, Evangelical Deaconess Associations were being organized in other cities across the land, and Deaconess Sisters from St. Louis were being sent to give professional leadership to many of the new deaconess institutions.

3-5. Protestant Deaconess Conference, 1908, Lincoln, Illinois. (Seated); Sisters Philippine Buehn, Magdalene Gerhold, Marie Stahlberg, Bertha Schlunk, Charlotte Boekhaus, Frieda Irion, Frieda Kaufmann, Caroline Pepmeier and Catherine Streib. (Standing): Supt. F. P. Jens, Pastor E. Bleibtreu, Mrs. Lydia Niebuhr, Pastor F. Reller, Sr. Beata Schick, Pastor G. W. Goebel, Sr. Winnie Lane, Pastor C. Bauer, Sr. Rosa Gerhold, Pastor Dr. J. Pister, president of the Evangelical Synod, Sr. Margaret Sievert, Prof. H. Hortsch, Sr. Hulda Echelmeier, Supt. Gustav Niebuhr, Sr. Louise Mernitz, Pastor Dr. J. Schneider, Sr. Lena Appel, Mr. C. Knorr, Miss Anna Gubler.

In order to strengthen the relationship between deaconess organizations in the Evangelical denomination, the First Conference of Evangelical Deaconess Homes and Associations was held at Deaconess Hospital in St. Louis in October 1909. Eight different institutions were represented by twenty-one delegates at this conference. They agreed to organize the Federation of Evangelical Deaconess Associations, and the Rev. Frederick P. Jens was elected to serve as the first president.

The Federation met annually, and in 1918 it published the basic guidebook, *Principles of Deaconess Work*, a translation by Rev. Jens of an earlier work in German. This English edition included additional brief histories and pictures of the work of thirteen Evangelical Deaconess Associations in the United States who were members of the Federation at that time. Later renamed the Federation of Evangelical Charities, this organization eventually became the Commission on Benevolent Institutions of the Evangelical Synod, a forerunner of the Council for Health and Welfare of the Evangelical and Reformed Church, now the Council for Health and Human Service Ministries of the United Church of Christ.[25]

Quarter-Century Achievements

By 1914 when the Deaconess Society in St. Louis celebrated its 25th anniversary, both the sisterhood and the hospital had prospered far beyond most expectations. A three-story annex for the east wing had been built in 1910 at a cost of $32,784 providing a new steam laundry on the lower level and rooms for more deaconesses above.

A commemorative 25th anniversary booklet, written by Superintendent Jens, included the 24th and 25th Annual Reports of the Deaconess Society, a history of deaconess work, and these achievements for the first twenty-five years:

Patients nursed in the hospital -	17,397
Patients served in private homes -	827
Patients given free care -	10%
Deaconesses in training -	144
Deaconesses serving in St. Louis -	47
Deaconesses serving in other institutions -	15
Budget for 1913 -	$55,029.93
Deaconess Support Fund -	$6,892.87
Value of entire property -	$180,000

3-6. Evangelical Deaconess Home and Hospital, with superintendent's home, left, and annex, right, 1914.

Many people had contributed to the success of deaconess work in St. Louis during the first twenty-five years, but Superintendent Jens reminded the members of the Deaconess Society, with his usual modesty, that "Above all, we owe the success of our work to the help of the Lord, our God."[26]

The Impact of World War I

There was little time, however, to rest on past accomplishments. In the summer

3-7. Deaconess Board of Directors, Twenty-fifth Anniversary, 1914.

of 1914, World War I began in Europe, and during the war years Deaconess Hospital faced new concerns.

With their strong German heritage and the use of the German language in many of their publications, members of the Deaconess Society and the hospital staff were careful, as were many German immigrants in St. Louis at that time, not to emphasize the German connection, and for good reason. One evidence of the emotional atmosphere in the city was that Berlin Avenue was renamed Pershing Boulevard, and there were reports that some people wanted to change the names of braunschweiger and bratwurst sausages to something sounding less traitorous.

No incidents against Deaconess Hospital were recorded, however, and the number of patients cared for annually doubled from 1914 to 1921 as did the number of operations performed. Costs also rose sharply and free care increased by one-third. The yearly gross income in 1921 also more than doubled to $122,780 and was $10,000 over expenditures.

Because of wartime frugality, the Deaconess Society did not publish statistics in printed annual reports from 1914 to 1920. The information for those years was given instead in a monthly periodical, the *Wohltatigskeitfreund* (Friend of the Needy), which was edited by Superintendent Jens and published jointly by Deaconess Hospital, the Evangelical Children's Home, and the Good Samaritan Home.[27]

Adoption of Hospital Standards, 1921

One of the reasons given for greater hospital occupancy in the early 1920s was the new attitude of the public toward hospitals, which had finally replaced the private home as the primary place for patient care, particularly for serious illnesses. As experts described it,

> The modern hospital's basic shape had been established by 1920. It had become central to medical education and was well integrated into the career patterns of regular physicians; in urban areas it had already replaced the family as the site for treating serious illness and managing death. Perhaps most important, it had already been clothed with a legitimizing aura of science and almost boundless social expectation.[28]

Equipped with a new Victor x-ray machine, a clinical laboratory, a pharmacy and two up-to-date operating rooms, Deaconess Hospital was well prepared to carry on its ministry of caring, healing and teaching in this new era.

> The result of these many new diagnostic and therapeutic aids was to effect cures of diseases formerly regarded as incurable, which in turn resulted in a notable increase in hospital occupancy.[29]

The increase in utilization of hospitals resulted in the realization that standards were needed in order to assure patients of the best quality of care. Anticipating this development, the American College of Surgeons drew up a "Minimum Standard" in 1918 which was a veritable constitution for hospitals. It set forth requirements for the proper care of the sick and its adoption was necessary for any hospital wishing approval for a medical education program.

In 1921 the board of directors and the medical staff of Deaconess Hospital, "desirous of having the work in the hospital conform to the standards set by the American Medical Association and American College of Surgeons," adopted resolutions requiring that those standards be enforced in the hospital.[30]

An Official Name Change

In another move toward standardization and modernization, and in an effort to disassociate itself from some of the negative aspects of a close German relationship, the Deaconess Society amended its constitution for the second time in 1921, thereby officially changing its name from the "Evangelischer Diakonissenverein von St. Louis, Mo." to "The Evangelical Deaconess Society of St. Louis, Mo."[31]

The English name had already been in use for many years in English-speaking situations. Official elimination of the German name emphasized the fact that deaconess work in St. Louis had become an American institution no longer primarily dependent on the German ethnic church community for support, yet closely related to the Evangelical Synod.

Superintendent Frederick P. Jens Honored

The close relationship of deaconess work to the Evangelical denomination was emphasized again in 1925 when Eden Theological Seminary awarded Superintendent Frederick P. Jens an honorary Doctor of Divinity degree "for outstanding leadership in deaconess institutions and the ministry of healing."

Among the Rev. Dr. Jens' achievements by that time, in addition to his service as the first superintendent and pastor of Deaconess Hospital, were his revitalization of the St. Louis Deaconess Sisterhood and School for Deaconesses, his leadership in the Protestant Deaconess Conference, his presidency of the Federation of Evangelical Deaconess Associations, and his editorship of the monthly periodical, *The Diakonissenfreund,* and its successors. He also edited, and translated from German, the *Principles of Deaconess Work,* adding historical information about Evangelical deaconess institutions in America which made it the primary training manual for deaconess work throughout the denomination.

At the same time, Superintendent Jens was known for his frequent appearances in the pulpits of Evangelical congregations speaking on behalf of deaconess work. He was also credited as the founding pastor in 1912 of Zion Evangelical Church of Union, Missouri.[32]

First Public Campaign for Funds, 1926

By 1926 the hospital facilities on West Belle Place were so overcrowded that many members of the Deaconess Society were convinced that the time had come to relocate on property purchased in 1918 on Oakland Avenue south of Forest Park.

In a special meeting of the Society on February 9, 1926, the board of directors was authorized to erect a Deaconess Home and Hospital on Oakland Avenue with living room for 100 deaconesses and a fully equipped hospital building with 175 patient beds. It was to be paid for with funds to be raised in a city-wide financial campaign.[33]

The goal of the campaign was $700,000, a tremendous sum of money in 1926, but preliminary planning encouraged the hope of success. An article published in the St. Louis Globe Democrat about a week before the opening of the campaign pointed out the public benefits of the proposed new hospital:

> In the new home that will be made possible through St. Louisians' response to the drive for $700,000 the work of the Deaconess Home and Hospital will be doubled. It will also be vastly improved for the new hospital's location is far away from the grime of the city, and in a neighborhood far away from the smoky and grimy atmosphere.[34]

The campaign was formally launched with a banquet for 1,500 volunteers at the City Club on September 24, 1926. Former Mayor Henry W. Kiel, who had accepted the chairmanship for the campaign, gave the keynote speech and urged the citizens of St. Louis to support this city-wide solicitation of funds. The next day the *St. Louis Globe-Democrat* reported:

> Amid the roar of a city gone mad over a pennant-winning baseball team, the campaign to raise $700,000 for the building of the new Deaconess Home and Hospital was launched last night.... The meeting was remarkable in many ways. It represented a union of 1500 men and women from all walks of life in the common cause. It was representative of the spirit of brotherhood and tolerance of the St. Louis citizenry in the common cause for humanity. There was a hospital to be built for the sick of St. Louis, and it was the duty of all loyal citizens to join hands to build it—that was the keynote of the speakers.[35]

The *St. Louis Times* and the *St. Louis Star*, two of the other major newspapers in the city at that time, likewise published lead articles about the campaign on September 24. The *Times* concluded its coverage with a statement from a letter written by former Mayor Kiel to thousands of those to be visited by the solicitors which said, "I am counting on your help. He who gives to a hospital gives to life itself."[36]

Conducted only from September 24 to October 4, this campaign was a great success in establishing Deaconess Hospital as a civic institution, and it reached a little less than 50 percent of its total financial goal in those first ten days. That was enough to allow plans for the new building to proceed on schedule.[37]

Membership in the American Hospital Association, 1927

Since Deaconess Hospital was now a civic as well as a church-related institution, and because changes in hospital management methods were occurring so rapidly that more information was needed to keep abreast of the times, the board of directors of the Deaconess Society passed a resolution at its meeting on July 21, 1927, that "our Deaconess Hospital shall join the American Hospital Association, if our superintendent favors such action."

The superintendent did favor this action, and in a meeting of the board of directors on September 15, it was decided that he and two of the Deaconess Sisters should attend the next meeting of the American Hospital Association scheduled for October in Minneapolis.

Disaster Services Tested

Two weeks later, on September 29, 1927, a devastating tornado swept through St. Louis. The original Deaconess Sisters' Home, which housed the chapel, the children's ward, the maternity department, the X-ray department, and rooms for some of the deaconesses and lay employees, was very heavily damaged. In the hospital itself, windows and skylights in the operating rooms and in other patient care areas were blown out completely. Miraculously, there were no lives lost among the 160 persons in the buildings at the time.

This major disaster was a severe test for the emergency services, the patient care services, and the management of the hospital. Insurance covered most of the tornado damage, and the board of directors authorized the beginning of repairs immediately.[38]

A $400,000 Loan Negotiated

The building committee, which included four members of the board of directors and the superintendent, held many consultations with members of the medical staff and with the deaconesses in charge of hospital departments. While repairs were made on the old building, plans were completed and submitted for the new building, which was projected to be a $1 million dollar venture.

In order to provide all of the necessary funds, a second city-wide financial campaign was conducted. It produced the gratifying sum of $223,207 which, in addition to the funds from the earlier campaign, allowed the building program to begin on schedule. A $400,000 loan was negotiated in 1929 so that, in spite of a staggering increase in costs, the main hospital building could be completed.[39]

Dedication of New Hospital, A Civic Event

The "magnificent new hospital on the hill," as it was described by many who attended the Dedication Service on Sunday, May 25, 1930, was built at a cost of $1,150,000 including equipment. The civic as well as the religious importance of this event was evident in that The Honorable Judge W. J. Neun, president of the St. Louis Board of Aldermen and vice-president of the hospital's first campaign for funds, gave one of the principal addresses.

3-8. Deaconess Hospital, 6150 Oakland Avenue, 1930.

Built to care for 225 patients eventually, and equipped to be as modern as possible, the new hospital was ready for occupancy in June 1930. The first three patients were admitted on June 10 and the transfer of all the patients from the old hospital on Sarah and West Belle was completed by June 26. Two floors of the hospital were used as housing for the Deaconess Sisters.[40]

Board of Directors and Administrative Staff Enlarged

To meet the challenges of operating a hospital twice as large as before, the Deaconess Society, which had 526 members by this time, approved some significant changes in management and administration.

3-9. 1930 Deaconess Board of Directors. Front: Mrs. H. Mangels, Miss Meta Peters, Sister Magdalene Gerhold, Miss Emma Kaechelen and Mrs. Bertha Brauss. Second row: Rev. O. Kienker, Rev. Theodore Oberhellmann and Mr. William Sodemann. Third row: Mr. H. Knickmeyer, Rev. Paul Press, President, and Mr. Oscar Grueninger. Fourth row: Rev. August C. Rasche, Superintendent F. P. Jens, and Mr. W. Geyer.

A new constitution adopted in 1930 enlarged the board of directors to sixteen to include four additional laymen. Four prominent St. Louis businessmen were elected: Mr. E. C. Hilmer, Mr. Charles Peters, Mr. F. A. Sudholt and Mr. H. E. Schultz. All four had given strong leadership in the second fund-raising campaign and their expertise in financial matters was seen as a way of strengthening the hospital, which had a debt of $400,000 on the new building.[41]

The administrative staff was also enlarged with the appointment of the Rev. Paul R. Zwilling of Louisville, Kentucky, as assistant superintendent. He was to serve as business manager of the institution, and the Rev. Dr. Jens was to be the general superintendent with the special task of continuing the duties of the pastor and chaplain in the hospital.

Assistant Superintendent Zwilling had served as a male nurse at Deaconess Hospital while a student at Eden Theological Seminary and he had developed a deep interest in the ministry of healing. Before assuming his new position on July 1, 1930, he took a short course in hospital management which was being offered at Deaconess Hospital in Chicago.

3-10. Administrative Staff, 1930. Assistant Superintendent Paul R. Zwilling, Director of Nurses Sister Beata Schick, Sister Superior Alvina Scheid and Superintendent Frederick P. Jens.

Completing the new administrative staff with Superintendent Jens and Assistant Superintendent Zwilling were Sister Beata Schick, director of nursing and nursing education, and Sister Alvina Scheid, the newly appointed sister superior.

A constitutional amendment adopted by the Deaconess Society in 1931 gave the sister superior voice and vote on the board of directors so that the sisterhood would be represented in policy decisions.[42]

Medical Staff Reappointed by Board, 1931

The transition from the old to the new hospital also brought changes in the medical staff.

There had been a hint at difficulties in the report of the president of the board of directors in 1930, but drastic action took place in March 1931 when the board asked the whole medical staff to resign! The issue seems to have been related primarily to the effort of some members of the staff to limit membership on the medical staff and thus control both the staff and the hospital.

Maintaining its constitutional authority, the board of directors proceeded to reappoint the medical staff as provided in amendments to the constitution of the Deaconess Society which were adopted at a special meeting held on May 27, 1931.[43]

Financial Hardships in the Great Depression

Meanwhile, the financial hardships of the depression had resulted in other management problems. On July 17, 1930, the board of directors found it necessary to borrow $60,000 "to meet current expenses." As the collection of hospital bills became more and more difficult, economies of every kind were adopted throughout the hospital in order to save money. The president of the board of directors reported that "a systematic, business-like conduct of all departments" had been secured and that all were more efficiently organized than ever before.[44]

The entire work force of the hospital in 1931 consisted of ninety-five Deaconess Sisters, the superintendent, the assistant superintendent, one roentgenologist, one pathologist, three interns, three externs and seventy-six lay employees. This was the largest staff on record up to that time, and 591 more patients were served that year than in any previous year in the history of the hospital.[45]

By the summer of 1932 hard times grew worse. One-fourth of the labor force in the nation was jobless and more than 1,400 banks failed, a trend that showed every sign of continuing. Superintendent Jens reported:

> Never before in the history of our Deaconess Hospital have we been in such financial straits as during the months of July, August and September 1932, nor so hard pressed in meeting our obligations.[46]

By way of explanation, the Rev. August C. Rasche, president of the Deaconess Society, reported that 22 per cent of the patients served during 1932 were charity or part-pay patients. He added, however, that "We dare not forsake the destitute sick."[47]

In a continuing effort to improve efficiency and reduce costs, two electrical generators were installed in the power plant in 1936 at a cost of $36,189.00 to supply the total electrical needs of the hospital, thus reducing the necessity to purchase power from an outside source.

By the end of 1936 it could be reported at the annual meeting of the Deaconess Society that "The financial status of the institution in general is substantial and sound."[48]

The Introduction of Health Insurance, 1936

One of the most significant contributions to the financial stability of both the hospital and its patients, however, was the board of directors' decision to have Deaconess Hospital become a member of the new Blue Cross Hospital Service Plan in 1936.

With increasing numbers of patients seeking medical care in hospitals each year and with many of them unable to pay for such care, the American Hospital Association endorsed the principle of group prepayment for hospital bills in February 1933 and then established standards for approval of such plans.

Based on the principle of group prepayment, the Blue Cross Plan enabled a large number of workers and their dependents to receive hospitalization in the institution of their choice for a nominal prepaid premium. At the same time, the Blue Cross Plan was of great assistance to Deaconess and other participating hospitals by stabilizing their income, by helping them develop uniform account-

3-11. Fiftieth Anniversary Board of Directors, 1939. Front: Mrs. Edward Harding, Mrs. John Mack, Rev. Dr. Paul Press, President, Mr. Emil Klick, Miss Emma Kaechelen, Miss Meta Peters. Back: Mr. William Samel, Mr. F. E. Hannemann, Mr. William Sodemann, Rev. Erich E. Leibner, Rev. H. C. Toelle, Rev. Arno H. Franke, Mr. S. C. Carlstrom.

ing and other business procedures to increase efficiency, and by "enabling them to continue on a high plane of professional excellence."[49]

"50 Years of Deaconess Ministry"

Professional excellence was always a high priority at Deaconess Hospital, and the Deaconess Society could point to many accomplishments as it prepared to celebrate the 50th anniversary of deaconess ministry in St. Louis.

Statistics for the first fifty years were impressive:

Patients cared for in the hospital	105,614
Patients cared for in their homes	1,005
Patients treated free of charge	10%
Deaconesses who entered sisterhood	453
Deaconesses in sisterhood, 1939	143
Deaconess Support Fund balance	$51,243
Deaconess Society Members	604

Property value, hospital buildings and equipment $1,150,000
Indebtedness $281,550
Projected yearly income $395,000

On Sunday, March 19, 1939, the 50th Anniversary of Deaconess Hospital and of the Deaconess Sisterhood was observed in the Evangelical and Reformed Churches of the St. Louis area. A rotogravure commemorative booklet, *50 Years of Deaconess Ministry*, with the fifty-year statistics, many pictures, a brief historical chronology and a suggested order of worship, was published for this occasion and widely distributed during the anniversary year.[50]

The Retirement of Superintendent Frederick P. Jens, 1939

On December 14, 1939, as the 50th anniversary year was coming to a close, the Rev. Dr. Frederick P. Jens informed the board of directors of the Deaconess Society that because of ill health he wished to retire as superintendent. He had seen Deaconess Hospital grow from a 40-bed facility with six Deaconess Sisters in 1898 to a modern, fully accredited health institution with 175 patient beds, 144 deaconesses, more than 100 lay employees, and a reputation for being both a civic and a church-related hospital providing health care and education of the highest quality.

3-12. Superintendent, Rev. Dr. Frederick P. Jens, 1940.

Throughout his forty-two years at Deaconess Hospital, Superintendent Jens served not only as an able and outstanding healthcare administrator and dedicated pastor, but also as a prolific writer and tireless advocate of deaconess work as a caring, healing and teaching ministry.

76

In recognition of his many years of devoted service to Deaconess Hospital, the board of directors appointed the Rev. Dr. Jens Superintendent Emeritus on January 20, 1940, and provided him with retirement benefits. Failing health made his retirement a brief one, however, and he died on July 7, 1940.[51]

The Rev. Paul R. Zwilling, Superintendent and Chaplain

After serving almost ten years as assistant superintendent, the Rev. Paul R. Zwilling was installed as acting superintendent of Deaconess Hospital on February 23, 1940, and he was appointed superintendent and chaplain on February 1, 1941.

Superintendent Zwilling's administration began with immediate attention and strong leadership for the fund-raising campaign to build a Sisters' Home, which had been authorized by the Deaconess Society at its annual meeting in December 1939. As described previously, this campaign was called an effort "For Greater Service," and it succeeded in raising $203,243.

Construction of the new six-story Sister's Home began in 1940 on property immediately west of the hospital. It was completed at a cost of $449,700 plus furnishings which were provided by the newly organized Deaconess Women's Auxiliary.

Dedication of the Sisters' Home on March 15, 1942, was the beginning of a new era of health care and health education at Deaconess Hospital. Facilities for the School for Deaconesses were excellent, and greater service to patients was made possible when rooms on the third floor of the hospital were vacated by the Deaconess Sisters who moved into their new home, described as "a dream come true" and "a prayer answered."[52]

3-13. Deaconess Sisters' Home and Hospital, 1942

A New Administrative Staff, 1942

Greater service to patients required more personnel throughout the hospital. This, in turn, resulted in more responsibilities for the administrative staff. Some significant changes in leadership followed.

Sister Superior Alvina Scheid requested less demanding duties and resigned in March 1942. As described earlier, the board of directors accepted her resignation with regret and honored her for devoted service to the sisterhood during the years of its largest membership and for her outstanding leadership in helping to nurture the founding of the Deaconess Women's Auxiliary.

Sister Olivia Drusch was installed as sister superior in July 1942 to succeed Sister Alvina. At the same time, Sister Hilda Muensterman was installed as director of nurses and director of the School for Deaconesses. Sister Ella Loew, who had been serving as night administrator, continued in that position.

To complete the new administrative staff, Mr. J. F. Mocker was appointed as an assistant to Superintendent Zwilling and as business manager, the first layman to hold that position at Deaconess. He had given outstanding financial guidance to the Greater Service Campaign and was highly regarded for his leadership ability.[53]

3-14. Sister Superior Olivia Drusch and Director of Nurses and Nursing Education Sister Hilda Muensterman, new members of the Administrative Staff, 1942.

3-15. Mr. J. F. Mocker, Business Manager, first lay member of the Administrative Staff.

World War II Scarcities

With the outbreak of World War II, the new administrative staff at Deaconess soon faced a scarcity of trained personnel in all departments of the hospital. Business manager Mocker stated that the personnel problem had given his office much concern and had "made heavy demands upon our loyal stand-bys in the office force who have stood by us through thick and thin.... The demand for war workers has unbalanced both our wage scale as well as our time table."[54]

Food shortages and food rationing were problems for the dietary department. Miss Margaret Graebner, chief dietician for Deaconess Hospital, served as a dietary advisor for the St. Louis Rationing Board beginning in April 1943, and she was given much credit for helping the board change forms to aid those on severe diets to receive sufficient food.[55]

Centralized purchasing, which was installed in 1944 throughout the hospital under Mr. Mocker's supervision, brought greater efficiency and resulted in significant cost reductions.

Meanwhile, with regard to obtaining other necessary supplies in the hospital, Mr. Mocker said that the slogan for almost every department had become, "Use it up...wear it out...make it do...or do without."[56]

Gerhold Hall Dedicated, 1947

To meet the growing shortage of trained nurses resulting from World War II, the Deaconess Society approved the School of Nursing for lay students in 1942 and accepted the first lay students in February 1943. Explaining the need for this new educational program and reassuring Deaconess Society members about the quality of nurse's training to be offered, the Rev. Arno W. Franke, president of the board of directors, said,

> The realities by which we are confronted demand of us more young women, who, though not deaconesses, have been trained under the direct and vigilant supervision of the Deaconess Order.[57]

With the World War II coming to a close, the Deaconess Society held a special meeting on June 14, 1945, and authorized the construction of an addition to the Sisters' Home to accommodate the growing student body.

Work began in August 1945 on the new building, estimated to cost about $314,000. Despite postwar shortages of some building supplies, it was completed and dedicated on September 28, 1947. Classrooms and a beautiful new chapel occupied the first floor. Rooms for student nurses and students in the School of X-ray Technology, newly established that year, were on the two upper floors. The building was named Gerhold Hall in 1951 in honor of Sister Magdalene Gerhold.[58]

3-16. Gerhold Hall, 1946.

The Retirement of Administrator Paul R. Zwilling

A new constitution adopted by the Deaconess Society in 1945 provided for the lay School of Nursing, an enlarged board of directors of eighteen members, a change making the superintendent's title "hospital administrator," and an

3-17. Administrator and Chaplain, Rev. Paul R. Zwilling, 1948.

80

age of sixty-five the mandatory retirement age for members of the administrative staff. This age limit reflected the passage of the Social Security Act of 1935, which made sixty-five the age for retirement with full benefits.

The Rev. Paul R. Zwilling was the first member of the administrative staff to reach sixty-five years of age under the new constitution of the Deaconess Society. In July 1947 he announced his retirement, to become effective as soon as a successor could be appointed.

Rev. Zwilling had given administrative leadership to Deaconess Hospital for eighteen years. He helped manage the hospital through the difficult depression years and in the transition involving the adoption of the first health insurance program approved at Deaconess Hospital, the Blue Cross Plan. Under his supervision, the Sisters' Home and Gerhold Hall were completed to provide space for greatly needed expansion. The founding of the Deaconess Auxiliary, the establishment of the School of Nursing for lay students, and the opening of the School of X-ray Technology were also important accomplishments during his administration.

In the larger healthcare community, Rev. Zwilling served as president of the Missouri Hospital Association in 1938, president of the American Protestant Hospital Association in 1939, and as president of the Commission on Benevolent Institutions of the Evangelical and Reformed Church in 1946.

The board of directors expressed gratitude to Rev. Zwilling and granted him retirement benefits   when his successor was installed.[59]

The Rev. Carl C. Rasche, Administrator and Chaplain, 1948

At the annual meeting of the Deaconess Society in November 1947 it was reported that the new administrator, the Rev. Carl C. Rasche, had been selected but that he could not accept the position until May. The Rev. Richard A. Miller, president of the board of directors, explained:

> There was hesitancy at first to approach Rev. Carl Rasche because of the invaluable contribution he is making in the work of Caroline Mission [as superintendent and pastor].   However, after much consideration and discussion, the committee decided that the matter should be discussed with Rev. Rasche, prayerfully seeking that God's will might be done.   After several

conferences with Rev. Rasche, he felt that it was a challenge and a call from God to accept. However, realizing his responsibility to Caroline Mission, he would consider it only under the condition he could remain at the Mission until next May so that its present fall and winter program might not be impaired. This condition has been accepted. We, who know Rev. Carl Rasche, his spirit and his abilities, feel that he will give our institution the leadership we need.[60]

3-18. Administrator and Chaplain, Rev. Carl C. Rasche, 1948.

The new administrator and chaplain began his duties at Deaconess Hospital on May 15, 1948, and he was officially installed on November 14. Although he had already had six years' experience in institutional administration following his graduation from Elmhurst College and Eden Theological Seminary and had previously completed a year of graduate study in Sociology/Group Work at Northwestern University, he took an intensive course in hospital administration in 1948 at St. Louis University to prepare further for his new position.[61]

High Occupancy and Higher Costs

The growing shortage of patient beds and rapidly rising hospital costs had both become matters of national and local concern when Administrator Rasche began his work at Deaconess.

The number of patients seeking hospital admission during the postwar years had increased dramatically as a result of many scientific medical breakthroughs and the introduction of group health insurance to help pay for the costs. There had been an increase of 1,254 patients served at Deaconess in 1947 over the previous year, and that increase was expected to double by the end of 1948.

At the same time, hospital costs and charges were also rising dramatically, with salaries alone having doubled and tripled since 1942 yet less than those paid by industry.

Operating expenses at Deaconess Hospital in 1947 were $8.24 per patient day, only a slight increase over the $7.59 of the previous year. That was considerably lower than the national average which was $11.39 per patient day in 1947, but hospitals were still operating at a deficit because of limited charges, and Deaconess Hospital was no exception.

To help make up this deficit, a new schedule of room rates was approved by the board of directors in November 1948. This increase in charges was projected as barely enough to produce the additional income needed to cover costs. Salary increases alone required about $25,000, due partly to a reduction of hours in the work week.[62]

The 40-Hour Week for All Employees, 1949

Recognizing the importance of good labor relation policies, and being committed to high standards and fairness in the workplace, the board of directors approved a 40-hour work week to be put into effect for all employees beginning January 1, 1949. Although some other hospitals in the St. Louis area had placed selected groups of employees on the 40-hour week, Deaconess Hospital was the first to have all of its employees on the 40-hour week program.[63]

Some Deaconess employees had given many years of loyal, continuous service to the hospital, often without regard to hours. At the Employee Recognition Dinner in 1949 the board of directors honored 78 employees who had served five years or more for a combined total of 780 years.

Four longtime employees received special honors in 1949 for faithful service of more than twenty-five years: Margaret Orgel, kitchen helper for 36 years; Dee Hutt, meat cutter and chef for 28 years; Arlie Groenemann, chief engineer for 26 years; and Fred Wilson, laundry supervisor for 25 years.

In response to this recognition, Dee Hutt spoke for all of these dedicated co-workers in health care when he said, "I enjoy being part of an institution rendering service to God and humanity."[64]

Board Elects Two Synod Representatives

In an effort to keep as many people as possible involved in the hospital's ministry of rendering service to God and humanity, the Deaconess Society had always maintained a close relationship with the church. In 1949 the Society was asked to strengthen that relationship further by approving as members on its board of directors two representatives, one a clergyman and the other a layman, to be elected with voice and vote for two-year terms by the Missouri Valley Synod of the Evangelical and Reformed Church.

In response to this request, the constitution and bylaws of the Deaconess Society were amended, and the Rev. Dr. Erwin H. Bode and Mr. Henry Decker were the first two synodical representatives to be elected to the board under this provision.[65]

Patient Receipts, $1 Million in 1949

With a stated capacity of 250 beds, an average of 264 adult and pediatric patients were nevertheless cared for daily during 1949 by converting some private rooms to semi-private facilities. This high rate of occupancy brought the total receipts from patients that year to more than $1 million for the first time at Deaconess Hospital.

The growing number of chronically and mentally ill patients and the over 100 percent occupancy rate encouraged the Deaconess Society to approve unanimously the plans in 1949 to proceed with the erection of a new building for such patients.[66]

Walter J. Stradal Directs $500,000 Campaign

The first step in the plans to erect additional facilities was to raise at least $500,000 by popular subscription to make the hospital eligible for matching government funds available from a Hill-Burton Grant.

Mr. Walter J. Stradal, an experienced journalist and fund-raiser, joined the hospital staff in 1950 as an assistant to the administrator to plan and direct this campaign.

Beginning in March 1951 as a quiet effort among friends of the hospi-

3-19. Mr. Walter J. Stradal, Assistant Administrator

tal, the building fund reached $361,000 by December. This was almost three-fourths of the goal, subscribed by 4,000 persons. Great rejoicing took place in 1952 when the $500,000 campaign went "over the top." It eventually reached $1,000,000!

This effort was the first of the hospital's campaigns up to that time to reach its complete goal within the original time frame much less double the amount. It was the largest contribution of funds ever secured in a single Deaconess effort and Mr. Stradal expressed appreciation for the whole Deaconess family when he said,

> Our thanks go to churches, church organizations, our Women's Auxiliary, the Medical Staff, Sisterhood, Alumnae, employees, and the School of Nursing students, for their help. And special thanks to the good folk of our community—business and professional men and women, and firms—who responded, many contributing to Deaconess for the first time.... We are proud, yes! We are grateful beyond expression![67]

A $794,194 Hill-Burton Grant, 1953

A Hill-Burton federal grant of $794,194 was received in November 1953 toward the construction of the new Deaconess Memorial Building (as it was then called) and groundbreaking occurred November 3.

A mortgage loan for $700,000 in 1954 enabled the board of directors to pay off the remaining $250,000 indebtedness incurred on the construction of Gerhold Hall and to help finance the cost of construction and equipment for the new expansion project.[68]

The 65th Anniversary, Biggest Year To Date

More patients were served and more babies were born at Deaconess Hospital in 1954 than in any previous year of the hospital's history. Moreover, the School of Nursing had its largest enrollment ever and accepted the largest freshman class in its history in September of that year.

The Rev. Dr. Elmer H. Hoefer, president of the board of directors, expressed gratitude in the annual report for 1954 for all who had served in the spirit of diaconia toward that accomplishment:

We praise God for the vision which initiated our great institution, and thank Him, that through these 65 years, there have always been dedicated hearts and hands willing to carry the torch of faith.

Changes in the administrative staff also occurred in 1954. Mr. Walter J. Stradal, who had so ably directed the building fund campaign as an assistant to the administrator, was appointed the assistant administrator. His responsibilities included not only the building fund and public relations but also some of the hospital departments previously managed by Mr. J. F. Mocker, who retired after twelve years of faithful service as business manager.

Sister Olivia Drusch was appointed the director of the School of Nursing and of nursing service replacing Sister Hilda Muensterman, who resigned to be married. Sister Frieda Ziegler was appointed as sister superior to replace Sister Olivia Drusch and the title, "sister superior" was changed to "executive deaconess."[69]

3-20. 65th Anniversary Board of Directors, 1954. Front: Mrs. Emma Moeller, Mrs. Amanda Stockhoff, Sister Olivia Drusch, Sister Frieda Ziegler, Mrs. Edgar Crecelius, Mrs. Jeanette Ehlhardt. Middle: President Rev. Dr. Elmer H. Hoefer, Rev. Dr. Erwin H. Bode, Administrator Carl C. Rasche, Assistant Administrator Walter J. Stradal, Mr. Dewey Carlstrom, Mr. William A. Friend. Back: Rev. Paul Rahmeier, Rev. Paul Stock, Rev. Paul Prell, Mr. Willis Ehrhardt, Mr. Conrad Mueller, Mr. Chester Bleikamp, Mr. Fred Kaiser.

Deaconess Memorial Building Dedicated, 1956

Fifteen hundred "friends of Deaconess" attended the dedication service for the new Deaconess Memorial Building on October 21, 1956, and an offering received that day amounted to $10,000. The first patient was admitted to the new facilities on November 27.

The four-story new building provided 84 beds for chronically ill patients and 74 for the mentally ill, increasing the total bed capacity to 410. This made Deaconess Hospital one of the larger hospitals in the St. Louis area and in the Evangelical and Reformed Church denomination at this time.

The addition of new patient beds necessitated the expansion of many other departments in the hospital as well. Renovation of the laboratory, the X-ray and the medical record departments, and the food service areas in the main hospital building were included as part of the expansion project, as were the laundry and the power plant.

A new Deaconess Memorial Chapel, adjoining the new building, honored the Deaconess Sisters and was constructed without the aid of federal funds. The cost of $75,000 was made possible by special gifts from friends of the hospital.[70]

3-21. Deaconess Memorial South Building, 1956.

Forty-seven additional development projects were completed in 1957 and another thirteen were in progress. Eleven sizeable projects, expected to cost about $3,136,000, were reported as still being urgently needed.[71]

Board-Appointed Chiefs of Service, A Turning Point

Early in 1958 the board of directors and the medical staff were informed by a surveyor for the Council on Medical Education and Hospitals of the American Medical Association that although Deaconess Hospital had excellent facilities and an outstanding medical staff, changes in the medical staff organization were urgently needed in order to maintain the hospital's accreditation as a teaching hospital.

To meet these recommendations, the board of directors, after careful deliberation and many consultations with the medical staff, approved revised Medical Staff Bylaws, Rules and Regulations effective October 1, 1958.[72]

The most immediate and drastic change brought about by the adoption of the new Medical Staff Bylaws was the provision for board-appointed chiefs of service and the creation of a medical administrative committee which was directly responsible to the board of directors for the proper medical practices and patient care carried on in the hospital. It was also charged with the responsibility of determining policies and procedures in medical education.

As a result of this drastic change in the medical staff organization, considerable sharp differences of opinion existed between the medical staff and the board of directors. But the board of directors maintained its constitutional authority, and the reorganization of the medical staff was a turning point, strengthening Deaconess Hospital as an outstanding institution both for patient care and for teaching purposes. It was fully accredited not only by the Joint Commission on Accreditation of Hospitals but its medical education programs were approved by the Council on Medical Education.[73]

Board of Directors Renamed Board of Trustees, 1959

With operating income for the hospital almost $3 million in 1959, and free service totaling more than $104,000 for the year, the Deaconess Society adopted revisions in its constitution which changed the name of the board of directors to the board of trustees, added two community members to the board bringing the total membership to twenty-eight and provided for the appointment of a controller in the finance office.

Mr. Harry J. Meinhardt, who had been a cost accountant in the finance office for nine years, was promoted to the newly created position of controller and was made a member of the administrative staff. Also new to the administrative staff in 1959 was Chaplain Ernest W. Luehrman, appointed by the board of trustees to succeed Chaplain Paul E. Irion, who had resigned to accept a position on the faculty of Lancaster Theological Seminary.[74]

1960 Annual Report Dedicated to Faithful Employees

Declaring that "our faithful employees are among the most important people at Deaconess," the board of trustees dedicated the 71st Annual Report of the Deaconess Society in 1960 "to our FAITHFUL EMPLOYEES." Ten had been employed at that time for more than twenty-five years:

Dee Hutt (chef)	39 years
Arlie Groenemann (chief engineer)	37 years
Edgar Barebo (porter)	30 years
Helen Engelage (cook)	30 years
Martha Lix (cook)	30 years
Frieda Deuschle (accountant)	29 years
Edna Stegner (pharmacy secretary)	29 years
Emma Gumper (cook)	28 years
Pearl Williams (cook)	28 Years
Erna Baltzer (finance officer)	27 years

Aware that the highest quality of patient care depends greatly on the total care given in the hospital, the board of trustees emphasized in the annual report for 1960 that those who provide "a good physical plant, the equipment, the food, house-cleaning, laundry and all of the ancillary services that make up the modern hospital program...are all making an extremely valuable contribution to good patient care."

Through the years many, many long-term dedicated Deaconess employees have been honored at annual Employee Recognition Dinners.

As tangible evidence of concern for good employee relations and fairness in the workplace, the board of trustees enrolled Deaconess employees in the Social Security Program in 1951, when such became possible for the first time for not-for-profit institutions. In January 1962 the Retirement Pension Program for employees was inaugurated.

3-22. Deaconess Employees Honored, 1957: with Administrator Carl C. Rasche(c.)- Dee Hutt, Arlie Groenemann, Fred Wilson, Margaret Orgel, Louis Urban, Helen Engelage, Martha Lix, and Edgar Barebo.

With more than 750 employees on the staff, the board of trustees appointed Mr. William C. Davidson in January 1963 as the first full-time personnel manager at Deaconess Hospital and as a member of the administrative staff.[75]

3-23. "Twenty-five Year Plus" Honorees, 1963: Receiving congratulations from Administrator Carl C. Rasche, left, are: Arlie Groenemann, Erna Baltzer, Mabel Wulff, Pearl Williams, Emma Gumper, Frieda Deuschle, Edna Stegner, and Marie Wieman.

Administrator Rasche Honored for Health Care Leadership

Administrator Carl C. Rasche was awarded the honorary degree of Doctor of Humane Letters in 1961 from Elmhurst College "in recognition of distinguished service rendered as Pastor, Hospital Administrator and Leader in the field of Social Service."

In addition to his duties at Deaconess, Administrator Rasche had represented the hospital locally and nationally. He served as president of the Council for Health and Welfare Services of the Evangelical and Reformed Church, now known as the Council for Health and Human Service Ministries of the United Church of Christ; secretary of the Board of Trustees, St. Louis Blue Cross Plan; president of the American Protestant Hospital Association; president of the Hospital Association of Metropolitan St. Louis; and as the chairman of the Committee on Accreditation of the Chaplain's Association, now the College of Chaplains. He was also named an Honorary Fellow of the Chaplains' Association in 1958.[76]

The Rev. Richard P. Ellerbrake, Associate Administrator, 1964

Deaconess Hospital was growing so rapidly that in 1962 the board of trustees agreed, on recommendation of Administrator Rasche, to appoint an assistant administrator trained in hospital administration.

The Rev. Richard P. Ellerbrake was appointed assistant administrator-elect in 1962 and was enrolled in the course at Washington University leading to a Master's Degree in Hospital Administration. An ordained clergyman in the United Church of Christ, he had served as the director of the Back Bay Mission, Biloxi, Mississippi, a United Church of Christ congregation and community center.

In June 1964 Rev. Ellerbrake was appointed assistant administrator of Deaconess

3-24. Associate Administrator, Rev. Richard P. Ellerbrake, 1964.

Hospital. In October 1964, under revisions in the bylaws adopted by the Deaconess Society, he was made associate administrator and associate pastor of Deaconess Chapel, continuing a long tradition of clergy leadership in the hospital administration.[77]

75th Anniversary Begins "Decade of Development"

Newspaper headlines November 15, 1964, announced: "Deaconess Looks Back — And Forward, HOSPITAL OBSERVES 75TH YEAR BY PLANNING $8 MILLION EXPANSION."

Several years of consultations, surveys and planning preceded the announcement of this expansion, called the "Decade of Development Program." Nationally-known hospital consultants, Booz, Allen and Hamilton, Inc., worked with the planning committee of the board of directors, and it was determined that although Deaconess Hospital occupied one of the finest and most strategic hospital sites in the metropolitan community, new space was urgently needed for ancillary and support services which had increased significantly during the previous five years.

3-25. 75th Anniversary Board of Directors, 1964. Left around table: Mr. Oliver G. Wetterau, Mr. Roy Chipps, Mr. Edgar Crecelius, Mr. Howard Weigel, Mr. Wendell Huntington, Administrator Carl C. Rasche, President Rev. Dr. Herbert H. Wintermeyer, Rev. Paul Press, Jr., Mrs. Alvin S. Hansen, Mr. Carl Holekamp, Jr., Mr. Russell L. Savage, Mr. Edgar E. Krieger. Back: Rev. Dr. Carl W. Klein, Rev. Lorenz Eichenlaub, Mrs. Esther Tibbles, Mrs. Alice Metz.

An Open House on Sunday, November 8, celebrated the achievements of "75 Years of Deaconess Ministry" and featured an address by the Hon. Dr. Walter H. Judd, former medical missionary and congressman. To express appreciation to all who had contributed to those achievements, a big band musical tribute by "Fred Waring and His Pennsylvanians" was presented at Kiel Auditorium through the courtesy of donors for 3,000 invited guests, the "Employees and Friends of Deaconess."

To help finance the Decade of Development Program, the Deaconess Society, which had 900 members in its 75th year, authorized a $3 million capital fund campaign at its annual meeting in December 1964. The remainder of the $8 million needed for the over-all cost of the project was to be met by a longterm mortgage.

Under the leadership of Walter J. Stradal, serving full time as director of development and public relations, the capital fund campaign passed the $2 million mark by the end of 1965, and new construction began. The campaign continued and soon reached a highly successful conclusion of over $3 million. In 1966, a $552,998 Hill-Burton Grant of matching funds from the federal government helped to complete the construction.[78]

Medicare, A Significant Innovation in 1966

Called by many "one of the significant innovations of our generation," Medicare became a reality on July 1, 1966, after intense study and preparation by governmental, hospital, medical and health insurance experts.

No one could predict accurately what the immediate response of the then 19 million people 65 years of age and older in the United States might be to this new program, much less whether or not the proposed payments from the government would be adequate. Many questions remained to be answered.

Payments made for Medicare services were at first extremely slow and in some cases less than half of billings. Some hospitals had to borrow funds to meet expenses. However, the percentage of occupancy at Deaconess Hospital increased only slightly as a result of Medicare. This was due in part to the fact that Deaconess was already serving a relatively higher percentage of patients 65 years of age and older as compared to other hospitals, and there was simply no more room. The small increase in occupancy was also due to the fact that, as Administrator Rasche reported at the end of the first three months, "the Utilization Review and Utilization Advisory Committees have received the

93

utmost cooperation from the Medical Staff and, as a result, unnecessary hospitalization has been kept to the very minimum."[79]

Deaconess Enters the Computer Era, 1968

With the purchase and installation of a Medelco "Total Hospital Information System" in 1968, Deaconess Hospital entered the computer era.

Unique to St. Louis hospitals, the Medelco system utilized the latest in Space Age and business technology. A data acquisition processing and retrieval system designed exclusively for hospital use, the Medelco system was used in conjunction with a National Cash Register mainframe computer installation.

The Medelco system consisted of punched cards coded for patient information and for medical and hospital instructions; optical card readers; teletype printers; and a solid state central processor which performed the functions of message control, printout control, bed information processor, charge information processing, and accounting. Information about the patient could thus be automatically communicated to all points in the hospital that needed to know and retain that information for future uses.

3-26. Homer Schmitz, Director of Data Processing, 1968.

The savings in time and human effort made possible by this new system were enormous, and these savings alone more than paid for the $286,000 cost of installation. The system contributed to a 1.4 day reduction in patient stay, resulting in savings to patients averaging $70 per stay.

By 1970 when the system was fully implemented, Deaconess became one of less than twenty hospitals in the country with this level of electronic sophistication. As such it became one of the focal points of medical information system technology, a world-class operation which was visited and evaluated by representatives of more than 175 hospitals from 38 states and 26 foreign countries.

Homer H. Schmitz, Ph. D., a graduate of Eden Theological Seminary and an ordained United Church of Christ minister, set up the new data processing system at Deaconess Hospital and he was appointed director of data processing in 1968. He subsequently was named executive director of management systems and then vice president and director of management services.

Since 1968, the data processing and communications system at Deaconess Hospital has been regularly updated. In 1976 MEDICS, a new hospital information and communications system, was installed to replace the Medelco-NCR System enabling Deaconess Hospital to retain its leadership role in information systems technology.[80]

Board-appointed, Full-time Chiefs of Service, 1968

The board of trustees appointed full-time chiefs of service on a contractual basis in 1968. Recommended by the medical administrative committee and supported by the medical staff, this action was taken in order to maintain the high patient care standards of Deaconess Hospital and accreditation for the medical education program.

The chiefs of service appointed under this provision were: Dr. Joseph C. Peden, Radiology; Dr. Henry C. Allen, Pathology; Dr. John H. Woodbridge, Medicine; Dr. William R. Cole, Surgery; and Dr. William D. Hawker, Obstetrics-Gynecology.[81]

Board of Trustees Enlarged

At its annual meeting on December 5, 1968, the Deaconess Society adopted changes in its constitution and bylaws to enlarge the board of trustees with six new board-elected community members and to provide for a board-appointed advisory council. In a break with long-standing tradition, neither membership in the United Church of Christ nor in the Deaconess Society was required for the six new board members, whose participation on the board was sought for greater community involvement.[82]

Decade of Development, a "Transformation"

Dedication of the new facilities made possible by the Decade of Development Program took place on Sunday, May 24, 1970, at which time the project was described as a "transformation, without and within, [which] fulfilled every expectation."

3-27. Deaconess Hospital, with new construction, 1970.

Members of the board of trustees, officers of the medical staff and members of the administration led the Ceremony of Dedication. The Rev. Dr. Fred C. Allrich, president of the board of trustees, gave thanks for the hospital's "rich heritage of good patient care," for all "who labored so diligently and gave so generously" and "for new opportunities of service made possible by the excellent and outstanding facilities."

A "Self-Guided Tour" enabled members of the Deaconess Society and guests, with the help of Deaconess Auxiliary members stationed at locations along the way, to see some of the extensive new facilities. Among the areas included were the new five-floor Ancillary Services Building, the coffee shop and gift shop, the professional library, and three patient care floors added to the South Building which brought the total bed capacity to 505.[83]

Revised Corporate Structure and New Titles

The tremendous growth of the hospital as a result of the Decade of Development Program and the need for more and more community contacts for fund raising brought the Deaconess Society to the decision in 1970 to seek experienced corporate lay leadership for the increasingly demanding and time-consuming position of board president.

Mr. Monte Shomaker, a prominent corporate leader and dedicated churchman, was elected president of the board of trustees in 1970, the first layman to hold this position.

3-28. Rev. Dr. Fred C. Allrich, President, Board of Directors, 1970.

3-29. Mr. Monte Shomaker, First Lay President, Board of Directors, 1970.

In a further move toward corporate structure and modern terminology, revisions in the constitution were adopted on October 14, 1971, changing the title of the president of the board to "chairman of the board." The titles of administrative staff members were also changed to comply with corporate terminology:

Carl C. Rasche, ...President and Chief Executive Officer
Richard P. Ellerbrake, ...Executive Vice President and Chief Operating Officer
Harry J. Meinhardt, .Vice President and Director of Fiscal Services
Ernest W. Luehrman, .Executive Chaplain

Sister Frieda Ziegler, ...Executive Deaconess
William A. Davidson, ...Executive Personnel Manager
Homer H. Schmitz, . .Executive Director of Management Systems
Ruth Triefenbach, ...Vice President and
                                          Director of Nursing Service
Robert N. Fridley, .Executive Director of
              the Deaconess Foundation and Public Relations
Robert A. Falconer, ...Executive Director of Education

Earlier in 1971 Sister Olivia Drusch retired from her position as assistant admin-istrator and director of nursing, and Mr. Walter J. Stradal retired as executive director of development. Both were recognized and highly commended for their outstanding contributions as members of the Deaconess administrative staff.[84]

3-30. The Administrative Staff, 1971. Seated left to right: W. Jerry Shriver, William A. Davidson, Robert N. Fridley, Homer H. Schmitz, Robert A. Falconer, Ruth Triefenbach, Harry J. Meinhardt. Standing: Sister Frieda Ziegler, Ernest W. Luehrman, Richard P. Ellerbrake and Carl C. Rasche.

The Deaconess Foundation, Serving through Giving

The board of trustees was also given authority, in the constitutional revision adopted October 14, 1971, "to establish a Deaconess Hospital Foundation and to approve bylaws under which said Foundation shall operate."

In keeping with these constitutional provisions, the Deaconess Foundation was formally established on February 2, 1972, and the Foundation board of governors was appointed by the Deaconess Society board of trustees.

The Foundation was directed to give specific attention to the following purposes, but was not limited by such:

1. The support and encouragement of research studies and special clinical centers for advanced study and treatment.

3-31. Harold Melser, Executive Director, Deaconess Foundation.

2. The support of the hospital's charitable clinics and care of the medically indigent.

3. The support of the hospital's teaching and education program.

4. The support of the hospital's continuous improvement of procedures, equipment and facilities for better patient care.

The executive director of the Foundation was made responsible to the president and chief executive officer of the hospital, and all gift receipts of the Foundation are maintained separately from hospital operating income. In 1983, corporate restructuring made the Deaconess Foundation a separate corporation with its own board of directors.

The Foundation's varied programs have resulted in the receipt of many significant gifts. Donors are acknowledged and honored annually in these levels of giving: Benefactor Associates for $100,000, Golden Associates for $50,000, Associates for $10,000, Friends for $5,000 and Patrons for $1,000.

Under the leadership of Mr. Harold Melser, executive director since 1981, assets and endowments, excluding campaign funds, have grown to more than

$6 million from donors who have responded generously to opportunities for "Serving through Giving."[85]

Change and Faithfulness

"Change" was the spirit of the times in 1974 when Deaconess Hospital celebrated its 85th Anniversary. Nuclear medicine, intensive coronary care, and kidney dialysis were among the new services being offered, and the 500,000th patient was admitted to the hospital that year.

The changing medical environment required 1,200 full-time and part-time employees in 200 job classifications at Deaconess in 1974, and almost 300 full-time students were enrolled in teaching programs designed to keep up with medicine.

3-32. Arlie Groenemann, Chief Engineer, 50 years.

What had not changed, however, was the faithfulness of many long-time Deaconess employees. Chief Engineer Arlie Groenemann held the record for long-time employment with fifty years' service at the time of his retirement in 1972. At the 85th Anniversary Employees' Banquet, 300 Deaconess employees were awarded jeweled service pins, presented annually since then, for specific levels of long-time "faithful service to the well-being of patients."[86]

Hospital Attorney Herbert W. Ziercher Honored

Mr. Herbert W. Ziercher also contributed greatly to the well-being of Deaconess patients while he served on the board of trustees and as the hospital's legal counsel for over 38 years.

The Deaconess Society honored Mr. Ziercher on December 4, 1975, at its 86th annual meeting and presented him with a copy of the "Lawgiver" by Edwin Russell. This statuette of a great statesman and lawgiver in Puritan America in 1778 was obtained from London where the renowned sculptor's work is displayed in Westminster Abbey and St. Paul's Cathedral. It symbolized the high

100

regard of the Deaconess Society for Mr. Ziercher whom Chairman Wayne D. Nusbaum of the Deaconess board commended as "one who has demonstrated the epitome of ability and sacrificial service...who donated the vast portion of his tremendous services to the hospital."[87]

Combating the High Cost of Liability Insurance

In 1975, the board of trustees was informed that the premium which the hospital paid for professional liability insurance would increase from $113,000 that year to $811,000 for less coverage in 1976.

3-33. Herbert W. Ziercher, Deaconess Hospital Attorney, 38 years.

Learning that other hospitals in Missouri were likewise experiencing astronomical premium rate increases for 1976, the Deaconess board of trustees instructed President Carl C. Rasche, to explore alternatives.

Under the sponsorship of the Missouri Hospital Association, a study group was formed and the Missouri Legislature was asked to enact Senate Bill 458 allowing formation of assessment insurance companies to write professional liability insurance. This bill was enacted on an emergency basis in June 1975 as a special law which is now codified as Chapter 383 of the Insurance Laws of the State of Missouri.

Twenty-seven hospitals in Missouri, including Deaconess Hospital, formed the MISSOURI PROFESSIONAL LIABILITY INSURANCE ASSOCIATION [MPLIA] in July 1976, and Carl C. Rasche was elected to serve as the first chairman of the board. In 1977 Senate Bill 245 allowed Chapter 383 companies the additional power to write general liability insurance for members. During 1977 Deaconess Hospital's malpractice insurance premium was reduced $400,000 in that one year alone.

ᒪimited to writing only professional and general liability coverages, and only for not-for-profit and governmental hospitals, MPLIA organized a subsidary company, PROVIDERS INSURANCE COMPANY [PIC], in 1981 to expand the insurance services offered to all Missouri hospitals and their healthcare related operations.

The Missouri Hospital Association estimated in 1985 that up to that time, the existence of MPLIA/PIC saved Missouri Hospitals the significant sum of $150 million in malpractice insurance premiums.[88]

The "Design for the '80s"

Deaconess was one of the busiest health care providers in the region in 1976. The bed occupancy rate for the four previous years was over 90 percent and growth in diagnostic and therapeutic services had been tremendous.   This encouraged the board of directors to make plans again for a major renovation and construction program, estimated to cost about $11,500.000.

After the necessary approvals were obtained from the United Church of Christ and from the Health Systems Agency of Greater St. Louis, the Deaconess Society approved a resolution on December 9, 1976, presented by Mr. H. E. Wuertenbaecher, chairman of the board of trustees, which gave the board authority to conduct a capital fund campaign, called a "Design for the '80s" and a "Blueprint of the Future."   Campaign literature said,

> Never before has medicine been able to do so much to ease pain, hasten recovery, and cure the once incurable. Technology abounds. Miracles are almost common-place.....Today's hospital has the awesome task of assembling the many and necessary supporting resources that allow medicine to keep pace with this decade's technological explosion.....Tomorrow is always on the doorstep.

Mr. Darryl R. Francis, former president of the Federal Reserve Bank of St. Louis and vice chairman of the board of trustees, served as general chairman of the $5 million capital fund campaign launched in 1977. It was completed successfully in 1979 with gifts totaling $5,066,663.[89]

The 90th Anniversary, A "Step into the Future"

Dedication of the new facilities made possible by the Desiugn for the 80s Program were held on Sunday, November 4, 1979, which was designated and celebrated as "Deaconess Sunday" in 285 congregations in the Missouri and Illinois-South Conferences of the United Church of Christ. Dedication ceremonies, led by chairman of the board, Larry A. Swaney, also celebrated the 90th Anniversary of Deaconess Hospital and the Deaconess Sisterhood.

Tours were then conducted through the new facilities, which enlarged the capacity of the hospital to 527 patient beds. Included were: a three-floor addition to the Ancillary Services Building; a three-level addition to the South Building for psychiatric and rehabilitation patients; a new seven-level parking garage for employees; and a hospital-wide renovation of most existing service areas.[90]

Reflecting the joy of achievement made possible by the Design for the 80s Program, the hospital's *90th Annual Report* concluded:

> We step into the '80s with enthusiasm, an enthusiasm that comes because of the many friends who share with us in this important work.

3-34. Deaconess Hospital, 1979, with new construction.

Mission Statement Adopted, 1979

Enthusiasm for the work of the future in health care and health education at Deaconess was given direction in a mission statement adopted by the board of trustees in November 1979, declaring that,

> Deaconess Hospital seeks to provide professional, compassionate health care and health education in a Christian setting.[91]

By focusing the objectives and purposes of the hospital within this brief statement, the board affirmed the historic Deaconess commitment to the ministry of caring, healing and teaching exemplified by the Deaconess Sisters.

Deaconess Archives Established, 1979

Mindful of the necessity to preserve appropriately the materials related to the Deaconess heritage, President Carl C. Rasche authorized the establishment of the Deaconess Archives in 1979. A memorial gift provided funds for the purchase of basic archival equipment, and the Deaconess Auxiliary continues to provide funding.

Under the leadership of Sister Velma Kampschmidt and Ruth W. Rasche, heritage materials and artifacts previously kept in a variety of departmental loca-

3-35. Deaconess Archives Museum.

104

3-36. Deaconess Archive Heritage Files.

tions and in the personal collections of the Deaconess Sisters, were gathered and organized for preservation in rooms now on the lower level of the Deaconess College of Nursing, where there is also a small medical museum and rare book library. Sister Elizabeth Lotz translated many early documents from German script to English.

The Archives are the repository for the records and history of the Deaconess Sisters, Deaconess Hospital, the Deaconess Society of St. Louis, Mo., and of Deaconess Associations once related to the Evangelical and Reformed Church. Recognized by the United Church of Christ Historical Council as one of the official archival collections of the church, the Deaconess Archives are staffed by an archivist and have become an important resource for women's history.[92]

Media Services Tell the Deaconess Story

A multitude of documentaries and publicity releases have been produced by the Deaconess Media Services since 1977 when closed-circuit television equipment was installed and the hospital's Channel 13 went on the air. Programs are produced to inform and educate patients, employees, students, alumni, volunteers, and support groups about the latest developments in health care and health education at Deaconess. On Sunday morning, worship services in the Deaconess Chapel are televised for patients wishing to view them in their rooms.

3-37. William L. Mathews, Media Specialist, Deaconess Media Services.

As in years past, monthly and quarterly periodicals, now entitled *Tempo, Focus* and *Deaconess*

Reports, are published to keep employees, donors and Deaconess Society members up to date. Brochures and newsletters, like *For Your Good Health, The Society Page* and *The Direct Line,* are issued as needed to tell the Deaconess story.[93]

Parking Pavilion, Medical Office Center and Deaconess Manor Added

A new 400-car parking pavilion for visitors and the medical staff adjacent to the hospital was completed at a cost of $2,218,000 in 1981 to provide better accessibility to the many new specialized services being developed in patient care at that time. Covered canopies were added to the walkways in 1989 and have added greatly to the comfort and convenience of patients and visitors.

The parking pavilion, in addition to an employees' parking garage completed in 1977, increased the hospital's total offstreet parking capability to 1,166 vehicles, another sign of the times.

In January 1982 ground was broken for a new medical office center, constructed by a private partnership on land adjacent to and leased from the hospital. This facility was opened in 1983 and was later purchased by the hospital to provide offices for forty to fifty physicians and space for the One-day SurgiCenter.

Likewise in January 1982 the board of trustees purchased Deaconess Manor, formerly Forest Park Manor, located immediately west of the School of Nursing. A state-licensed skilled nursing facility, the Manor specializes in round-the-clock care for more than 100 convalescing, chronically ill and aged patients, thus meeting another urgent healthcare need of the 1980s.[94]

President Carl C. Rasche Retires, 1982

Having served as chief executive of Deaconess Hospital for thirty-four years, President Carl C. Rasche announced his wish to retire on February 1, 1982. The board of trustees approved his request and honored him with the title of President Emeritus. He was also named Pastor Emeritus of the Deaconess United Church of Christ.

"A Salute to Carl C. Rasche," was given at a luncheon in his honor on January 22, 1962, held at the St. Louis Sheraton Hotel in Convention Plaza and attended by more than 400 hospital, civic and church leaders. Mr. Larry A. Swaney, immediate past chairman of the Deaconess board of trustees, served as master of ceremonies and described some of the many areas in which the honoree had represented Deaconess Hospital, stating:

> Mr. Rasche's career has been distinguished by a myriad of accomplishments in national, state and local health and welfare organizations.... He has served as president of the Council for Health and Welfare Services of the Evangelical and Reformed Church (now the United Church of Christ); of The American Protestant Hospital Association; and of The Hospital Association of Metropolitan St. Louis; as Chairman of the Board of Trustees of the Missouri Hospital Association, of the Board of Directors of the Missouri Professional Liability Insurance Association and of the Committee on Accreditation of the Chaplain's Association (now the College of Chaplains); as a Delegate to the House of Delegates of the American Hospital Association; as a Member of the Executive Committee of the Educational Commission for Foreign Medical School Graduates; and as a Member of the Board of Directors and a Consultant to the New York Board of the Christian Medical College and Hospital, Vellore, South India. He has been honored as a Fellow of the Chaplain's Association, (now the College of Chaplains), with

3-38. Carl C. Rasche, President and Chief Executive Officer, 1982.

107

the Distinguished Service Award of the United Church of Christ Commission on Health and Welfare (now the Council for Health and Human Service Ministries); the Distinguished Service Award of the Missouri Hospital Association; with the Doctor of Humane Letters degree from Elmhurst College [and the Doctor of Divinity degree soon to be awarded by Eden Theological Seminary].[95]

It was also noted in the Luncheon Program that under President Rasche's leadership, "Deaconess Hospital has evolved from a 252 bed facility into a 527 bed, full-service teaching hospital with a budget of $59 million planned for 1982."

Commenting about his thirty-four years at Deaconess, President Rasche attributed his accomplishments to "team effort," saying, "I have really been blessed to have been a member of so many great teams." One of the most enduring and important members of the Deaconess team was Miss Lois Schatzmann, who was introduced and applauded at the luncheon as President Rasche's executive secretary for thirty-two years.

3-39. Lois Schatzmann, Secretary to the President, 1950-1982.

Appreciation for President Rasche's many years of service to the St. Louis community was expressed in an editorial by the *St. Louis Globe-Democrat* on January 25, 1982, which stated:

> Rev. Dr. Carl C. Rasche...has attained local, state and national recognition as a leader in the field of hospital administration.

> St. Louisans are grateful to him for his determination to maintain Deaconess as a quality hospital inside the city.[96]

The Deaconess Auxiliary had a reception for President and Mrs. Rasche at the hospital on Sunday afternoon, January 24, at which time a generous gift from the Auxiliary was given to the Carl and Ruth Rasche Scholarship Fund, established as a continuing tribute to them in the School of Nursing.

A "Service of Praise and Thanksgiving for the Ministry of Carl C. Rasche," scheduled for Sunday afternoon, January 31, could not be held because St. Louis was completely paralyzed that weekend by the worst snowstorm in the city for seventy years.

President Rasche retired on February 1, 1982, stating that he did so "with a sense of joy," and that with the hospital under the direction of his successor, the Rev. Richard P. Ellerbrake, "things are going to go forward better than ever before."[97]

The Rev. Richard P. Ellerbrake, President and CEO, 1982

Well-prepared for his new position with twenty years of experience as assistant administrator, associate administrator and then as executive vice president and chief operating officer of Deaconess Hospital, the Rev. Richard P. Ellerbrake was appointed president and chief executive officer and he began a new era of strong executive leadership on February 1, 1982.[98]

One of the first major changes initiated in the management under President Ellerbrake's leadership was the further restructuring of the Deaconess corporate organization.

3-40. Richard P. Ellerbrake, President and Chief Executive Officer, 1982.

109

At a special meeting of the Evangelical Deaconess Society held on June 1, 1983, resolutions were adopted which changed the traditional relationship between the Deaconess Society and Deaconess Hospital. It was explained that:

> Following the example of private industry, the hospital shed its traditional stance as a single corporate entity and opted for restructuring as one subsidiary of a multi-faceted parent firm, the Deaconess Health Services Corporation. This new parent company directs and coordinates activities of Deaconess Hospital and other DHSC subsidiaries. Through the parent-subsidiary structure, Deaconess will offer more services to the St. Louis area, strengthen the quality of traditional services in this very competitive environment and add to its financial strength.[99]

The Deaconess Health Services Corporation, 1983

Under the new corporate structure, the board of trustees of Deaconess Hospital was renamed the board of directors and, as such, was one of the several subsidiary boards of directors under the Deaconess Health Services Corporation.

3-41. Chairmen, Deaconess Health Services Corporation Boards, 1984. Back from left: A. J. Reimers, Deaconess Manor; Merle T. Welshans, Deaconess Foundation; Larry A. Swaney, Deaconess Advisory Council; Wm. M. Fogarty, M.D., Deaconess Preferred Care. Front from left: Richard P. Ellerbrake, President and Chief Executive Officer; Kenneth A. Marshall, Deaconess Health Services Corporation; William E. Winter, Deaconess Hospital.

It was predicted by President Ellerbrake and Chairman of the DHSC Board William E. Winter that as a result of this new structure,

> The prospects for achieving above-average, uninterrupted growth at Deaconess are excellent. This is due partly to a long-range planning policy that allows strategic change as dictated by fluctuations in the environment and social climate of the community.[100]

Specialized Services, A Matter of Survival

Few could predict, however, the combination of drastic financial, medical and social changes which would soon alter the environment and impact on hospitals in the 1980s.

Larry Millner, Ph. D., vice president of planning and marketing at Deaconess Hospital, explained:

> Traditionally, hospitals earned 80 percent of their revenue from inpatient care, and 20 percent from outpatients. When new medical techniques shortened time spent in the hospital and turned many inpatient surgeries into outpatient operations, hospitals found themselves with too many beds and too little revenue.[101]

The average length of hospitalization at Deaconess Hospital was reduced 13 percent in 1983. This made it necessary for Deaconess, like other hospitals, to develop more specialized services not only to keep up with new medical technology but in order to make ends meet.[102]

"Diagnostic Related Groups"

The government's implementation in October 1983 of 468 "Diagnostic Related Groups" and the Medicare and Medicaid limits on reimbursements that go with them made a most disturbing and far-reaching financial impact on hospitals.

Under the DRG system, each time a Medicare patient is hospitalized, the government pays the hospital a pre-determined amount for that specific illness, regardless of whether the cost of care is more or less than the set amount. Since older patients usually make up the largest number of inpatients, most hospitals recognized that new sources of revenue and new types of patients had to be found as Medicare reimbursements decreased.

Deaconess was the first St. Louis hospital to use this Medicare prospective payment plan because its fiscal year began October 1st. As a result of careful planning and expert consultation, combined with a long tradition of cost-effective patient care, which has kept charges among the lowest in the St. Louis area, the changeover at Deaconess proceeded smoothly.[103]

Deaconess College of Nursing Approved

Also proceeding smoothly in 1983 was the transition of the Deaconess School of Nursing to become the new Deaconess College of Nursing. In recognition of the important link between quality patient care and health education, the board of directors of the Deaconess Health Services Corporation approved the establishment of the College, the first hospital-based program of this type in the area and the second in the nation.

The traditional three-year nursing program leading to R.N. certification continued to be offered with an optional fourth year for those who wanted a Bachelor of Science in Nursing degree in the College.[104]

President Richard P. Ellerbrake Honored

Cited "for outstanding leadership in the healthcare ministry," the Rev. Richard P. Ellerbrake was honored by his alma mater, Eden Theological Seminary, and was awarded a Doctor of Divinity degree in 1985. In addition to serving as the president and chief operating officer of Deaconess Hospital, he served as chairman of the Missouri Committee to the U.S. Commission on Civil Rights and the St. Louis Human Relations Commission; the board of the American Protestant Health Association; the Council for Health and Human Service Ministries of the United Church of Christ; the Mid America Transplant Association; and the Regional Transplant Association Foundation.

President Ellerbrake likewise served with distinction as a member of the board of directors of Interhealth; Ventures; the Missouri Hospital Association; Health Systems Agency, St. Louis; the Missouri Professional Liability Insurance Association; Hospital Services Group/Missouri Hospital Plan; the Missouri Patient Care Review Foundation; the Hospital Association of Metropolitan St. Louis; Group Health Plan of St. Louis; Group Health Foundation; and as secretary of the Association for Clinical Pastoral Care, Inc.[105]

An $8.1 Million Improvement Program

A two-year, $8.1 million improvement program, approved at a special meeting of the Deaconess Society in October 1984 and also approved by the St. Louis Heritage Commission and by the Board of Public Service, was completed in 1986 to give Deaconess "a whole new look."

Designed to improve the aesthetic as well as the functional capabilities of the hospital, this project included the modernization of 177 patient rooms with private bathroom facilities; a new, contemporary look for the front of the hospital; a new bridge connecting the third floor of the hospital to the Deaconess Medical Office Center; and remodeling of the main lobby.

In this new modern environment, inpatient care increased eleven percent and emergency patients increased seven percent in 1986 as compared to 1985. Expenditures also increased, but not as much as income. The annual report for 1986 stated that $5,740,000 was "left over for improving patient care in the future."[106]

New Department of Religion and Health

A new department of religion and health was established at Deaconess Health Services in 1986 with the appointment of the Rev. Lee W. Tyler as the first minister of religion and health.

The responsibilities of the minister of religion and health, as the liaison between the hospital and the United Church of Christ, are "to strengthen the bond between the Deaconess family and United Church of Christ congregations, other institutions and individuals; to enhance United Church of Christ understanding throughout the Deaconess community; and to support the Deaconess Society."[107]

3-42. Rev. Lee W. Tyler, Minister of Religion and Health, 1986.

In 1989 the department of religion and health was also given responsibility for supervising a new one-year, full-time volunteer program, the Diaconal Ministry, which was introduced as a centennial gift from Deaconess Health Services to institutions of the United Church of Christ.

Corporate Structure Streamlined Further

To streamline the structure of the Deaconess Health Services Corporation further, a plan of reorganization was approved at the annual meeting of the Deaconess Society in November 1986, transferring many responsibilities to the renamed Deaconess Health Services Corporation (DHSC) Board of Directors. This eliminated one layer of corporate structure.

3-43. Rev. Jerry W. Paul, Executive Vice President and Chief Operating Officer, 1986.

Members of the Deaconess Society were informed that under this new plan they would continue as members of the new Deaconess Health Services Corporation. The reorganization also reflected "a desire to strengthen management structure by placing more duties formerly performed by the board of directors in the hands of management, so that the board of directors serves truly in an oversight capacity."[108]

In the new corporate structure, management was represented on the Board of Directors of the Deaconess Health Services Corporation by President and Chief Executive Officer, Richard P.

3-44. Dennis W. Kruse, Vice President of Finance and Treasurer, 1986.

114

Ellerbrake, and by Secretary/ Executive Vice President and Chief Operating Officer, Jerry W. Paul, who had served as an administrative intern and resident at Deaconess. He holds a master's degree in health administration from Washington University School of Medicine, a bachelor's degree from Elmhurst College and a master of divinity degree from Eden Theological Seminary. Dennis W. Kruse, Vice President of Finance, served as Treasurer.[109]

"Stepping Stones to the Future"

A multiplicity of exciting new patient care programs and related facilities were approved by the board of directors and initiated during the late 1980s. Sometimes described as "stepping stones to the future," these new programs placed Deaconess Health Services in a strong position to begin a second century of health care and education in St. Louis.

The Deaconess Child Care Center, opened to meet the child care needs of Deaconess employees in 1984, was a first in the community and Deaconess was named one of the best employers in St. Louis by the *St. Louis Magazine*, which cited the Center.[110]

A Guide for the Future

Based on the long-established Deaconess heritage of caring, healing and teaching, and in the spirit of the purpose adopted by the founders of Deaconess

3-45. DHSC Board of Directors, 1989. From left back: James R. Elsesser, L. John Gable, Rev. Dr. C. Dwayne Dollgener, H. E. Wuertenbaecher, Jr., Bob E. Senseman, Paul B. Convery, M.D., Tehmton S. Mistry, M.D., Jerry W. Paul. Seated from left: Ralph W. Streiff, Nell Pinckert, President Richard P. Ellerbrake, Chairman A. J. Reimers, Robert C. Wolford, Rev. Carleton E. Norton.
Not pictured: Louis C. Bailey, Rev. Martha Ann Baumer, William P. Grant, Ralph Korte, Gertrude McKenney, John A. Shiell, Charles H. Sincox, M.D., Edythe Meaux Smith, John L. Ufheil.

Hospital in 1889, the board of directors of the Deaconess Health Services adopted a revised mission statement in 1989 to serve as a guide for the centennial celebration and for the future:

> Life of quality for all through value-centered health care and health education offered in the compassionate spirit of Jesus Christ.[111]

Chapter Four

THE MEDICAL STAFF
AND MEDICAL EDUCATION
"To Provide the Best Possible Care"

Finding a good doctor in 1889 was not easy. State licensing was not required and virtually anyone could hang up a sign and go into the practice of medicine. Many who did so had very little if any basic medical training.

> A century ago, being a medical student in America was easy. No one worried about admission, for entrance requirements were lower than they were for a good high school. Instruction was superficial and brief. The terms lasted only sixteen weeks, and after the second term the M.D. degree was automatically given, regardless of a student's academic performance. Teaching was by lecture alone. Thus, students...would often graduate without ever having touched a patient.[1]

There were fifteen medical schools listed in St. Louis in 1889 when the first Deaconess Home and Hospital was opened on Eugenia Street. Some of those schools were well regarded but most were proprietary, which meant that they were owned by doctors who operated them for profit. Three were based on homeopathy, once a very popular approach to healing, but it was declining rapidly in the 1880s as scientific medicine advanced.[2]

Because most medical schools in America were of such questionable quality in the 19th century, many young doctors went abroad to study if they could possibly afford to do so. Medical schools were part of the highly advanced university system in Germany, considered at that time to be "the medical mecca of the world." And before that time, more than 700 Americans had studied medicine in Paris. A diploma or degree from Europe was, therefore, an indication of more advanced medical training.[3]

Membership in the St. Louis Medical Society was another indication of a doctor's training and ability. The Society was organized in 1836 by seven "medical gentlemen" who founded a medical library and promoted the highest professional standards of their day. Membership in the Society was not only considered an honor but was limited to those who could meet the high professional standards set by the group.[4]

In this healthcare environment one hundred years ago, it is understandable that much of the American public was skeptical of doctors. Except for severe injury or the sudden onset of alarming symptoms, even the wealthy seldom called a physician immediately.[5]

When needed, the family doctor treated everyone from grandparents to newborns. Childbirth, childhood diseases, minor surgery, everyday injuries and chronic illnesses were all his responsibility and were usually treated in the patient's home. Most family doctors in St. Louis in the late 1880s made their house calls travelling by horse and buggy, but some used the new electric streetcars which by that time were said to have become the fastest way to get around town.[6]

Wherever they went, or however they travelled, doctors could always be recognized because they carried the indispensable "tools of their trade" in a small black bag. Varying somewhat in its contents depending on its owner, the doctor's black bag in the 1880s usually contained a stethoscope, a thermometer, a scalpel and small bottles of medication:

> The doctor's bag was filled largely with drugs: pills, salves and powders.... Opium soothed pain and allayed diarrhea, digitalis was useful in certain heart conditions, quinine exerted a specific effect on malaria, and fresh fruits relieved scurvy.... Aspirin(although not under that name) had just come into widespread use in the treatment of fevers and rheumatism...and mercury did have some effect on syphilis.... In addition, the majority of physicians carried sugar pills,

4-1. Dr. A. R. Shreffler at Deaconess Hospital with his modern black bag, 1930.

placebos to reassure the anxious and demanding patient that something was being done.[7]

But even more reassuring to some patients in the sickroom at that time was just the doctor's presence. Nothing was more important than his ability to inspire confidence. He brought hope, and as one eminent physician described it, "Hope is itself a kind of medicine."[8]

Finding good doctors who were highly qualified and at the same time willing to take time to work with the Deaconess Sisters in caring for the poor in St. Louis in 1889 seemed impossible. Yet that is exactly what the members of the Evangelical Deaconess Society proposed to do when they founded the first Deaconess Home and Hospital on Eugenia Street. It was well known that only the best available medical care would be acceptable to the Deaconess Sisters. Familiar as they were with the superior quality of medical training and practice in Germany where modern deaconess work had originated, they demanded no less for their patients.[9]

The First Deaconess Medical Staff, 1889

Dr. Henry H. Summa, described earlier as one of the charter members of the Evangelical Deaconess Society, was exactly the type of doctor needed to work with the Deaconess Sisters. Born in Germany, he had come to the United States as a youth. In 1875 he graduated from the St. Louis Medical College, one of the two most highly regarded medical schools in the city. It later became the Washington University School of Medicine. Licensed in both Missouri and Illinois, Dr. Summa became a member of the St. Louis Medical Society in 1882, and he was recognized as a very competent physician who had developed a large and desirable practice. His office was located on North Eleventh Street near St. Peter's Evangelical Church, where he is thought to have been a member.[10]

Dr. A. F. Bock, like Dr. Summa, was a highly regarded member of the St. Louis Medical Society. Born in Waterloo, Illinois, where his father was the first physician to settle in that district, he was confirmed in the Evangelical faith in 1862 and became a member of St. Paul's Evangelical Church in Waterloo. After graduating from the "City University of St. Louis" in 1864, he was sent to Europe for his medical education at the Universities of Vienna and Wurzburg, both prestigious centers of learning. Following his graduation in 1868, he spent one year touring in Europe where he observed advanced scientific medical methods and became acquainted with the excellent nursing care given by the Deaconess

Sisters. Returning to St. Louis, he rapidly acquired a large family practice and soon began to devote special attention to surgery. Alert to the new advances in scientific medicine, he is credited with having performed the first suprapubic operation for vesical calculus west of the Mississippi, and of having given the first injection of diptheria antitoxin in St. Louis.[11]

As previously mentioned, in a joint meeting with the board of directors of the Deaconess Society on September 23, 1889, Dr. Summa and Dr. Bock agreed to alternate monthly as house physicians and to teach the first probationers at the new Deaconess Home and Hospital on Eugenia Street. Dr. Bock took charge the first month and became chief of staff, a position he held for fifteen years until his retirement in 1904.[12]

Building on this base of scientifically trained, highly qualified members of the medical profession, the Deaconess Medical Staff was quickly enlarged to include Dr. Arthur E. Ewing and Dr. John Green Sr., who brought their many eye patients to the hospital. Like Doctors Summa and Bock, Doctors Ewing and Green were members of the St. Louis Medical Society and they had both completed medical post-graduate work in Germany, where they too had become acquainted with deaconess work.

Dr. Ewing was a graduate of Dartmouth College and he practiced law in Alabama before graduating from the St. Louis Medical College in 1883. His post-graduate studies in medicine were conducted at Kiel, Germany, after which he returned to St. Louis and was associated with Dr. Green and Dr. M. H. Post Sr., who limited their practice to diseases of the eye. Dr. Ewing became head of the Department of Ophthalmology of Washington University School of Medicine in 1902 and served in that position until 1921, when he became professor emeritus. It was said of him, "Much to his own detriment he gave no cognizance or heed to money," which may explain his willingness to care for the poor and to serve on the first Deaconess Medical Staff.[13]

Dr. Green, the fourth member of the first Deaconess Medical Staff in 1889, was born in Worcester, Massachusetts, and was a descendent of the second governor of the Massachusetts Bay Colony. After graduating from Harvard College with both A.B. and B.S. degrees in 1856, he received his M.D. degree from Harvard and was admitted as a Fellow of the Massachusetts Medical Society by examination in 1858. He spent two years studying in London, Paris, Berlin and Vienna before beginning his practice in Boston. During the Civil War he served as Acting Assistant Surgeon, U.S.A., after which he returned to Europe for special study in ophthalmology in London, Paris and Utrecht. He then established himself in practice in St. Louis in 1866. Later associating in practice with Dr. Ewing and Dr. Post, he became a "special professor of ophthalmology" at Washington University and part of a team which is said to have "stood for ophthalmology and ophthalmology at it best." It was he who admitted the first patient to the new Deaconess Home and Hospital on Eugenia Street.[14]

Modest Facilities for First Staff

The building at 2117 Eugenia Street was well equipped as a home for the Deaconess Sisters, and its eleven rooms could accommodate a limited number of patients. There were, however, at first

4-2. Dr. A. F. Bock, First Deaconess Chief of Staff.

4-3. Dr. Arthur E. Ewing, Member, First Deaconess Medical Staff.

4-4. Dr. John Green Sr., Member, First Deaconess Medical Staff.

121

no operating rooms or special treatment facilities. If there was a surgical case, operating equipment was rigged up around a patient's bed as was the practice of that day when surgery was often performed in the patient's own home.

The first operating room was equipped by Dr. Ewing and Dr. Green for their many eye cases. This contribution, in addition to their services to the poor, led to their description as "early friends of the institution."[15]

Staff Development in a New Location

Though records from the early years are scant, it is evident that the first Deaconess Medical Staff and the Deaconess Sisters gave their patients such outstanding care that those seeking their services soon outgrew the small hospital's modest facilities.

When a location for a new hospital was found on West Belle Place, the medical staff was very much involved in the expansion project. The record says that "Dr. Ewing gave his time and advice in devising the plans of the new hospital building" and that "he loaned large sums of money as they were needed." As a result of his expert and generous assistance, the new three-story Deaconess Home and Hospital at 4117 West Belle Place was modern in every respect with "two thoroughly aseptic operating rooms" and space for forty patients.

With the facilities for treating so many more patients at the new location, the medical staff recruited more new members. By 1894, Dr. H. W. Hermann, a neurologist; Dr. Walter B. Dorsett, a gynecologist; Dr. J. R. Lemen, a heart and lung specialist; Dr. Hugo Summa, a pathologist; and Dr. John B. Shapleigh were on the staff. Each of these new Deaconess Medical Staff members was a member of the St. Louis Medical Society. This is a strong indication that the high qualifications and professional excellence of the first four staff members attracted other physicians of like quality, a significant factor in staff development.[16]

Strained Relations

Several years of steady growth and harmony then followed for deaconess work in St. Louis, but a crisis developed in 1897.

The resignation of Sister Katherine Haack as the sister superior and her departure with thirteen other Deaconess Sisters in her support resulted in a severe shortage of nursing personnel in the hospital. Strained relations between the medical staff and the board of directors then developed.

The whole medical staff supported Sister Katherine, and they sent a letter to the board of directors, dated December 14, 1897, in which they not only commended the sister superior's leadership and listed her many accomplishments but wherein they also expressed their great displeasure at not having been consulted by the board in this sensitive matter.

> The Hospital has been a success both financially and as a hospital, and we cannot understand why such action was taken without first advising with your medical staff.... As we have been absolutely faithful in the discharge of the trust you reposed in us and have done all in our power to aid and assist you, we feel deeply wounded at your utter neglect of us in this matter.[17]

As a result of this first serious difficulty between the members of the medical staff and the board of directors, some members of the staff transferred their patients to other hospitals, others admitted no new patients, and Dr. Shapleigh resigned.   Only three patients finally remained in the hospital and the future of deaconess work looked very doubtful.[18]

Medical Staff Rules and Regulations, 1898

Once the immediate management crisis was solved with the appointment of Sister Magdalene Gerhold as sister superior and the Rev. Frederick P. Jens as superintendent and pastor of the hospital in May, 1898, the board of directors gave attention to clarifying and mending its relationship with the medical staff.

Handwritten in German script, a document setting forth the duties and rights of the medical staff was prepared which began with this explanation:

> In order "to bring about a more harmonious relationship between the medical staff and the institution" the board of directors of the Deaconess Society adopted these "Rules and Regulations" in 1898:
> ### Duties of the Staff

> All members of the medical staff are expected to treat all charity or ward patients free of charge.

Staff members are expected to have their patients, as much as possible, hospitalized in our institution and to abide by the rules of the house. The admitting procedure also must be in keeping with regulations set up by the hospital.

It is the duty of all staff members to participate in the educational program of the deaconesses under the leadership of the superintendent and head deaconess.

Every staff member is requested to stop by at the superintendent's office and to register that he has done so.

The board of directors appoints Dr. A. F. Bock as the chief of the staff and asks him to give the names of a number of doctors for possible staff membership.

The staff members are expected to set up their organization especially in regard to new membership and changes, under the leadership of the board of directors.

The medical staff is requested to meet every three months.

Rights of the Staff

Members of the staff have the right to expect that house patients are placed according to the character of their illness and that the doctor be notified as to their placement.

Members of the staff may bring in poor and needy for care. The medical staff has the right, through the chief of the staff, to bring in recommendations and suggestions with reference to the care of patients and to express their opinion about functional areas in the hospital.

Members of the staff and their services to patients will be recognized in the Annual Reports. Their relationship to the hospital will be given due respect.[19]

Among the earliest such documents of its kind, these "Rules and Regulations of 1898," as adopted by the board of directors and the members of the Deaconess

Medical Staff, did result in the strong new cooperative effort necessary for institutional growth. By 1899 there were more new members on the staff and they were prominently recognized in the annual report on the same page with the members of the board of directors, the executive committee and the Deaconess Sisters:

STAFF OF PHYSICIANS

A. F. Bock, M.D., president . . . . .Surgeon
J. Campbell Smith, M.D., secretary . . . . .Laryngologist
H. W. Hermann, M.D. . . . . .Neurologist
W. B. Dorsett, M.D . . . . .Gynecologist
J. R. Lemen, M.D . . . . .Heart and Lungs
W. A. Shoemaker, M.D. . . . . .Oculist and Aurist
H. D. Brandt, M.D. . . . . .General Medicine
J. F. Keber, M.D. . . . . .Dermatologist
Amand Ravold, M.D. . . . . .Pathologist and Bacteriologist
J. C. Koehler, M.D. . . . . .Intern[20]

This list indicates that all of the major medical specialties, which were developing rapidly at that time of revolutionary scientific discoveries, were represented on the Deaconess Medical Staff before the turn of the century. There was also an intern on the staff, signifying the beginning of the medical education program at Deaconess Hospital.

The Medical Education Program, 1899

Serving in a hospital as an intern at the turn of the century was, as it is today, a method of supplementing one's medical education. Beginning in the 1830s, some hospitals selected "house pupils" to reside in the hospital, before or after getting an M.D. degree, and to assume responsibility for managing cases. By 1884 in some large, city hospitals such house pupils accompanied the staff in their daily visits to the sick, received their orders, kept a record of the cases and their treatment, reported all violations of medical discipline, and were supervised in their work.[21]

At Deaconess Hospital in 1899 the duties of the first intern, Dr. J. C. Koehler, were described by the superintendent in this way:

Our assistant house physician is on duty both day and night and is ever ready to render assistance to any physician or his patients.[22]

This 24-hour-a-day schedule for the intern assured patients and members of the medical staff alike that a qualified physician was always nearby for an immediate response to emergencies or any unusual medical development. This was very reassuring to patients and their families at a time when most people still resisted hospital care if at all possible. But from the intern's perspective, it was often a grueling, miserable workload. Yet it also included teaching responsibilities, as reported in the superintendent's report for the following year.

> The course of lectures in medical and surgical nursing was given regularly to the deaconess nurses, because we were fortunate in securing the services of an efficient intern, Dr. J. C. Koehler, who finished the first year's course with the freshman class. Unfortunately, he was obliged to resign his position after seven months on account of failing health.[23]

Failing health was not an uncommon experience for interns in hospitals at that time. By the 1890s they were described as being overworked and overstressed, and teaching was an additional load that sometimes proved to be too much.

> In 1892, members of the surgical staff at the Massachusetts General Hospital pleaded with the trustees to increase the number of house officers. The responsibilities of the house staff had become so great that "few men finish the hospital curriculum without some illness plainly due to the weight they have been carrying.[24]

The requirement that the intern (or house physician) teach anatomy and physiology in the School for Deaconesses continued, however, for many years in the generally accepted pattern of medical education in that day.

Before the time of hospital accreditation, the role of the intern was not always clear even to members of the medical staff, and the issue came up again and again. Years later, as recorded in the "Minutes of the Deaconess Medical Staff Annual Meeting", May 24, 1912, the qualifications of an intern were still being discussed:

> The question of an intern for the hospital was then taken up and discussed at some length....Dr. W. A. Shoemaker moved, seconded

by Dr. Babler, that if, in its wisdom the board of directors deemed it best to enter into a contract with an experienced physician, i.e. (one who has had at least one year of hospital training) rather than a recent graduate without hospital experience, as intern for the hospital, it would meet with the hearty approval of the medical staff. Motion carried.

There was at that time no standardization of terminology and no generally accepted approach to such supplementary medical education. The terms "house pupil," "intern," "resident," "house physician" and "resident physician" were sometimes used interchangeably to describe the same experience. Regardless of the terminology, however, such an assignment was considered to be an excellent opportunity to receive intensive clinical training at the bedside, valuable experience not offered in most medical schools.[25]

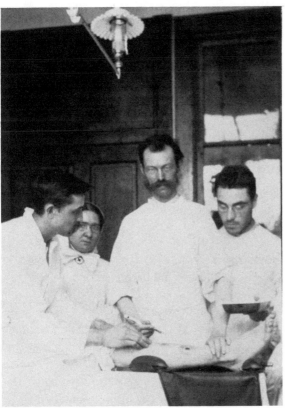

4-5. Dr. A. F. Bock, (center), Sister Magdalene Gerhold and Interns, Dr. Herbert Beedle and Dr. D. S. Werth, in Deaconess Operating Room, 1901.

All of the members of the Deaconess Medical Staff had some responsibilities for the teaching program in the School for Deaconesses. They not only fulfilled their duty in accordance with the Rules and Regulations of 1898 "to participate in the educational program of the deaconesses" but they apparently did so with thoroughness. Superintendent Jens stated in the hospital's annual report for 1899 that "Our deaconesses who nurse the patients have had a thorough theoretical and practical training...."

In 1908 a three-year curriculum of lectures representing all of the departments of medicine and surgery was adopted by the medical staff as the course of study for the deaconess nurses. Each member of the staff was then assigned specific courses having to do with his particular department and the number of lectures to be given in each category. A heavy schedule, it was nevertheless adopted repeatedly with additions in the following years.[26]

Medical Staff Recognition and Appreciation

It is apparent that the board of directors of the Deaconess Society kept its agreement made in the Rules and Regulations of 1898 to recognize the services contributed by the members of the medical staff. In the annual report for 1899 Superintendent Jens wrote:

> It would have been impossible for us to do such a large amount of work if the physicians and surgeons of our Hospital Staff and other doctors would not have assisted us so faithfully in the treatment of the charity patients, and in giving the course of lectures on nursing to the sisters.

The Courtesy Staff

The superintendent's reference to "other doctors" who brought patients to the hospital refers to a "courtesy staff" which had been given privileges at Deaconess Hospital. This is explained in the introduction to the *11th Annual Report of the Evangelical Deaconess Society* where it was stated, "Patients are at liberty to select the physician or surgeon of their choice, whether he is a member of the staff or not."

One year later, in 1900, there was a list in the annual report of 45 physicians whose patronage was gratefully acknowledged for having recommended their patients to the hospital. By 1901 a similar list included 128 physicians. This annual listing continued through 1908 when there were 228 physicians named. By that time the number had become so large that the annual reports from then on stated simply,

> We also wish to thank all physicians and surgeons who have sent patients to our hospital. We only regret that our hospital was often so crowded, that we could not accommodate patients sent by members of our staff as well as by other doctors.[27]

128

The high occupancy rate was good for balancing the hospital budget, but already in that early period of hospital development there was a growing shortage of patient beds.[28]

First Medical Staff Minutes, 1904

The "Rules and Regulations of 1898" served both the medical staff and the hospital exceedingly well. The first official meeting of the staff, however, was not convened until six years later. The first Deaconess Medical Staff Minutes were recorded on November 17, 1904, on the first page of a small bound record book entitled *Minutes of the Meetings of the Medical Staff of the Evangelical Deaconess Hospital.* The following members of the medical staff were present for this meeting: Dr. W. B. Dorsett, Dr. L. H. Hempelmann, Dr. W. Hermann, Dr. J. R. Lemen, Dr. Amand Ravold, Dr. J. Campbell Smith and Dr. W. A. Shoemaker. In the absence of Dr. A. F. Bock, president of the staff, the meeting was called to order by Dr. J. R. Lemen.

The stated object of this meeting was: "to elect officers for the ensuing year and propose a constitution and by-laws for the guidance of the medical staff." Dr. J. R. Lemen was unanimously elected president, Dr. W. B. Dorsett, vice-president, and Dr. Amand Ravold, secretary-treasurer.

The absence of Dr. Bock and the election of Dr. Lemen (his cousin) as the new president of the staff imply that Dr. Bock, after fifteen years as president, chief of staff and surgeon, had retired. He had written a letter of resignation to the board of directors three years earlier but it had not been accepted.

Following the election of officers, a motion was made and passed that a committee be appointed to draw up a constitution and bylaws and report at the next meeting. The minutes conclude with two further short entries which state that the meeting was adjourned subject to call of the president, and that a joint meeting of the medical staff and the hospital board of directors was then held to elect three physicians to the staff: Dr. H. L. Nietert, Dr. A. J. Koetter, and Dr. J. F. Shoemaker. In 1905, Dr. Bransford Lewis was elected to the Deaconess Staff to head the new department of Genito-Urinary Diseases.[29]

Medical Staff Constitution and Bylaws, 1911

There was no great haste in the preparation of the first medical staff constitution and bylaws proposed in 1904. The second entry in the Deaconess Medical

Staff Minutes is dated February 27, 1911, at "9 o'clock P. M." The late hour suggests that a greatly overworked staff was called together to discuss an urgent issue.

The stated object of this meeting was to consider the adoption of the constitution and bylaws which had been drawn up by the committee appointed in 1904. Dr. Dorsett, chairman of the committee, read the proposed document, whereupon a motion "to appeal [repeal] the old rules, which had been adopted in 1898 and substitute for them the Constitution and Bylaws just read by Dr. Dorsett" was unanimously carried.

Though it is never mentioned in the Deaconess Medical Staff Minutes by name, the Flexner Report, *Medical Education in the United States and Canada,* was published the previous year (1910) and had created a new awareness for the standardization needed in medical schools and in teaching hospitals. As a result, many hospitals across the land which wished to have a medical education program hastened toward better medical staff organization and the adoption of standards for accreditation.[30]

The "object" of the Deaconess Medical Staff in 1911, as stated in the constitution and bylaws was:

> to promote the welfare of the Deaconess Hospital in its noble work
> of caring for the sick and disabled; to encourage and assist the
> Deaconesses in their effort to acquire a proper knowledge of nurs-
> ing of the sick that may be entrusted to their care.

Important new provisions, as compared to the Rules and Regulations of 1898, were: (1) all departments of medicine and surgery were to be represented on the medical staff, (2) official notices of meetings had to be mailed out to all members one week in advance of the date, (3) annual dues of $1.00 were to be paid by all members, (4) officers had to be elected by ballot by a two-thirds majority of the members present, (5) vacancies and additions to the staff were to be filled by the board of directors on the unanimous recommendation of the staff, and (6) any member accused of unprofessional conduct could be expelled from the staff by a two-thirds majority vote of all the members present at a regular or special meeting of the staff.[31]

Medical Staff Departments, 1911

The seventeen members of the Deaconess Medical Staff in 1911 represented thirteen medical specialties which had been developed by that time:

General Surgery	Dermatology
General Medicine	Neurology
Obstetrics and Gynecology	Proctology
Ophthalmology	Pathology
Otology	Genito-Urinary Surgery
Laryngology	Roentgenology
	Bacteriology[32]

In 1914 when it became advisable to amend the constitution and bylaws of the medical staff before a second printing was ordered, a department of pediatrics was added and Dr. T. C. Hempelmann was appointed as the first pediatrician on the staff.[33]

Meanwhile, taking seriously their stated constitutional purpose "to promote the welfare of the Deaconess Hospital in its noble work," the medical staff adopted resolutions in 1912 which were sent to the hospital board of directors regarding (1) the need for an intern with experience, (2) the immediate need for a resident pharmacist, and (3) the location and equipment of a pathology laboratory.

These recommendations resulted in prompt action by the board of directors. Superintendent Jens announced at the next annual meeting of the medical staff on September 29, 1913, that an intern and a druggist had been appointed and that the new pathology laboratory had been completed and was in use.[34]

"Minimum Standard" Adopted, 1921

Hospitals continued to grow rapidly, and in 1918 the American College of Surgeons developed a "Minimum Standard" which, as described earlier, set forth requirements for the proper care of the sick. In 1919, the Council on Medical Education and Hospitals of the American Medical Association published the "Essentials for Approved Internships." In 1920, inspections were begun and hospitals were graded to determine their accreditation for the proper education and training of interns and residents.[35]

In order to have the work in the hospital conform to the standards set by the

American Medical Association and American College of Surgeons, the board of directors and the medical staff of Deaconess Hospital adopted the following rules in March 1921:

1. The history of each patient must be written 48 hours after the admission to the hospital.

2. No patient will be admitted to the operating room until the history has been written.

3. Each operator shall write out the operative findings and a brief history of the operation immediately after the same.

4. Any physician who neglects or refuses to comply with these rules shall be denied the privileges of the hospital.

5. We are absolutely opposed to the secret division of fees and will deny the privileges of the hospital to any physician known to practice "fee splitting."[36]

The first inspection for accreditation of the intern and resident training program at Deaconess Hospital was described by Sister Elizabeth Schaefer, the medical records librarian, who wrote in her "Progress Notes of the Medical Records Librarian" in 1925:

...suddenly Dr. MacEachern [of the American Medical Association and the American College of Surgeons] announced himself for an inspection of the new record department. He really got behind the files!

Accreditation for Teaching, 1928

By 1928 the American Medical Association had adopted the provision that a "teaching hospital" must have at least three interns. Deaconess Hospital had four interns at that time and it was accredited.[37]

The first documented report to the hospital after an American Medical Association inspection was recorded in the "Minutes of the Board of Directors of the Deaconess Society" for January 17, 1929, which read:

A letter from the American Medical Association was read showing the findings of their inspection.... This report showed that our hospital is operating practically with few exceptions, up to their standards.

One year later Superintendent Jens stated in his annual report to the Deaconess Society for 1930 that:

The Deaconess Hospital is recommended by the American Medical Association for intern service and is fully accredited by the American College of Surgeons.

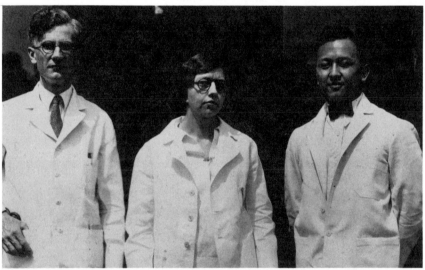

4-6. Deaconess House Staff, 1930. Left to right: Dr. Joseph H. Smyth, Dr. Gladys Huscher (first woman intern at Deaconess) and Dr. David Katsuke.

Staff Support for Hospital Relocation

When it became apparent that Deaconess Hospital had grown so much that expansion was no longer possible at West Belle Place and plans were proposed for a new hospital to be built on Oakland Avenue, the medical staff was very supportive.

In the campaign for funds to finance the new building, Dr. H. L. Nietert was the chairman of the doctors' division. As architectural plans were developed for the construction of the new facilities, an advisory committee of the medical staff worked with the building committee and "rendered incalculable service" in making it modern in every respect.[38]

Dr. L. H. Hempelmann, president of the medical staff, presented one of the addresses in the dedication ceremonies for the new hospital on May 25, 1930, and a note in the Dedication Bulletin expressed appreciation "to all physicians and surgeons who have been so loyal and helpful to us."[39]

A beautiful art glass window depicting Christ, the Great Physician, was the center of attention in the front lobby of the new hospital. A memorial gift, it commemorated Dr. Edmund A. Babler, a prominent surgeon and leader on the Deaconess Medical Staff. He had served patients and the Deaconess Sisters with great skill and generosity for many years at the old hospital, but his sudden death in 1929 denied him the privilege of serving in the new building. The

4-7. The Deaconess Medical Staff, 1930. Front: Doctors Joseph C. Peden, E. Lee Dorsett, H. G. Lund, A. R. Shreffler, L. H. Hempelmann. Middle: Doctors H. L. Nietert, E. Brockelmann, George B. Winter, Dr. E. H. Rohlfing, Carl T. Eber. Back: Doctors C. H. Shutt, Francis Reder, Fred C. Simon, Charles Klenk.

Babler window remains in the hospital as a symbol of the healing ministry and has been located since 1970 in the lobby of the Deaconess Memorial Chapel.[40]

Medical Staff Reorganization, 1931

With excellent, up-to-date facilities in which to serve twice as many patients as before, the Deaconess Medical Staff was, however, soon involved in internal controversy.

As previously reported, the Minutes of the Board of Directors in 1930 hint at "difficulties" and record discussions about the assignment of the large number of charity patients seeking care in the hospital, the fees of the pathologist, and the need to add many more new qualified members to the medical staff despite opposition from some of its members who were thought to be seeking control.

Universal state licensing laws for physicians had been enacted by 1930 and reforms in medical education and in medical practice were being adopted in many institutions to meet the new standards. But there were also slogans heard like, "Fewer and better doctors."[41]

The difficulties within the Deaconess Medical Staff intensified and it became necessary for the hospital board of directors to act. As a result, on March 19, 1931, the board asked for the resignation of all active medical staff members so that the staff could be reorganized. Following this action it was reported that:

> With few exceptions all of former members of the medical staff could be reappointed and many new names of well-known physicians and surgeons have been added to the roster. Today the Deaconess Hospital has the largest active staff in its history. Appointments of the staff are on an annual basis. Officers are elected from the staff as a whole, and in addition, each department is provided with a chairman. These officers constitute an executive committee which confers with the staff committee on problems of hospital policies.[42]

Dr. L. H. Hempelmann was elected as president of the reorganized medical staff, with Dr. Otto Koch as vice president and Dr. E. H. Rohlfing, secretary and treasurer. The strong, respected leadership of these officers brought harmony again to the staff and the members were assigned to active, consultant, associate and general staff divisions.[43]

Throughout the reorganization of the medical staff, the medical education program at Deaconess Hospital continued to be accredited and remain strong. Dr. Henry Scott, who served as senior resident in 1933, was among the senior resident physicians who were awarded Deaconess Hospital "keys" in addition to certificates upon completion of their service.[44]

Staff Committees Appointed

As the medical staff grew larger during the 1930s, the executive committee of the staff found it increasingly difficult to carry out the many duties assigned to it. To share the load, the president appointed these five standing committees in 1936 and annually thereafter:

4-8. Deaconess Senior Resident's Key. Awarded to Dr. Henry Scott, 1933.

1. Records committee.
2. Intern committee.
3. Library committee.
4. Special committee.
5. Bylaws committee.

In 1937 a liaison committee was added and a program committee was appointed in 1947.[45]

Staff Divisions Adopted, 1940

In 1939, the fiftieth anniversary year, there were 62 physicians and surgeons on the active staff, 19 on the consulting staff, 49 on the associate staff, and 103 on the general staff, for a total membership of 233.

To keep up with this significant growth and the ever-increasing numbers of specialties developing in the practice of medicine, the medical staff adopted a further revision of its constitution and bylaws in 1940 which designated five membership classes:

1. Active Staff: Members under 65 years of age with responsibilities for service to charity patients and teaching, all new members to be diplomates of an American board.

4-9. Deaconess Medical Staff, Fiftieth Anniversary, 1939.

2. Senior Active Staff: Members over 65 years of age who are relieved of all active duties and dues.

3. Associate Staff: Physicians or dentists who are specializing in their chosen field and are possible candidates for the active staff.

4. Courtesy Staff: Physicians or dentists who are privileged to treat patients in Deaconess Hospital and are in none of the above classifications.

5. Honorary Staff: Physicians or dentists receiving honorary recognition for faithful, long-continued or meritorious service to Deaconess Hospital.

Four new departments of medicine were also included for the first time in the bylaws of 1940: physical therapy, neurology, neurological surgery, and plastic surgery. With these four additions, there were then sixteen departments of medicine at Deaconess Hospital and active staff members were required to specialize in one of these departments.[46]

Neuro-Psychiatry Department, a "First" at Deaconess

Though not established as a separate department, the practice of psychiatry began at Deaconess Hospital in 1934 when Dr. A. H. Deppe became a member of the general staff. He was, reportedly, the first physician in St. Louis to treat private psychiatric patients in a private hospital. Others who practiced psychiatry at that time did so in government hospitals.

137

Dr. Deppe became a member of the department of neurology of the active staff at Deaconess in 1937, and in 1946 the department of neurology became the department of neuro-psychiatry.[47]

Wartime Service and Staff Shortages

Soon after World War II began in Europe, its impact was felt at Deaconess Hospital and in the Deaconess Medical Staff. By 1941, 24 members of the staff had been called into military duty. Their number increased each year until 1945, when 71 were named in the hospital's annual report as being "IN OUR COUNTRY'S SERVICE." Dr. Edgar L. Tversky was listed as missing in action and Dr. Fred S. Butler and Dr. Hans Kleine as having given their lives.[48]

The end of the war in 1945 brought the return of most of the members of the Deaconess Medical Staff, but new difficulties arose as post-war shortages of trained personnel were felt, particularly in the diminishing number of interns available for house service.

The growing importance of the Deaconess Medical Education Program had been reemphasized in the statement of purpose of the medical staff in the constitutional revision of 1940 with the addition of the phrase, "and to instruct interns." But in 1948 the Rev. Carl C. Rasche, new administrator of Deaconess Hospital, reported to the board of directors:

4-10. Deaconess House Staff, 1942. Dr. C. E. Mueller, with arms crossed, center. Dr. Robert Keller, second from right front.

138

The fact that there are almost twice as many opportunities for internship as there are interns graduating from the approved medical schools as of July 1, 1949, is directly reflected in the forthcoming intern staff of the Evangelical Deaconess Hospital. We had hoped for nine interns and one chief resident. However, we were successful in gaining only three interns.... Our teaching program, which the medical staff has developed for the interns, concentrates on general practice and in so doing has gained favorable recognition. It is anticipated that in the next few years we shall be able to attract sufficient interns to staff our institution adequately.[49]

Dr. Edwin H. Schmidt, one of the interns attracted in 1948 to Deaconess Hospital, was notified of his acceptance in the medical education program by a telegram from Administrator Rasche which read:

Your application for internship at Evangelical Deaconess Hospital St. Louis Missouri is approved. We welcome you to our staff. Compensation will be sixty dollars stipend per month plus full maintenance. A contract will follow your acceptance.[50]

A New Statement of Purpose, Rules and Regulations, 1949

Concerned about the care of all patients in the increasingly complex hospital environment, the medical staff adopted new bylaws, rules and regulations in 1949 which included an expanded statement of purpose:

1. To insure that all patients admitted to the hospital, or treated in the outpatient department, receive the best possible care.

2. To provide a means whereby problems of a medico-administrative nature may be discussed by the medical staff with the board of directors and the administration.

3. To initiate and maintain self-government.

4. To provide education and to maintain educational standards.[51]

A Full Staff as Nuclear Medicine Begins

Though high qualifications for membership and strict rules and regulations for hospital procedures might have been deterrents for staff growth, the Deaconess Medical Staff continued to grow steadily. The administrator reported in 1950:

> It is understandable that when a hospital has an outstanding repu-
> tation for nursing care, good food, a friendly environment, and
> good medical care, more and more doctors will want to bring
> their patients to that hospital. In the course of this year, many
> more doctors have applied for the privilege of bringing patients to
> Deaconess Hospital than we could possibly add to our Staff. The
> problem which is involved is not that of discrimination against doc-
> tors in order to maintain a so-called "closed staff," but rather we
> have a "full staff" which is determined by the limited number of
> beds available.[52]

One year earlier Dr. Stanley Burns, president of the medical staff, reported that at that time, "Some eighteen branches of medical science are [now] repre-sented on the active staff." These included new departments of anesthesia and general practice, which were added in 1949. The appointment of the first full-time medical anesthesiologist, Dr. John P. Eberle, in 1950 was indicative of the scientific strides being made in medical practice and patient care.

The installation of a radio-active isotopes laboratory in 1951 under the control and supervision of a consultant committee added to the diagnostic facilities available at Deaconess Hospital and marked the beginning of nuclear medicine for the Deaconess Medical Staff.[53]

The Joint Commission on Accreditation, 1953

Meanwhile, the Deaconess Medical Education Program was fully accredited and those in charge of it were commended. Dr. Roy Mitchell, chief resident in 1951, reported:

> I am happy to say that Deaconess Hospital's intern and resident
> training program is exceptionally good for the person who is
> really anxious to learn and is willing to use the possibilities that are
> present. The large amount of pathological material, the willing-
> ness and ability to teach on the part of the medical staff, as well as
> the ward rounds and conferences, supplemented by a fully
> approved medical library, offer the very best in a rotating, general
> practice internship and residency.[54]

To strengthen the medical education program further, the board of directors appointed Dr. Jesse Younger as the first paid part-time director of intern and residency training in 1952. Dr. H. A. Goodrich, president of the medical staff, reported that the staff gave its "heartiest approval" to this appointment and stated that the members would fulfill their responsibility in supporting the program.[55]

Even more changes were soon necessary, however, in order for Deaconess to meet the standards for teaching hospitals required by the new Joint Commission on Accreditation of Hospitals. In 1953 Dr. Arthur Wright Neilson, president of the medical staff, reported that it was imperative for the members of the active staff to participate in the professional meetings and that each medical staff member had to assume proper responsibility in teaching interns and residents under the supervision of the director of intern and residency training. In response to this report, the active medical staff voted in October 1953 to adopt "certain regulations and requirements as specified by the new Joint Commission on Accreditation of Hospitals."[56]

In 1955 Dr. Clarence E. Mueller, president of the medical staff, reported that during the past year the bylaws committee had undertaken "the laborious task" of writing a revision of the bylaws, rules and regulations to fulfill the require-

4-11. Deaconess House Staff, 1951. Front: Dr. Ilse Weihe, Dr. Roy Mitchell, chief resident, Dr. Kathleen Egner. Second row: Dr. Chun-Lu-Tsai, Dr. Francisco Licon, Dr. Edward Nemethy. Third row: Dr. Theodore Feierabend, Dr. George Korgel, Dr. Roland Kappesser, Dr. Felix Jobson, Dr. Talivadis Kisle.

ments of the Joint Commission on Accreditation of Hospitals, thereafter referred to as the JCAH.

Revised bylaws were approved by both the active medical staff and the hospital board of directors in April 1955, and in 1956 Deaconess Hospital was fully accredited by the JCAH and fully approved for its internship and general practice residency program by the Council on Medical Education and Hospitals of the American Medical Association. Interns were paid $150 to $200 monthly, first year residents received from $225 to $275 and second year residents, $275 to $325, plus full maintenance, which meant quarters, board and laundry, and two weeks of vacation annually with pay.[57]

New Staff Facilities and Services in Memorial Addition

The new Deaconess Memorial addition to the hospital, previously described as completed and dedicated in October 1956, added 144 more patient beds, bringing the total to 410. It also provided new facilities for treating patients with psychiatric and chronic diseases and for the medical staff and medical education program. Dr. Edward M. Cannon, president of the medical staff that year, spoke for the staff when he said:

> Members of the medical staff are truly grateful for the new Medical Staff Meeting Room.... This room, with modern teaching equipment including a sound movie projector and micro-projector, will be the new location for medical staff and scientific activities. In close proximity to the meeting room are the new medical library, conference room and autopsy room, comprising an excellent center for the expanded teaching program.[58]

In January 1958 Dr. Harry L. Acker, an accredited physiatrist, became the first full-time director of the rehabilitation service, which was located in the new Deaconess Memorial addition. Dr. Birkle Eck, president of the medical staff, welcomed Dr. Acker on behalf of the staff with the observation that "this department will flourish under the leadership of such a highly-trained, enthusiastic physician."[59]

Board-Appointed Chiefs of Service, 1958

Circumstances surrounding the hospital's teaching program and its status as a teaching hospital brought the necessity for more drastic changes in 1958. As mentioned in a previous reference on "Management," a surveyor of the Council on Medical Education and Hospitals observed that changes in the medical staff organization were urgently needed in order to improve the medical education program. In response, sharp differences of opinion developed between the medical staff and the hospital's board of directors. The principal contention centered around the board's decision to appoint five chiefs of service after consultation with the joint conference committee, made up of members of the medical staff and the board of directors. Some members of the medical staff considered this to be interference in the staff's time-honored prerogative of electing its own department heads.

After many discussions and meetings, and after conferring frequently with the executive committee of the medical staff, the board of directors appointed these members of the staff as chiefs of service in 1958:

Surgery: . . . . .Dr. Arthur R. Dalton
Medicine: . . . . .Dr. James P. Murphy
Ob/Gyn: . . . . .Dr. William D. Hawker
Radiology: . . . . .Dr. Joseph C. Peden
Pathology: . . . . .Dr. Henry C. Allen

Following the appointment of these chiefs of service, a medical administrative committee was activated in accordance with revised Deaconess Medical Staff Bylaws, Rules and Regulations. Any member of the medical staff who disagreed with this action was given the opportunity to resign from the staff. None did so, and Dr. Bert Klein declared in his report as president of the staff in December 1958, "The Medical Staff will continue to uphold the high standards of this progressive institution of which we are honored to be members."[60]

The Medical Administrative Committee, A Turning Point

Within this new medical staff organizational pattern it was now possible to develop a team approach to patient care and a strong medical education program as well. The medical administrative committee [the MAC] was responsible for the professional care given to patients in the hospital. As the policy-making committee of the medical staff, it also dealt directly with the hospital board of directors.

4-12. First Board-Appointed Chiefs of Service, 1958. Left to right: Dr. Joseph C. Peden, Radiology; Dr. Henry C. Allen, Pathology; Dr. Arthur R. Dalton, Surgery; Dr. James P. Murphy, Medicine; Dr. William D. Hawker, Obstetrics-Gynecology.

The members of the first MAC at Deaconess Hospital were:

Dr. Arthur R. Dalton, ...Chief of Surgery, Chairman
Dr. James P. Murphy, .Chief of Medicine
Dr. William D. Hawker, .Chief of Ob-Gyn
Dr. Bert H. Klein, ...President, Medical Staff
Dr. Guerdan Hardy, ...President-elect, Medical Staff
Dr. Henry C. Allen, ...Chief of Pathology
Dr. Joseph C. Peden, ...Chief of Radiology
Rev. Carl C. Rasche, ...Administrator, Secretary[61]

During its first year the MAC met twenty-one times. Reporting to the board of directors in October 1958 on the progress being made, Administrator Rasche explained:

> The basic achievement involves decision making on the basis of facts rather than having final decisions predicated on philosophical arguments.... The fact that the members of the MAC report directly to the board regarding credentials and policy matters makes it necessary for the committee members to be much more conclusive in their judgments than heretofore.[62]

144

Serving as a medical education committee, the MAC supervised the program of the three medical education directors, Dr. Cesar A. Gomez, Dr. Robert H. Ramsey and Dr. Frank J. Valach; increased the house staff to twelve rotating internships and twelve residencies; and established three-year residencies in surgery, medicine and obstetrics-gynecology.

The MAC also served as a credentials committee and during its first year it recommended to the board of directors that twenty-six doctors be appointed to the medical staff. It also made twenty-five recommendations to the board of directors regarding hospital management and the board, after careful consideration, concurred in every recommendation given.

Functioning with both responsibility and accountability, the MAC became a strong organizational base for the growth and development of patient care, medical education and hospital operation. By the end of 1960 the administrator could report that:

> During the course of the past year the medical staff conducted excellent departmental and general staff meetings with resultant benefits to the patient-care program of the hospital. We are also fortunate to have a medical staff organization which makes possible the solving of problems involving professional judgments with a minimum of friction. To this end the medical administrative committee, which has been charged by the board of trustees with responsibility for the professional care given in the hospital, deserves the highest acclaim.[63]

Medical Staff Members Honored

Also deserving the highest acclaim were eighty members of the Deaconess Medical Staff who were honored at a 75th Anniversary Board of Trustees-Medical Staff Dinner at the hospital on September 30, 1964.

Among those receiving special honors for twenty-five or more years of service to Deaconess were Dr. Robert Mueller, Dr. Harold A. Goodrich, Dr. Daniel L. Sexton, Dr. Joseph C, Peden, and Dr. Henry P. Thym.[64]

Full-time Director of Medical Education, 1964

Under the excellent leadership of the MAC great progress was made in the med-

4-13. Special Medical Staff honors at the 75th Anniversary in 1964 were presented by (from left) Rev. Dr. Herbert H. Wintermeyer, trustee president, and Administrator Carl C. Rasche to : Dr. Robert Mueller, 39 years; Dr. Harold A. Goodrich, 33 years; Dr. Daniel L. Sexton, 33 years; Dr. Joseph C. Peden, 44 years; and Dr. Henry P. Thym, 35 years.

ical education program, and in 1962 there were twenty-four interns and residents at Deaconess Hospital. But with a growing nationwide shortage of medical school graduates in the 1960s, it became increasingly difficult for community teaching hospitals such as Deaconess to recruit sufficient numbers of house staff officers to maintain an accredited medical education program.

In order to strengthen Deaconess Hospital further as a teaching hospital, in March 1964 the board of trustees appointed Dr. John H. Woodbridge as the first full-time director of medical education and research and as director of the heart station. He also became a member of the MAC.

Under Dr. Woodbridge's leadership, the three-year residency program in medicine was approved in 1964, the four-year residency in surgery was approved in 1965, and the three-year residency in obstetrics-gynecology in 1966. The remuneration for house staff officers had increased to $400 monthly for interns, $450 for first year residents and $500 for second year residents, all with full maintenance and two weeks vacation with pay.[65]

Full-Time Chiefs of Service, 1968

The medical staff, under the leadership of Dr. Dean Sauer, gave significant financial support to the hospital's Decade of Development Program, which was completed in 1968. A new ancillary services building, a new outpatient division, and an increase in patient beds from 410 to 505, previously described as part of this modernization program, helped to transform the hospital into a large medical complex.

In order to meet new organizational needs in this growing medical environment, the Deaconess Medical Staff unanimously adopted revised bylaws in June 1968.

As provided in the revised bylaws, and as recommended affirmatively by the medical staff and the MAC, these full-time chiefs of service were appointed by the board of trustees in 1968:

> Dr. John H. Woodbridge . . . . Chief of Medicine
> Dr. William R. Cole . . . . Chief of Surgery
> Dr. William D. Hawker . . . . Chief of Ob/Gyn
> Dr. Joseph C. Peden . . . . Chief of Radiology
> Dr. Henry C. Allen. Chief of Pathology[66]

In this new organizational pattern, Dr. Woodbridge and Dr. Cole were appointed by the board to serve as co-directors of the medical education program.[67]

4-14. Medical Education Co-directors. Left, Dr. William R. Cole, Chief of Surgery. Right, Dr. John H. Woodbridge, Chief of Medicine. Center, Rev. Dr. H. Wintermeyer, President, Deaconess Board of Trustees. 1968.

147

Dr. James P. Murphy Appointed to Board of Trustees

In a further effort to give the medical staff representation at the highest policy-making level of the hospital, the board of trustees appointed Dr. James P. Murphy, president of the medical staff, as a member of the board in September 1968.

Dr. Murphy was the first medical staff member to serve on the board of trustees, and his participation was described as "outstanding in every respect."[68]

Medical Education Program Extended Off-Site

4-15. Dr. James P. Murphy. First Medical Staff President to hold membership on Deaconess Board of Trustees.

"New Potentials," "New Opportunities," and "New Tasks" were the terms used to describe what Dr. Charles N. Nicolai, president of the medical staff in 1969, said he sensed as "a new aura of expectancy" prevailing at Deaconess Hospital.

One of the new potentials was the opportunity for new stimuli in the educational and research programs as a result of an association of Deaconess Hospital with the University of Missouri School of Medicine. This came after a year of careful and persistent dialogue between Deaconess representatives led by Dr. Arthur W. Neilson, chairman of the MAC, and representatives of the University of Missouri School of Medicine, which assumed responsibility for the direction of the hospital's educational programs offering certification in national accrediting organizations. When this association with Missouri University proved to be too difficult to maintain because of the distance between Columbia and St. Louis, an association with St. Louis University Medical School was established.[69]

Describing how the medical education program at Deaconess Hospital enhanced the whole environment of the hospital, Dr. Neilson reported:

> In "grand rounds," classroom conferences, and corridor conversations a stronger feeling of intellectual inquiry is present. For the attending physician and instructor who is assigned a role in the teaching function, there is great satisfaction in working with

148

bright, young doctors, nurses and technicians. All continually strive for excellence. For the patient, this new environment has produced an improved quality of care.[70]

By 1971 there were more than 360 physicians on the Deaconess Medical Staff and there were 38 interns and residents enrolled in the medical education program, the highest number ever up to that time. They staffed gynecology clinics at St. Louis State Hospital and obstetric clinics in Kinloch. They also participated in eye care and ob-gyn programs at the Neighborhood Health Center. The Deaconess outpatient department provided clinics in surgery, medicine, ob-gyn, pediatrics, diabetes, dermatology, cardiology, physical medicine and rehabilitation as well as diagnostic clinics.[71]

4-16. Deaconess House Staff, 1971: Dr. Robert C. Kingsland, Chief of Medicine, front left; Dr. Raymond O. Frederick, Chief of Surgery, front right; Ms. Mae Novotny, secretary, middle left; and Carl C. Rasche, President and CEO, top center.

Board Certification for All New Staff Members, 1973

Reaffirming the belief that the doctor is a primary factor in providing high quality patient care, the Deaconess Medical Staff adopted bylaws in 1973 requiring that:

> All physicians appointed to the medical staff after July 25, 1973, must be certified by a board approved by the American Board of Medical Specialties or other board deemed its equivalent in the

149

judgment of the board of directors, or must be an active candidate for board certification.[72]

All members of the Deaconess Medical Staff appointed since 1973 are board certified or actively pursuing such certification, except for a few whose exceptional circumstances led the board to waive this requirement.[73]

Women Physicians, Deaconess Medical Staff Leaders

Among the more than 370 members of the Deaconess Medical Staff in 1973 who met these high standards of board certification were a growing number of women physicians, some of whom served as officers.

The number of women physicians in the United States remained small until the early 1970s when the feminist movement facilitated their entry into the profession. As a result, the proportion of women among medical school graduates increased from 11 percent in 1973 to 28 percent in 1984.

Women physicians served on the courtesy staff at Deaconess Hospital, however, as early as 1902, when Dr. Caroline Skinner was the first to be named. She continued to serve patients at the hospital for many years in an era when women made up less than 3.5 percent of all medical schools graduates.

In 1903 Dr. Adelheid Bedal also became a member of the Deaconess courtesy staff. Dr. Bedal arrived in St. Louis in the 1890s, and she is described by medical historians as one of several competent women physicians "whose credentials, skills and service to St. Louis helped to expand opportunities for women, especially in public health and institutional settings." In 1903 she was one of the first three women to be admitted to the St. Louis Medical Society. All three had received their medical education elsewhere because Washington University Medical School in St. Louis did not accept women students until 1918, when it admitted two. St. Louis University Medical School did not admit women until 1948.[74]

4-17. Dr. Adelheid Bedal. Member, Deaconess Courtesy Staff, 1903.

Internships were equally difficult for women medical graduates to find. In St. Louis City Hospital, internships were once highly prized because of the broad experience they provided, but they were closed to women until World War II. At Deaconess, however, as reported earlier, one of the three interns in 1930 was Dr. Gladys Huscher, the first woman physician to be accepted in the Deaconess Medical Education Program. In 1989 there were fifteen women among the sixty-five members of the house staff.[75]

4-18. Dr. Katherine Crawford. Vice President, Deaconess Medical Staff, 1968.

Dr. Katherine Crawford was elected vice president of the Deaconess Medical Staff in 1968. Appointed to the active staff in the department of surgery in 1958, Dr. Crawford represented that department on the medical staff executive committee in 1966 and was the first woman physician to serve on that committee. She had the added distinction of being the first woman surgeon in St. Louis to be elected to membership in the St. Louis Surgical Society.[76]

Dr. Ruth C. Comens, chief of the department of anesthesiology, was elected president of the Deaconess Medical Staff in 1975, the first woman physician to hold that position and to become a member of the board of trustees of Deaconess Hospital. She had served with distinction on the active staff in the anesthesia department since 1953.[77]

Dr. Susan Luedke was appointed director of the Deaconess Oncology Service in 1980, and in 1989 she served as a member of the board of directors of Deaconess Preferred Care. Her leadership on the medical staff continues the

4-19. Dr. Ruth C. Comens. President, Deaconess Medical Staff, 1975.

distinguished service of many outstanding women physicians throughout the years at Deaconess Hospital.[78]

Diagnostic Related Groups, New Challenges

The government's development of diagnostic-related groups (DRGs) and the Medicare and Medicaid limits on reimbursements that go with them brought new challenges for the Deaconess Medical Staff and Hospital in the 1980s.

4-20. Dr. Susan Luedke. Director, Deaconess Oncology Service. 1989.

Under the DRG system, described previously as a challenge to the hospital management as well as to the medical staff, the government paid hospitals a pre-determined amount for health care, regardless of whether the cost of that care was more or less than the set amount. This DRG system placed great pressure on physicians to limit costs, such as drugs and tests, while the patient remained in the hospital, and it limited the patient's stay to the time allowed in order for reimbursement to be equitable.

With the full cooperation of the members of the medical staff, the transition to this new system went smoothly at Deaconess.[79]

Specialization in the 80's

As Medicare reimbursements shrank under DRG's and as new medical techniques shortened the time patients must spend in the hospital, converting many inpatient procedures to outpatient programs, Deaconess Hospital, like other hospitals, soon found itself with too many beds and too little revenue.

In response to this development and to new healthcare advances, many specialized programs, described in greater detail in the chapter on "Patient Care," were introduced during the 1980s at Deaconess under the direction of members of the medical staff. The Deaconess Sleep Disorders Laboratory, the Deaconess Alcoholism Program, the Chronic Pain Program, the BASH Treatment and

Research Center for Eating and Mood Disorders, and the Deaconess Institute for Sexual Medicine were among these specialized programs. They have not only enhanced cost-effectiveness and promoted more specialization among physicians, but they have also strengthened the Deaconess Medical Education Program. Interns and residents serve patients in many of the new services.[80]

Medical Education and the Challenge of the 90s

The explosion of scientific knowledge throughout the 1980s, the proliferation of specialized medical programs, and the public's expectations of accuracy in diagnosis and treatment made it necessary for physicians to get as much training as possible. Some students became hesitant, however, about beginning a career in medicine because of discouraging malpractice trends apparent in medical practice. As a result of this and many other factors, there was a decrease in medical school applicants.

Dr. M. Robert Hill, director of medical education and chief of medicine at Deaconess Hospital since 1981, explained:

> The high cost of medical school, exorbitant malpractice insurance premiums and the increasing burden of Medicare regulations, such as the DRG reimbursement program and other bureaucratic problems have caused many to take a dim view of the future of medical education.[81]

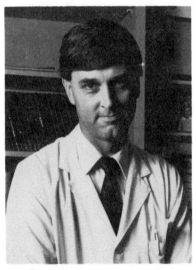

In 1989, however, the Deaconess Hospital Medical Education Program had sixty-five interns and residents enrolled, the largest number ever in the hospital's history. Dr. Hill explained further:

> We encourage our residents to gain an appreciation of the good they can do. Most of the difficulties associated with medical practice are not quite as significant when the whole picture is considered.[82]

4-21. Dr. M. Robert Hill, Director of Medical Education and Chief of Medicine, since 1981.

153

The whole picture for Deaconess interns and residents may include a one-year transitional internship during which young doctors rotate through the major medical areas to gain experience and explore the possibilities for specialization. Or, a straight internship leads them directly into post graduate work in a specialty. Most then continue their training in a specialized residency program of which Deaconess now has three, medicine, family practice and podiatry.[83]

The residency in internal medicine under Dr. Hill has traditionally been the first choice for medical school graduates. In 1989 there were 38 residents in that three-year program at Deaconess Hospital while two more were in their fourth year as chief residents. Internal medicine residents study and care for acutely ill, adult patients.

A new residency in family practice under Dr. David C. Campbell, chief of family medicine, was one of only two such programs offered in the St. Louis area in 1989 and eleven physicians were enrolled in that three-year program. Family practice residents rotate among the major medical disciplines such as internal medicine, surgery, orthopedics, obstetrics-gynecology, pediatrics, psychiatry, and dermatology to learn how to give comprehensive care to patients regardless of sex or age. About 40 percent of their training time is spent in outpatient departments.

Medical education at Deaconess Hospital remains strong because it has, according to Dr. Hill, the three important components of a successful teaching program: (1) good recruiting, (2) excellent faculty and (3) the goodwill of the

4-22. Deaconess House Staff and Instructors. 100th Anniversary, 1989.

attending staff. It also provides excellent experience with a large variety of illnesses.

Throughout almost 100 years, benefits to Deaconess Hospital and to the Deaconess Medical Staff from a strong medical education program have been: "better patient care, improved cost-effectiveness, an enhanced hospital reputation, and quality medicine."[84]

The Medical Executive Committee

Major responsibilities for leadership in the Deaconess Medical Staff now reside in the medical executive committee [known as the MEC] as provided in a revision of the bylaws adopted in December 1982 and in further revisions approved by the hospital board of directors in July 1988. This committee includes the medical staff president; president-elect; chiefs of the eight departments; the elected representatives from the departments of obstetrics-gynecology, medicine, surgery, and psychiatry; and the hospital president, who serves with voice but without vote.

The MEC meets at least once a month and is responsible to the board of directors for recommendations on all professional matters in the conduct of the hospital; serves as the credentials, accreditation, and medical education committees; and receives and acts upon the reports of all medical staff committees. The members of the MEC aid in the enforcement of medical staff bylaws, rules and regulations and for implementation of sanctions where they are needed.[85]

In a report to the board of directors, Dr. Tehmton S. Mistry, president of the Deaconess Medical Staff in 1987, described the strength of the staff in this way:

> In a sense, the Deaconess Medical Staff is a microcosm of our country. We are richly endowed with talented physicians of different geographical, racial and cultural origins. We are also experiencing a growing collaboration and peaceful coexistence between physicians belonging to different philosophies of healthcare delivery. This delicate balance, this unity amidst diversity is not an accidental occurrence. It has been nurtured by a succession of leaders from the hospital. Indeed the spirit of harmony between administration and doctors, and within the medical staff itself, is one of the unique assets of this hospital which we should cherish.[86]

A Celebration of "Tradition and Change"

To celebrate the cherished traditions and assets of Deaconess Hospital and to honor members of the Deaconess Medical Staff, almost 500 guests attended a Medical Staff Centennial Gala at the Adam's Mark Hotel in St. Louis on April 22, 1989.

In this festive setting, Dr. James P. Boedeker, president of the staff, served as the master of ceremonies. Many longtime staff members were present to recall important events in Deaconess Medical Staff history.

"Change" was the theme of the featured speaker, Former U.S. Ambassador to the United Nations Jeane J. Kirkpatrick, who called current world trends "really dramatic and exciting."[87]

The Deaconess Medical Staff has seen many dramatic and exciting changes in medicine and medical practice during the past 100 years. Some medical historians now say that "recent advances made in imaging technology or 'machine vision,' [which] enable doctors to see inside the body without the trauma of exploratory surgery [have resulted in] more progress in diagnostic medicine in the past fifteen years

4-23. Dr. James P. Boedeker, Deaconess Medical Staff President and Master of Ceremonies, 100th Anniversary Centennial Gala.

4-24. Dr. Paul Convery, Deaconess Medical Staff Past-president, with Jeane J. Kirkpatrick, speaker, Centennial Gala.

156

than in the entire previous history of medicine."[88]

Focus for the Second Century

Looking toward a new century of more dramatic changes in health care and health education, the Deaconess Medical Staff reaffirmed in 1989 its traditional primary purpose:

> To provide that all patients admitted to the hospital or treated as outpatients receive the best possible care.[89]

4-25. 1989 Deaconess Medical Executive Committee. Left to right, top: Executive Vice President Jerry W. Paul; Paul J. Ritter, M. D.; Philip J. Schmitt, M.D.; M. Robert Hill, M.D.; Jorge A. Viamontes, M.D.; Henry D. Onken, M.D.; Kate DeClue, Ph D.; James S. Compton, M.D.; Frederick E. Youngblood, M.D.; President Richard P. Ellerbrake; Barry D. Brown, M.D.; Horatio D. Marafioti, M.D.

Chapter Five

PATIENT CARE
"The Primary Function"

The primary function of the hospital, the one that has never been lost sight of throughout the whole of its evolution, is to care for the sick and injured.[1]

A poor sick woman, alone and in need of nursing care, was the person who set into motion the series of events in 1889 which led to the organization of The Evangelical Deaconess Society of St. Louis, Mo., the establishment of the Deaconess Sisterhood and the founding of Deaconess Hospital. The purpose of the founders, as stated in their charter, was "1st. To nurse the sick," and that has been the primary function of Deaconess Hospital ever since.[2]

Home Care, the First Choice in 1889

Patient care is the total care given a patient. One hundred years ago it was most often provided in the patient's own home by a family member or close friend on a one-to-one personal basis.[3]

In 1889 there was little that could be done for a patient in a hospital that could not be provided equally well at home. Only the destitute or the gravely ill were ordinarily taken to an institution for patient care.

> For the middle class, a bed among strangers in a hospital ward was a last resort.... The hospital was a place to be avoided— often a place in which to die....Even surgery was most frequently undertaken in the patient's home.[4]

Accident victims were also usually taken to their own homes first for treatment if at all possible.

> It was common...for most folks to be taken home [from the scene of an accident] to await recovery or death. Naturally, the better the conditions and facilities, the better chance a person had to cheat the undertaker.[5]

158

To facilitate patient care in the home, many households at that time had "recipe books" which included home remedies for everything from asthma to earache, a sore throat, or "nerves." One such widely used book, *Mother's Remedies*, was written by a physician who gave more than 1,000 recipes, including those for many popular patent medicines. Remarks followed each remedy giving the medical virtue or active principle of the ingredients prescribed.[6]

Tuberculosis was by far the greatest single killer of adults in 1889, and gastrointestinal ills (summer diarrheas) were the greatest cause of death among children. Every year there were also epidemics of typhoid fever, malaria, measles, smallpox and diphtheria. Doctors made house calls, but it was a widely held belief that most ailments were, in the terminology of the day, "self-limited." In the great majority of cases a patient could expect to recover with or without a physician's treatment. Life expectancy, however, was only a little over forty years for the population generally and it was even less than that in large cities.[7]

The First Deaconess Patients

Since home care was the preferred care of the times, the first two Deaconess Sisters began their work in St. Louis in August 1889, by going to the patients' homes to give patient care. The record says,

> One [deaconess] went out into the homes of the sick—charging 50 cents for a 24-hour day —while the other maintained the [Deaconess] Home.[8]

Most patients in need of the Deaconess Sisters' care at that time were very poor so they were given home care for whatever they could pay.

5-1. Sister Philippine Buehn, on Home Care Assignment.

159

Sometimes it was only a few cents, but that was accepted in order to maintain the person's dignity and to encourage him or her to follow orders and take any medications prescribed.

Since many home care patients required around-the-clock nursing, the Deaconess Sisters could often be seen leaving the Deaconess Home with their overnight bags and baskets of food.

Home care was not an easy assignment. Florence Nightingale once wrote:

> Nursing the poor sick in their homes is no amateur work. To do it as it ought to be done requires knowledge, practice, self-abnegation, and...direct obedience to, and activity under, the highest of all Masters, and from the highest of all motives.[9]

The Deaconess Sisters were well prepared for such assignments. Their primary study guide, *The Principles of Deaconess Work*, devoted an entire chapter to "Nursing in Private Homes." Careful instructions were given not only for specific nursing procedures in a limited home environment but also for the conduct and behavior of the deaconess within a family setting. She was cautioned, "Do not allow yourself to tell of family affairs" and "Do not neglect to go out into the fresh air during the day, if in any way possible, particularly when you are obliged to sleep in the same room with the patient."[10]

Demanding as it was, nursing the patient was sometimes not the only responsibility on home care assignments. The deaconess nurse was also expected to do all of the work in the sickroom. Airing the bed, cleaning the room, and washing bandages were part of patient care. If the patient was the mother of the household, the care of the children and the preparation of meals usually became her duties as well.

The First Deaconess Inpatients

On October 9, 1889, just a little more than two weeks after the first physicians and surgeons offered their services to the Deaconess Home on Eugenia Street, the first patient was admitted to the hospital by Dr. John Green Sr., the well-known ophthalmologist previously described as a member of the Deaconess Medical Staff.[11]

160

The record shows that this first inpatient came from out of town and she remained for two months. Apparently she had a serious eye condition requiring surgery. Although the facilities in the first Deaconess Home and Hospital were described as being very modest, surgery was possible. It was usually of a relatively minor nature, however, because at that time the technical problems of blood loss, shock, and infection had not yet been solved.[12]

Whatever the reason, the first Deaconess inpatient remained in the hospital more than forty days, the average length of stay in hospitals at that time. All but one of the other nine patients admitted from October through December 1889 stayed for at least a month, and two were accompanied by "guests" who remained with them. All but one were discharged as "improved" or "cured."

The Deaconess reputation for good nursing care soon brought many more patients to the Deaconess Home and Hospital, and sixty-one were admitted in 1890. By the end of the first full year of service, so many patients were seeking admission that the Deaconess Society authorized the search for a new location where larger, permanent hospital facilities could be built.[13]

"Modern" Patient Care in the 1890s

5-2. Deaconess Sisters' Home and Hospital, 4117 West Belle Place, with horse-drawn ambulance at front door, 1893.

161

The sign on the front of the new hospital buildings on West Belle Place and Sarah Street read: "Evang. Deaconess Home and HOSPITAL." Dedicated on January 15, 1893, these new facilities could accommodate forty patients and fifteen deaconesses. In this institutional setting, now officially designated as a HOSPITAL, a new era of patient care began.

Considered "modern" at that time, the new three-story hospital on West Belle Place was described as having "25 private rooms and 25 ward beds...two thoroughly aseptic operating rooms and well equipped bath rooms with hot and cold water on each floor of the building, which are free to all patients." At the same time, it was said to be a "quiet, more homelike place" with good, wholesome, well-cooked meals, personal attention, cleanliness and "every comfort at our command at the most reasonable prices."[14]

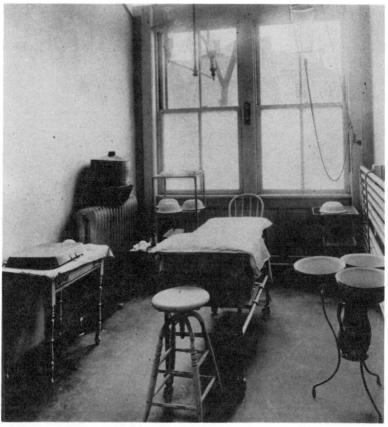

5-3. Deaconess Operating Room,. 1893.

More than 200 patients were admitted in 1893, double the number cared for during the previous year on Eugenia Street. In 1894 the patient census increased to 240, and 113 surgical operations were specifically reported that year for the first time.[15]

The Germ Theory and Modern Surgery

"Thoroughly aseptic [germ-free] operating rooms" were the result of bacteriological discoveries made during the 1880s. A host of diseases, like cholera, diptheria, pneumonia, tuberculosis, typhoid fever, tetanus, influenza and bubonic plague, many of which were among the great scourges of the human race, had been proved to be of bacteriologic origin.

The germ theory was credited as being to medical thought of the nineteenth century what the theory of evolution was to biological thought, and it ushered in the era of modern surgery. In early aseptic operations, scrupulous cleanliness was the rule and buckets of antiseptics were used to sterilize both the instruments and the doctors' hands.

With the introduction of rubber gloves, the autoclave and sterilized dressings during the 1890s, surgery became more and more successful and the number of operations increased steadily. By the turn of the century, it was said that "the very word 'operation' was to the lay mind almost synonymous with 'hospitalization.'"[16]

Speaking of her experience as an operating room nurse supervisor "in the old days," Sister Magdalene Gerhold recalled that:

> At first we boiled everything...and we used sterilized water in the operating room...it was taught that nothing could be made more sterile than bare hands and arms adequately scrubbed.... We used sea sponges. No use to number and keep track of them, for only two were used. They were put in a solution for the next operation....[17]

Scrupulous cleanliness was not new to the Deaconess Sisters. They had always practiced what some called "scrubby Dutch" housekeeping as well as meticulous nursing procedures. As reported earlier, this was confirmed by the members of the medical staff who stated in a letter to the board of directors in 1897:

163

The cleanliness of the Hospital has been above criticism and beyond reproach, an imperative necessity to the success of a hospital.

In surgical and medical work no institution can boast of greater success. The best surgeons in the city have been at home in the operating rooms, feeling absolutely sure that every precaution was being taken for the security and safety of the patient.[18]

Appendectomies were the operations most often performed at Deaconess Hospital in 1899 with gynecological operations a close second. This followed a national trend at that time. The term "appendicitis" was introduced in 1886 at Massachusetts General Hospital where an analysis of the disease paved the way for its proper diagnosis and successful surgical treatment. With the development of aseptic operating rooms, the body cavities were no longer forbidding obstacles, and in some hospitals appendectomies became so numerous that critics "were already warning against excessive and unnecessary resort to the scalpel."[19]

In spite of great surgical advances, however, preoperative procedures at the turn of the century were enough to discourage unnecessary abdominal surgery. Recalling further her experience in the operating room, Sister Magdalene Gerhold described some of the standard procedures.

In the old days before an abdominal operation, a patient was required to enter the hospital three days beforehand. The patient was then dosed with calomel, then Epsom salts, and completely dehydrated. He was allowed no water for 24 hours.

To prepare a patient for an operation, the part was liberally anointed with soap, left on overnight, cleaned off with bichloride, then vigorously scrubbed with a stiff brush which often left the skin raw and susceptible to ulceration along the line of stitches.[20]

Long periods of recuperation were necessary for most patients hospitalized in the 1890s, but by 1899 the average length of stay in Deaconess Hospital decreased to twenty-six days.[21]

Labor-intensive Patient Care

Whether post-operative or non-surgical, patients at the turn of the century usually remained bedfast throughout most of their hospitalization. Doctors at that time placed strong emphasis on rest, diet and medication as important for recovery regardless of the illness. Nursing care in such a setting was very labor-intensive with each patient requiring almost constant attention.

Typhoid fever was the most frequent non-surgical disease treated at Deaconess Hospital in 1899, and typhoid patients required particularly long periods of care. Although the bacteriological cause of the disease was known, little could be done to treat it, and recovery was very slow.

The bedside care given by the Deaconess Sisters, both for private room patients and for those in the wards, provided not only basic hands-on nursing procedures but a comforting, encouraging presence which was conducive to healing. Spiritual ministry was part of their approach to caring for "the whole person."[22]

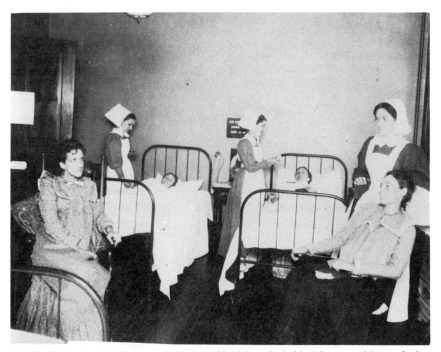

5-4. Ward Room for Four Patients, 1902. Sister Magdalene Gerhold, right, supervising probationers with patients.

An Early Patient Handbook

The transition of patient care from the home to the hospital brought much more hope for healing but it was not without its problems.

Charity patients accounted for almost one-third of the care given by the Deaconess Sisters in the late 1890s. Though this service was in keeping with the Deaconess Society's original purpose of providing care for the sick poor, abuses had occurred. In 1899 the new superintendent, the Rev. Frederick P. Jens, reported,

> If the nearest relatives or friends are not able to pay something...it ought to be the duty of the church congregation from which they come to donate a certain amount for such charity work.... In several instances, charity patients have been sent to us from different places and later on we learned that incorrect statements had been made as to their financial ability, and although promises were made to send us some remunerations...we never heard from them, except in some cases even ungrateful slander.[23]

To overcome these difficulties and to help the public come to a better understanding of the hospital's role in healing, "TERMS" for admission were adopted and published for the first time in the hospital's annual report in 1899.[24]

Hospitalization was still so new and misunderstood at the turn of the century that some patients arrived unannounced from out of town and others came by train to Union Station and then had difficulty finding Deaconess Hospital in the unfamiliar city. Still others came with too little or too much clothing for a hospital stay which averaged twenty-two days in 1902. To help such patients, another page was included in the annual report that year with pertinent information about "How To Get To The Home And Hospital" and "What To Bring With You."[25]

As might be expected, the steady increase in patients brought a corresponding increase in visitors. While the annual report for 1902 still emphasized Deaconess Hospital as "a quiet, more homelike place," the large influx of visitors was changing that atmosphere so rapidly that the first "RULES FOR VISITORS" were also published that year.[26]

By 1907 it became necessary to adopt "RULES FOR PATIENTS" as well in order to maintain a proper atmosphere for healing. With the publication of those

TERMS.

1. Application for admission to the Evangelical Deaconess Home and Hospital must be made at the office of the house.

2. Charges are, $5.00 per week in the wards, and from $7.00 to $15.00 in the private rooms, payable ONE WEEK IN ADVANCE. These charges include board, light, fuel and ordinary nursing care, but they do not cover the expenses of a special attendant day and night, wines, liquors, etc. The charges for the use of the operating room are $5.00.

3. Chronic cases, those having contagious or infectious diseases or suffering from mental aberation or alcoholic mania are not eligible for admission. It is desirable that every applicant shall bring a physician's certificate of his condition.

4. Application for the admission of charity patients must be made to the President, in person or by letter, he only having authority to admit them.

5. It is absolutely necessary that those persons, through whose means charity cases are admitted into the hospital, shall assume the responsibility of POSSIBLE funeral expenses.

6. Persons of all creeds, and of no creed are admitted, and receive the same quality of nursing and care, but the hospital is a Christian household, and the services held in the chapel are those of the German Evangelical Church. Every patient however is privileged to receive the ministrations of whatever form or faith he may profess or prefer.

5-5. Terms for Admission, 1899.

RULES FOR VISITORS.

The visiting hours are: On week days from 10:00 to 12:00 A. M., and from 2:30 to 5:00 P. M.; on Sundays from 2:30 to 5:00 P. M., and at no other time, except in cases of special emergency.

Nothing in the way of eatables or drink shall be carried to the patients without the approval of the person in charge of the floor.

Loud talking, or loitering about the office, halls or stairways, is not allowed.

Visitors are requested to leave the house promptly and quietly at the close of the visiting hours.

5-6. Rules for Visitors, 1902.

RULES FOR PATIENTS.

1. Patients are not allowed access to the wards or private rooms unless by special permission, nor are they allowed to leave the premises without permission of the sister in charge of their department.

2. Patients and visitors must not deface walls or funiture, sit on sides of beds, talk loud in wards or halls, nor spit on floors.

3. Those who have received the physician's dismissal will not leave the Institution permanently without reporting to that effect at the office.

4. Smoking within the Hospital is prohibited; also the use of wines or spirituous liquors, unless prescribed by the physician.

5. Profane or indecent language; or the expression of immoral or infidel sentiments, will not be tolerated.

6. The feeing of sisters or employees is not allowed.

7. Convalescents are desired, as far as possible, to be present at the services in the Chapel.

8. The Hospital cannot be held responsible for loss of money or any valuables, unless deposited at the office.

5-7. Rules for Patients, 1907.

rules, the hospital's annual report that year began to take on the appearance of the modern "Patients' Handbook."[27]

Some patients and visitors considered the enforcement of such rules a troubling trend toward regimentation and impersonalization, and it is interesting to note that Deaconess annual reports after 1904 no longer emphasized the "quiet, more home-like atmosphere" of the hospital. Critics of other hospitals at that time spoke of them as becoming "monolithic medical factories," but most people at Deaconess accepted the new regulations as part of the price of progress brought about by the new scientific atmosphere of medical care.[28]

Innovative Pediatric Care

The life of one young patient brought to Deaconess Hospital in 1901 was transformed by the scientific progress being made in plastic surgery, which was then a very new specialty practiced only in some larger urban areas. Although there was no pediatric department at Deaconess at that time, children were admitted in unusual cases.

Deaconess Hospital of St. Louis reports having nursed more sick children during the past month than any month in the last few years. Among them was an orphan boy from the Northwest of Missouri. He was twelve years old and was born literally without ears. The cartilage of the ears had grown to the head. The doctors first loosed this cartilage and bent it forward. Then they cut the skin which had grown over the passage to the ear drum, trying first one ear. He can now hear some and begins to speak.[29]

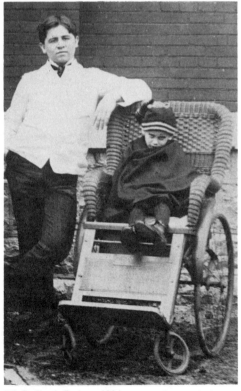

5-8. Pediatric Patient, 1904.

Of the 551 patients admitted to the hospital in 1901, there were

22 under 10 years of age. Since no special pediatric equipment was available at that time, young patients sometimes used equipment not intended for them.[30]

Babies born in the hospital in the early 1900s were usually placed in a basket alongside the mother's bed unless she insisted on having the baby in bed with her. Sometimes even more creative "cribs" were improvised.[31]

Only obstetrical patients with serious complications ordinarily entered hospitals for delivery. As a result, only seven births were recorded at Deaconess Hospital in 1900 but by 1904 there were eighteen. There were also eight abortions recorded at Deaconess in 1904 but, according to the Deaconess Sisters, such procedures were performed only to save the lives of the mothers.[32]

First Baby Incubator in St. Louis

Eight of the eighteen babies born at Deaconess in 1904 were premature. One of them, weighing only two-and-one-half pounds, was among the first so small to survive in St. Louis. That was a newsworthy event which occurred because of the availability at Deaconess Hospital of the first baby incubator in the city.[33]

The baby incubator was invented in Europe in the 1890s and was a scientific, medical breakthrough in infant care. More of a curiosity, however, than an acceptable new approach to premature infant care in hospitals, incubators had been popular attractions in several International Fairs beginning in Berlin in 1896.

After saving the life of the premature infant at Deaconess Hospital, these baby incubators were moved on June 1, 1904, by the Imperial Concession Company to an elaborate building which by then had been completed for them on the World's Fair grounds in Forest Park. With the medical attention of Dr. Joseph B. Hardy and the help of Dr. John Zahorsky (later a

USE INCUBATOR TO SAVE LIFE OF VERY SMALL BABY.

Infant Said to Be Doing Well and to Have Chance for Life.

One of the smallest babies ever known by St. Louis physicians to survive birth is struggling for life in an incubator at the Deaconess hospital and Dr. Joseph B. Hardy, the physician in charge, states that the chances for the infant becoming a lusty child are excellent. The baby was born Thursday afternoon. It was placed at once in one of the incubators of the Imperial concession company, and last night was giving every indication of gaining victory over death. The infant is 11 inches long and weighs but 2· pounds and 7 ounces. Its arm is about the size of the little finger of a man's hand and its head is not of greater circumference than an average-sized orange.

The concession company's incubators, fourteen in number, are being operated at the Deaconess hospital, pending the completion of the concern's building on The Pike at the World's Fair. This will be ready in about ten days.

5-9. Newspaper Report of First Baby Incubator in St. Louis, May 1904.

170

5-10. Baby Incubator Exhibit, 1904 World's Fair. (Missouri Historical Society Photo Collection, used with permission).

member of the Deaconess Medical Staff), the lives of many premature babies were saved in those incubators during that summer.[34]

The cost of maintaining each infant in an incubator was then $15.00 per day. With most wage-earners receiving from only $4 to $5 pay per day, few babies' parents could afford such care. The costs at the Fair were covered by huge crowds of visitors who paid twenty-five cents each to view the exhibit and marvel at scientific progress.

> The INFANT INCUBATOR to many persons was the most interest-
> ing exhibit to be seen at the Exposition. This interest had partic-
> ular reason for existing in that the exhibition was a practical show-
> ing of the latest and most successful scientific means for nurturing
> and saving immature infants....[35]

After the World's Fair closed, the baby incubators were moved from St. Louis to other cities for exhibition. Deaconess Hospital, like most hospitals, could not afford to keep such expensive equipment at that time.   But the Deaconess image as a hospital on the forefront of scientific patient care had been enhanced by the baby incubator experience.

New Diagnostic Tools

As a result of the medical discoveries being made in the 1890s, new diagnostic tools were becoming available for patient care in the hospital soon after the turn of the century.

The first X-ray examination at Deaconess was recorded in 1907 and the charge was $9.00. A new X-ray room was included in the new hospital building which had been built in 1906 to care for 100 patients.

Although X rays had been discovered in 1895 by German physicist, Wilhelm Roentgen, X-ray examination was not generally available for patient care until some years later. Its use necessitated large and elaborate equipment which only larger hospitals could afford to install, and specially trained personnel were required to operate it safely. One of the first practitioners in Boston, unaware of how hazardous X-rays could be, suffered severe, unhealing burns and died at an early age.

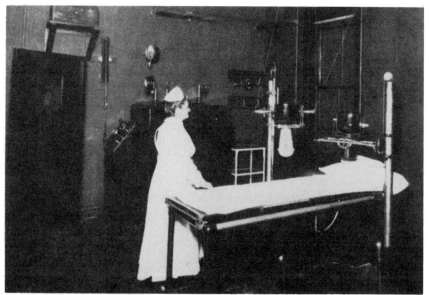

5-11. First Deaconess X-ray Room, 1907. Sister Katherine Streib, Supervisor.

172

5-12. First Deaconess Laboratory, 1906.

Sister Katherine Streib took the special training required and was in charge of the first Deaconess X-ray room, which cost $54.44 to maintain in 1907.[36]

The first pathologist and bacteriologist, Dr. Amand Ravold, was appointed to the Deaconess Medical Staff in 1898, but it was said that only the use of a thermometer and taking urine samples for analyses were an accustomed part of hospital routine before the end of the century.

By 1906 laboratory analysis had become a more important part of patient care, and the first laboratory was built at Deaconess as part of the new hospital building on West Belle Place. The cost of maintaining that laboratory the first year was $65.00.[37]

There were also two new operating rooms in the new hospital, and 843 operations were performed in 1907, surgical patients accounting for more than half of the 1,319 patients admitted to the hospital that year.[38]

Patient Entertainment in 1907

Patient care was made more pleasant during a long convalescence when a library was opened in 1907 in the new hospital building. The record says,

We are especially indebted to Dr. Bransford Lewis for his present to the hospital of a large beautiful mahogany library case and for his work in founding a library for patients. It has grown to several hundred volumes and is used very gratefully by the majority of patients whose condition allows them to read.[39]

Since the length of patient stay averaged 20.2 days in 1907, the library was an instant success. The librarian reported that 1,719 books were read during the first year alone.[40]

Higher Costs, Another Sign of the Times

Patient care in the new hospital building was not only more modern and more entertaining, it was also more   costly. An increase in charges in 1907 was a sign of the times and the beginning of a continuing trend.

Charges are $7.00 per week in the wards, $9.00 in rooms with two beds, and from $15.00 to $25.00 in the private rooms, payable one week in advance.[41]

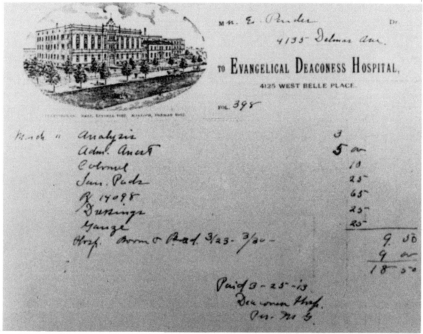

5-13. Patient Bill, 1913.

To attract middle class patients as well as the sick poor and the more affluent who could afford private rooms, Deaconess Hospital offered semi-private patient care for the first time in 1907.

In 1913 these room rates were unchanged, as was the charge of $5.00 for the operating room, but the itemized bill of one semi-private patient included a $3.00 fee for laboratory analysis:

Occupational Therapy in 1913

Former patient, Mr. Joe Ponder, wrote that he received much more than primary patient care while he was in the hospital in 1913:

> Dr. Babler was my doctor...and he took 30 stitches in my arm.
>
> The nurses [Deaconess Sisters] were great as they let me dry dishes for them and taught me the German alphabet along with some German language. I had a great time along with getting well. It was also great to ride in the horse-drawn ambulance.[42]

Occupational therapy was not a specialized service at that time, but as this patient reveals, the Deaconess Sisters were always alert to new opportunities for promoting recuperation and recovery.

Specialization and a New Kind of Medicine

The distinction between physicians and surgeons was already being made in urban areas when Deaconess Hospital was first opened in 1889. Ten years later in 1899 Deaconess patients could be treated not only by Dr. Bock, the surgeon and president of the medical staff, but also by a "laryngologist, neurologist, gynecologist, heart and lungs specialist, oculist and aurist, dermatologist, pathologist and bacteriologist." In 1914 the Deaconess staff included additional specialists in "otology, proctology, genito-urinary surgery, and roentgenology."[43]

These specialties in medical practice helped to project the powerful image of the hospital as a scientific institution, and patient care became increasingly disease-oriented. More lives were saved, and the average length of stay at Deaconess was reduced to 13.7 days in 1920, half of what it had been in 1900. This was true even during the great influenza epidemic of 1918-1920, when there were so many patients in the hospital that the hallways were often full of beds.

The isolation of insulin in 1921 for the control of diabetes and the introduction of a diet of raw liver to control pernicious anemia were among further new medical advances of the 1920s which brought dramatic, effective treatments for these hitherto fatal illnesses. New methods of prevention and treatment were also found for contagious diseases such as scarlet fever. Cod liver oil was discovered as a preventative for rickets, and vitamins were named for the first time and studied as important for good health. Surgery brought the most patients to the hospital, however, and new anaesthetic substances were beginning to make brain and chest surgery possible.

In 1920-21 only one death was recorded at Deaconess Hospital from typhoid fever, one from tuberculosis and two from pneumonia. As a result of the new immunization against diptheria there were no cases of that dread disease. Meanwhile, the number of births increased to 76 and surgical admissions outnumbered medical cases with significant increases in appendectomies (255), tonsillectomies (312) and hysterectomies (106). By 1920 medical technology had provided new tools as well as a new rationale for centering acute care in the hospital. "Prospective patients were influenced not only by the hope of healing, but by the image of a new kind of medicine—precise, scientific and effective."[44]

"Quality Assurance" in 1921

The rapid growth of hospitals in this new scientific environment, as described earlier, led to the hospital standardization movement, and in March 1921 the Deaconess board of directors and medical staff adopted the American Medical Association's "Minimum Standard" for the proper care of the sick. It was explained that,

> The focus of all effort in Hospital Standardization is the patient. It is with the object of giving him the best professional, scientific, and humanitarian care that the entire program is conducted and that such stipulations as the following are required of the approved hospital: that it have an organized, competent, and ethical medical staff; that the staff hold regular conferences for review of the clinical work; that fee-splitting be barred; that accurate and complete clinical records be kept of all patients treated; and that adequate diagnostic and therapeutic facilities, including a clinical laboratory and an X-ray department, be provided.[45]

Deaconess Hospital was approved in compliance with these standards after its first examination and has received approval regularly ever since.[46] Although the Minimum Standard of 1921 did not specifically require a full-time pharmacist in the hospital, the Deaconess board of directors and medical staff interpreted the requirement, "adequate...therapeutic facilities," to include a full-time registered pharmacist. As described previously, Sister Mary Feutz was appointed to that position after her graduation from the St. Louis College of Pharmacy in 1921.

So many potent new pharmaceuticals were being developed as a result of medical experience in World War I and the influenza epidemic of 1918 that the St. Louis College of Pharmacy had introduced already in 1919 a new course entitled "Biological Therapeutics" stating that "physicians were coming to rely more and more on the professional cooperation of pharmacists in obtaining information concerning the employment of these remedies."[47]

5-14. Deaconess Pharmacy, 1921. Sister Mary Feutz, Pharmacist.

A Full-time Superintendent of Nurses

In 1923 patient care was organized at Deaconess Hospital under the supervision of the first full-time superintendent of nurses, Sister Sophie Hubeli, who received special training for this new position.

Until that time, Sister Superior Magdalene Gerhold supervised all patient care divisions of the hospital in addition to her supervisory duties in the Deaconess Sisterhood, the School for Deaconesses and the Deaconess Home.[48]

5-15. Sister Sophie Hubeli, First Deaconess full-time superintendent of nurses, with staff: (Left to right) Sisters Ida Bieri, Selma Hess, Beata Schick, Matilda Matthes, and Martha Roglin, night supervisor.

The efficiency of nursing service under Sister Sophie Hubeli's supervision was demonstrated, as previously mentioned, when the tornado of 1927 devastated St. Louis. During the first three days after that storm, 126 patients were treated at Deaconess in the emergency room. Meanwhile, as debris was removed and repairs were made throughout the hospital, nursing service continued to care for 100 inpatients, and no lives were lost at Deaconess because of this disaster.[49]

New Patient Care Facilities, 1930

In June 1930, nursing service was expanded to care for 175 inpatients when Deaconess Hospital relocated to its new seven-story hospital building at 6150 Oakland Avenue.

Set on a hill overlooking Forest Park, the new hospital had rooms for almost twice as many patients as the old one on West Belle. There were also two large up-to-date operating rooms, smaller operating rooms for eye, ear, nose and throat surgery, separate rooms for cystoscopic examinations, physiotherapy treatments, and orthopedics, and a new obstetrical department, clinical laboratory, X-ray room, and pharmacy.

The purchase of an electrocardiograph and diathermy machine in 1931 added still further to the diagnostic and therapeutic facilities available at the new location. A few years later, a new deep X-ray therapy machine was installed at a cost of $4,500, the gift of a generous contributor who gave an additional $40,000, the interest from which was to be used exclusively "for the [nonsurgical] treatment of indigent patients suffering from the dread affliction of cancer."[50]

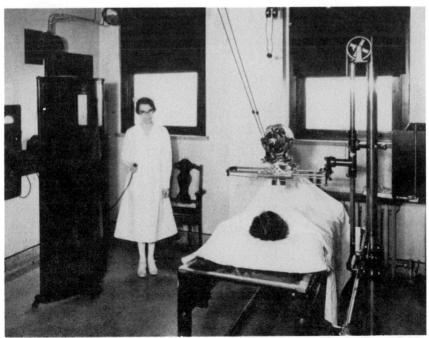

5-16. X-ray Room, 1930. Sister Flora Pletz, X-ray Technician.

5-17. Laboratory, 1930. Sister Clara Weltge, Laboratory Technician.

Sister Beata Schick, Director of Nurses, 1930

The larger patient census required a larger hospital staff. The number of lay employees was therefore increased from fifty-two in 1930 to seventy-six in 1931.

To supervise nursing service in the greatly expanded facilities, Sister Beata Schick was appointed "director of nurses," a new title in 1930. As reported elsewhere, she was also appointed director of nursing education and as a member of the hospital's administrative staff.[51]

In 1933, Sister Ella Loew was appointed to the new position of "hospital night supervisor," an indication of the growing workload in nursing service.[52]

5-18. Sister Beata Schick, Director of Nurses, 1930.

180

Health Insurance Benefits, 1936

The growing financial problems during the Great Depression in the 1930s, as described earlier, led the American Hospital Association to endorse the principle of group prepayment for hospital bills in 1933 and to established standards for such plans.

When Deaconess Hospital became a member of the Blue Cross Plan for health insurance in 1936, many patients found for the first time that they could afford hospitalization benefits. As a result, there were 533 more admissions in 1937 over the previous year at Deaconess and it was reported that "During the last months of

5-19. Sister Ella Loew, Night Supervisor, 1933.

the fiscal year a number of patients could not be admitted on account of lack of beds."[53]

100,000th Patient Admitted in 50th Anniversary Year

The 100,000th patient was admitted to Deaconess Hospital in 1939, the hospital's 50th anniversary year, and by that time more than 1000 patients had been given care in their own homes, particularly in the early years.

One indication of the progress made in patient care in the United States from 1889-1939 was revealed in healthcare statistics which reported that the average length of life had been increased during that period of time from forty to fifty-nine years and the annual death rate reduced from 17.2 to 10.6 per 1,000.

Moreover, deaths recorded from childhood diseases, pneumonia and tuberculosis declined significantly while deaths from heart disease doubled and those from cancer tripled.

At Deaconess Hospital in 1939 there were 124 more surgical patients, 74 more X-ray examinations and 2918 more laboratory examinations recorded over the previous year, suggesting that more and more patients saw the hospital as a place of diagnosis and healing and that they could afford such care.[54]

Sister Hilda Muensterman, Director of Nurses, 1942

Sister Hilda Muensterman, who had completed study at St. Louis University for a bachelor of science degree in nursing education, was appointed director of nurses in 1942 to succeed Sister Beata Schick, who died after a serious illness.

5-20. Sister Hilda Muensterman, Director of Nurses, 1942, presiding at nurse supervisors' meeting.

Deaconess Sisters held the key positions in nursing service and throughout hospital departments until 1946, but this staffing pattern became increasingly difficult to maintain during World War II. The steady increase in the number of patients, wartime personnel shortages and a decline in the number of deaconesses entering the sisterhood made it necessary for Sister Hilda to begin recruiting nurses from other schools of nursing and from among the first lay graduates of the new Deaconess School of Nursing in 1946.

Lay leadership in nursing service necessitated the reorganization of patient care services to include written personnel policies and job descriptions, details which had previously been included as part of the Deaconess Sisters' training and work assignments.[55]

World War II and Patient Care Benefits

Although World War II brought shortages in personnel and supplies, the war was also indirectly responsible for some major medical discoveries and improvements in patient care. Dried blood plasma, mixed with sterile water, became available to hospitals after it was found that this method saved the lives of war casualties until they could be taken to emergency centers for surgery. Blood banks were established soon thereafter, the first one at Deaconess beginning in 1948. At the same time,

> Penicillin went into production on a vast scale and was used to treat pneumonia, wound infection, meningitis, gonorrhea and syphilis. And wartime research produced new drugs to combat malaria, and new insecticides, notably DDT, which drastically reduced deaths from typhus.[56]

Also introduced in the 1940s were new medical technologies such as the iron lung respirator for polio patients and an automatically controlled baby incubator for premature infants. Both were very expensive at that time and were the gifts of Deaconess donors.[57]

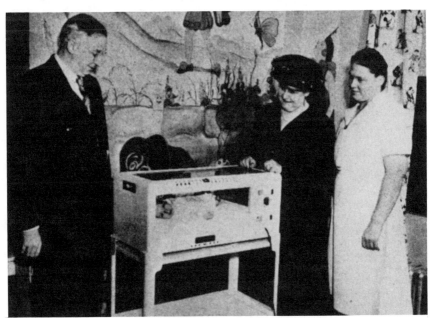

5-21. Sister Marie Lee, Pediatric Supervisor, with Mr. and Mrs. Albert Lishen, donors of new baby incubator, 1947.

183

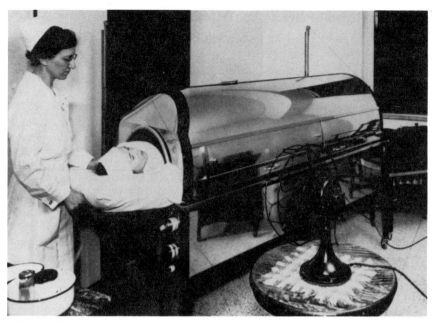

5-22. Sister Bertha Grollmus, with patient in iron lung, donated by the Hilmer family, 1947.

Another indirect result of the war was the training of the first patient care volunteers at Deaconess to help alleviate the severe shortage of professional help. Trained Red Cross volunteers began serving in patient care areas in 1942 and by April 1943 there were 35 Red Cross Aides contributing 670 hours a month to patient care.[58]

Nursing Service, A Separate Department in 1948

In 1948, after careful planning and research, nursing service was made a separate department at Deaconess Hospital. Sister Hulda Weise was appointed assistant director of nursing service and she was given full responsibility for all nursing service under the guidance of Sister Hilda Muensterman, director of nurses and director of the School of Nursing.

The objectives of the nursing service department were:

1. To give adequate and efficient care to all patients in the hospital.

2. To maintain a high standard of working conditions through good personnel policies and other activities of employer-employee relationships.

3. To motivate the employee to achieve his or her goal through education, and leadership by job promotion and in-service programs.[59]

Clinic for Indigent Outpatients Opened, 1948

Throughout its history, Deaconess Hospital is said never to have turned away persons in need of medical care, and a so-called "dispensary" was occasionally mentioned in some reports. There was no established clinic for indigent outpatients, however, until 1948.

The rapidly growing demand for patient care in the hospital at that time, combined with an acute shortage of patient beds, led Administrator Carl C. Rasche, in consultation with the medical staff, to recommend the opening of the first Deaconess Outpatient Clinic. The board of directors approved, and in July 1948 this new patient care facility was established in conjunction with the emergency department.[60]

Chronic and Mental Illnesses, No. 1 Health Problem in 1950

With the availability of the so-called "miracle drugs" and many other new medical breakthroughs such as isoniazid, which made tuberculosis a curable disease, the No. 1 health problem in the United States by 1950 became chronic and mental illnesses. As a result, the shortage of patient care beds became even more severe. Of the 4309 general hospitals in the United States at that time, only 112 provided care for even the mildest mental disturbance, and only six of the 29 St. Louis hospitals (Deaconess being the first) had psychiatric facilities.

In 1952, the Deaconess Mental Hygiene Outpatient Department was opened, separate from the inpatient services, in a renovated residence on Oakland Avenue next to the hospital, the first of its kind in any general hospital in the United States.[61]

5-23. Dedication of Mental Outpatient Department, 1952. Left to right; Sister Elizabeth Lotz, Psychiatric Supervisor; Dr. Harold A. Goodrich, Medical Staff President; Dr. Arthur Deppe, Mental Outpatient Department Director; Sister Hilda Muensterman, Director Of Nurses; Carl C. Rasche, Administrator.

Sister Olivia Drusch, Director of Nursing Service, 1954

Sister Olivia Drusch, M.S.N.E., was appointed director of nursing service and director of the school of nursing in 1954 to succeed Sister Hilda Muensterman, who resigned from the Deaconess Sisterhood to be married.

With Sister Hulda Weise and Sister Mary Kramme as assistant directors of nursing, the nursing service department in 1954 included:

Head Nurses 14
Staff Nurses 59
Nurses' Aides 54
Ward Clerks 8
Orderlies 7
Part-time Nurses 20

In 1955 Sister Hulda Weise was appointed associate director of nursing service after she received her M.S.N.E. degree from St. Louis University.

5-24. Sister Olivia Drusch, Director of Nursing serice, 1954, (third from right front) with nursing service supervisors. Front row: Sister Elizabeth Lotz; Sister Hulda Weise, assistant director; Sister Mary Kramme, assistant director; Sister Superior Frieda Ziegler, pharmacist; Sister Olivia; Mrs. Elizabeth Evans; Sister Kate Nottrott. Middle row: Miss Marianne Gehlbach; Mrs. Bonnie Sue Collier; Miss Ruth Price; Miss Gloria Doll; Miss Lena Boettcher; Mrs. Sylvia Eilers; Miss Bernice Haag; Mrs. Emmogene Lageman. Top row: Miss Shirley Lehde; Miss Shirley Hasebrink, Mrs. Betty Gore; Sister Amanda Wulff; Sister Marie Lee; Sister Ida Bieri; Mrs. Gladys Engelbrecht; Miss Sandra Saunders.

By this time, the average length of stay for patients at Deaconess had been reduced to only a little more than ten days. While in the hospital, however, more

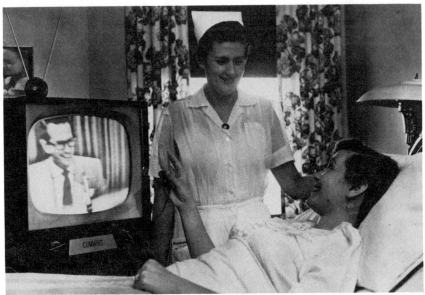

5-25. Television Installed for Patients. Sister Marilou Mitchell with patient, 1953.

patients were likely to be critically ill and in need of treatment such as piped oxygen, which was installed in all patient rooms in 1953. Meanwhile, the installation of television and wall mounted electric fans was added for patient comfort.[62]

South Memorial Building for Mental and Chronic Patients

A whole new phase of patient care began at Deaconess in 1956 when the new South Memorial Building was dedicated for the care of chronic and mental patients.

Included in the new building, which increased the number of patient care beds to 328, were a new psychiatric and mental hygiene outpatient department and a rehabilitation service with new physical therapy and occupational therapy departments.

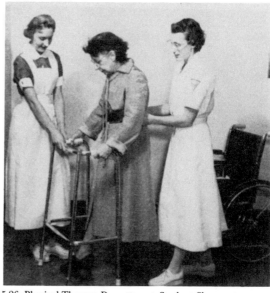

5-26. Physical Therapy Department. Student Sharon Schickedanz and Supervisor Ann Brown assist patient.

Noting that as patient care became more scientifically advanced it had also become more costly during the previous ten years, Administrator Carl C. Rasche stated that Deaconess had two employees per patient in 1956, and that the average total cost per patient per day was $23.70, with $14.26 of that amount required for salaries alone.[63]

All Patient Care Areas Get a New Look

Advanced patient care in the rehabilitation and psychiatric services stimulated comparable modernization throughout the whole hospital. In 1957 new delivery rooms and nurseries updated the department of obstetrics and gynecology. Although not required at that time for accreditation by the Joint Commission on Accreditation of Hospitals, a recovery room was added to the department of surgery in 1957.[64]

188

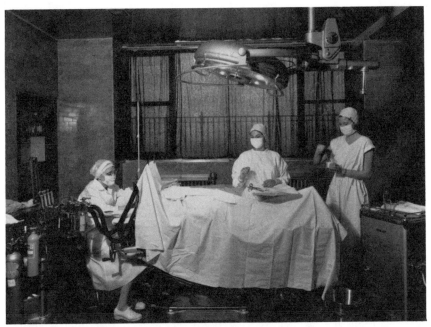

5-27. New Surgical Lights in Modernized Operating Rooms, 1956.

To help patients cope with the greater complexity of the many new medical services being offered, a department of medical social service was inaugurated at Deaconess Hospital in 1957 under the direction of Mrs. Dorothy McKelvey.

At the same time, the Deaconess Outpatient Clinic for Indigent Patients was moved in 1958 to a renovated residence on Clayton Avenue, adjacent to but separate from the hospi-

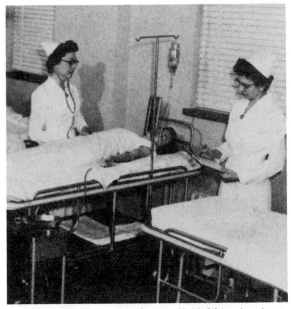

5-28. The Recovery Room, 1957. Sister Hulda Weise, Associate Director of Nurses, amd Sister Pauline Becker, Recovery Room Supervisor, with patient.

tal. In this new facility 2,183 patients were served the first year, 3,122 in 1959, and many more each year thereafter.[65]

Meanwhile, to improve patient care further and to help control rapidly rising costs, a new Group Nursing Program was inaugurated in 1961 and enthusiastically received by patients, doctors and nursing service personnel. In this new program, groups of up to three patients were served by one private duty nurse for which each patient paid the nurse one-half the usual private duty charge.[66]

Medicare and Medicaid Patients

When health care became available in 1966 under the government's Medicare and Medicaid Programs for large segments of the population, particularly the poor and the elderly, such patients accounted for more than half of Deaconess Hospital's occupancy on any one day, and they have done so ever since.

At the same time, a proliferation of voluntary and commercial health insurance programs added significantly to third-party payment for patient care. In this new environment, the quality of patient care became a concern not only for the hospital, the medical staff and the patient but also for government agencies, other insurers and the community, adding still further to the increasing complexity of patient care services.[67]

Computerization Speeds Services

To achieve greater accuracy and speed of communication, Deaconess patient admissions, records, orders for treatments, billings and discharges were all computerized in 1968 with the new Medelco Hospital Information System, part of the aforementioned 11.5 million Decade of Development Program.

This program also expanded the hospital facilities to 505 patient beds in air-conditioned rooms, added a new ancillary services building, and provided a new coffee and gift shop for the convenience of patients and visitors.

In 1969, as Deaconess Hospital celebrated its 80th anniversary, patients in the hospital could watch space technology enabling a man to walk on the moon while they themselves were being treated with new medical miracles, among them many new drugs, 85 percent of which were unknown ten years earlier.[68]

Ruth Triefenbach, Vice President and Director of Nursing Service

In 1971, the Deaconess board of trustees appointed Miss Ruth Triefenbach, M.S.N.E., vice president and director of nursing service, to succeed Sister Olivia Drusch, who retired.

Miss Triefenbach was the first layperson appointed to direct the Deaconess Department of Nursing Service and the first to be designated a vice president. A graduate of the Deaconess School of Nursing, she had completed further graduate studies and had worked closely with Sister Olivia Drusch for many years.

As previously described, the title of vice president was in keeping with the hospital's revised constitution and corporate structure in 1971. By that time the depart-

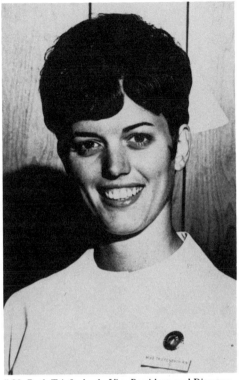

5-29. Ruth Triefenbach, Vice President and Director of Nursing Service, 1971.

ment of nursing service included more than 500 nurses and technicians, who cared for 16,221 inpatients annually in 505 inpatient beds with an average occupancy rate of 88.3 percent for the year.[69]

The 500,000th Patient

When the 500,000th patient was admitted in February 1974 during Deaconess Hospital's 85th anniversary year, patients could be treated with a new theratron 80 cobalt therapy machine, or they might have received care in the new Deaconess Eye Care Center. Microsurgery, nuclear medicine in the form of radioactive isotopes, kidney dialysis in the new hemodialysis and renal transplant center, special care in the intensive coronary medical-surgical care units, or minor surgery in the one-day surgery center were also among the new services available to Deaconess patients in 1974.

Another cause for celebration was that patients could count on a hospital stay averaging less than ten days in 1974. Meanwhile, deaths in the hospital from all illnesses had decreased 59 percent since 1945.

Many patients at Deaconess have been spared exploratory surgery since the installation in 1976 of the full-body computerized axial tomography (CAT) scanner, which enables diagnoses to be made of pin-point diseases otherwise difficult or impossible to detect. A new birthing room, with the latest scientific equipment nearby in case of emergencies, was opened in 1977 to provide greater comfort and home-like surroundings for obstetrical patients. And laboratory analyses for all patients at Deaconess were made possible at lower cost and within three minutes with the installation of a new automatic clinical analyzer, the first in St. Louis.[70]

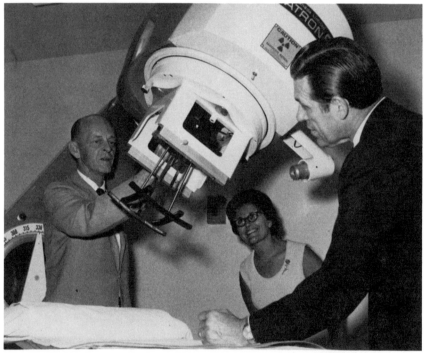

5-30. Theratron 80 Cobalt Unit, 1974. Dr. Francis O. Trotter, Director, Department of Radiology; Mrs. Donna Pohlman, President, Women's Auxiliary, donor of unit; and Carl C. Rasche, President and CEO.

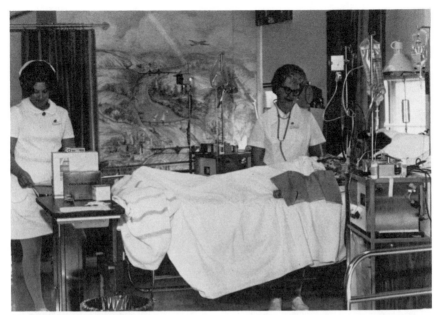

5-31. Hemodialysis Center.

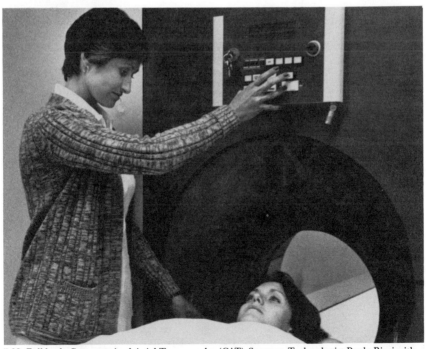

5-32. Full-body Computerized Axial Tomography (CAT) Scanner. Technologist Paula Ricci with patient, 1976.

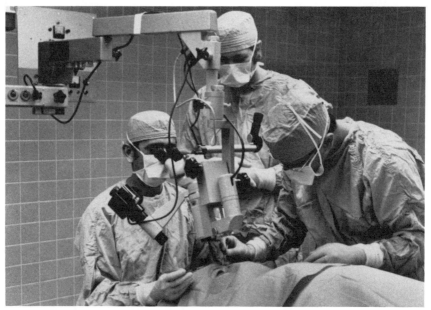

5-33. Surgeons Using Microsurgery.

5-34. Coronary Care Unit Nurses' Station.

Patient Care "Designed for the '80s"

Miraculous as these scientific advances in patient care already seemed to be, in 1976 Deaconess Hospital announced a new building and renovation program, called a "Design for the 80s," in order "to provide the tools and services essential to effective, modern medical practice...in a day of spiraling economy and overwhelming need."[71]

Despite the spiraling economy, Deaconess patients received care at a charge of $25 less per patient per day than the average hospital in St. Louis in 1976, and the demand for new services and more patient beds continued to increase. For the previous four years there had been an average daily occupancy of more than 90 percent at Deaconess, and there were tremendous increases in diagnostic and therapeutic services: 51.8 percent in occupational therapy, 52.1 percent in the psychiatric department, 66 percent in nuclear medicine, and 84.9 percent in hemodialysis.

In November 1979, the new and renovated patient care facilities, made possible by the Design for the '80s Program, were dedicated in celebration of the 90th Anniversary of Deaconess Hospital and the Deaconess Sisterhood. There were then 527 patient care beds, many new patient care services and a new parking garage for visitors, medical staff, volunteers and employees.[72]

"Our Specialty is You"

With up-to-date facilities for patient care throughout, Deaconess   Hospital began   its 90th decade   of service by reaffirming its longtime purpose in a new mission statement:

> "To provide professional, compassionate health care and health education in a Christian setting."[73]

Promising "to keep a personal touch in everything we do" in the increasingly impersonal world of scientific progress and medical specialization, the Deaconess board of directors and staff assured patients in the hospital's annual report for 1980 that "Our Specialty is You."

This promise, based on the Deaconess tradition of caring as an integral part of healing, resulted in the establishment of many more new specialized patient care programs throughout the 1980s. Designed to provide the highest quality and most up-to-date care and, at the same time, to cut the high cost of sophisticated medical technology and help meet the requirements of new Diagnostic Related Groups for Medicare reimbursement, these new programs offered patient care in concentrated areas of specialization within the hospital and in a variety of outpatient facilities located conveniently in the metropolitan community.

Some of these new programs arose out of existing patient care services: the Deaconess Oncology Unit (1980), the Coronary Prevention and Rehabilitation Service (1980), Home Health Services (1984), the One-day SurgiCenter (moved to Deaconess Medical Office Center in 1985), Pediatric Services (reopened in 1987), and the Cancer Screening Center (1988).

Changing social attitudes toward emotional and behavioral illnesses encouraged the opening of the Deaconess Sleep Disorders Center (the first in St. Louis, 1980), the Alcoholism Program (1981), the OptiFast Weight Management Program (1984), the BASH Eating and Mood Disorders Program (1985), the St. Louis Program for Substance Abuse (1988), and the Institute for Sexual Medicine (1988).

Other new services at Deaconess Hospital in the 1980s included an Audiology Service (1981),the Deaconess Manor Skilled Nursing Facility (1982), the Cardiac Catheterization Laboratory (1986), the Park Central Institute (for head and neck surgery, 1987), Podiatry Services (1987), and Family Medicine (1987).

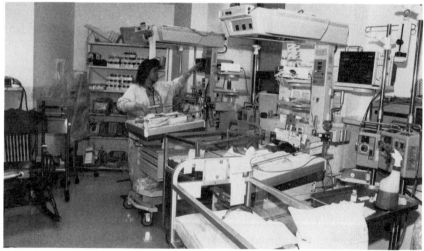

5-35. The Deaconess Nursery, 1988.

196

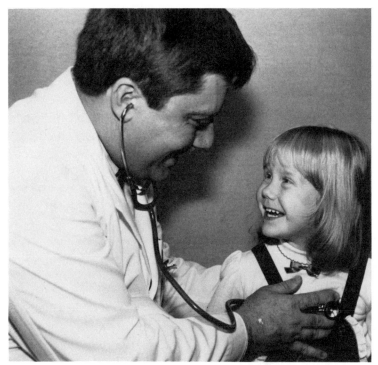

5-36. Dr. David Campbell, Chief of Family Medicine, and patient.

Off-site outpatient services were established at the South County Dialysis Center (1983), at MedCenters in Eureka (1983), in Fairview Heights (1984), in Chesterfield (1985), at the Tri-County SurgiCenter (1986), and the Magnetic Resonance Imaging Center, with St. Mary's Hospital (1986).

Community service programs were also developed: the Physician Referral Service (1980), affiliation with the health maintenance organization, known as the Group Health Plan (1981), the LifeDial Emergency Response Program (1982), the Preferred Provider Organization, now known as Deaconess Preferred Care (1984), and Orchard House, a retirement community in Webster Groves (1988).[74]

Deaconess Centennial Patients

Deaconess Hospital admitted 19,843 patients in 1989, the largest annual admission in the hospital's 100 year history. More than half, 10,985, were medical/surgical cases. Of the remainder, OB patients and newborns accounted for a total of 6,140.

With heart disease and cancer now the greatest causes of death in the United States, most hospital patients require more aggressive treatment and a greater variety of services in a shorter time period than ever before. As a result, the average length of patient stay at Deaconess in 1989 was 7.7 days, compared to 40 days 100 years ago.[75]

Healthcare costs were higher, with the average of $255 per patient day at Deaconess in 1989. But that care was still a comparative bargain.

> The Missouri Hospital Association has reported that if you want to have a baby, a heart attack or a stroke, you can't do it less expensively than at Deaconess. If you have an aching back, you can't get it fixed more economically than at Deaconess.[76]

Life expectancy in the United States now averages seventy-five years, almost twice what it was when Deaconess was founded in 1889. Moreover, in keeping with the hospital's stated mission, Deaconess patients in the centennial year could expect to receive the best care possible, "offered in the compassionate spirit of Jesus Christ."[77]

The Deaconess Patient Care Services Department

The nursing service department at Deaconess was reorganized in 1987 and renamed the Deaconess Patient Care Services Department. Mary Catherine DeClue, who has a bachelor of science and master of science in nursing, and a doctorate in education, was appointed vice president of patient care services. In that position, she also served as a member of the hospital administrative staff and on ten committees: Institutional Planning, Pharmacy, Medical Records, Safety, Infection Control, Critical Care, Quality Assurance, Quality Review, Emergency and Anesthesia.[78]

The Deaconess Patient Care Services Department directs and coordinates the activities of all of the members of the total patient care team. Reaffirming its 100-year-old Deaconess tradition, the department stated its philosophy as:

> We believe that the primary function of the department of Patient Care Services is the welfare of patients and their families.[79]

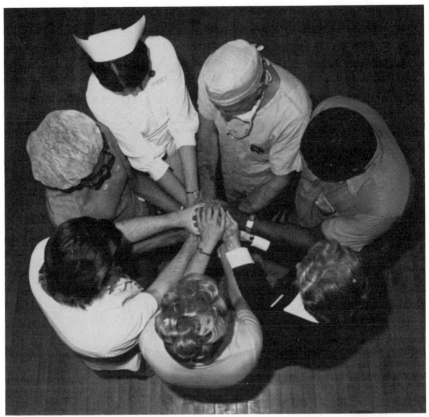

5-37. The Deaconess Patient Care Team.

Chapter Six

THE DEACONESS SCHOOLS AND COLLEGE OF NURSING
"Educating To Care"

Deaconesses throughout the world were known for their excellent education long before 1889, when the first School for Deaconesses was established in St. Louis. Recognizing that the quality of caregiving depends greatly on the quality of the education provided for caregivers, deaconess educators have always required academic excellence, thorough clinical training and spiritual growth.

In 1851 Florence Nightingale travelled from England to Germany to study with the deaconesses in Kaiserswerth where, as described earlier, she received her only formal nurse's training. Impressed with deaconess training methods, she declared,

> Nursing is an art; and if it is to be made an art, it requires as exclusive a devotion, as hard a preparation as any painter's or sculptor's work....[1]

The St. Louis School for Deaconesses, 1889

The Evangelical Deaconess Society of St. Louis also adopted the Kaiserswerth model for healthcare education and declared in 1889 that one of its purposes was "to found and support a deaconess home where deaconesses shall be educated and trained," making Deaconess a teaching hospital from the very beginning.[2]

There were no state licensing laws for nurses or boards of accreditation for schools of nursing in Missouri in 1889, so the credentials of Sisters Katherine Haack and Lydia Daries depended on their own training under deaconess educators. That they were ably qualified as teachers was soon acknowledged by the members of the first Deaconess Medical Staff who wrote:

> The training of nurses [deaconesses] who were capable and willing has been exceptionally fine, and all that could be desired. The nurses trained under her [Sister Katherine] have everywhere

200

been received without question, and their work has been entirely satisfactory.[3]

Called "probationers," Sisters Sophie Brunner and Charlotte Wellpot were the first students in the School for Deaconesses. Instructions in nursing procedures were given by means of the apprentice method, which enabled the training to proceed much more rapidly on an individual basis rather than with the classroom approach of later years.

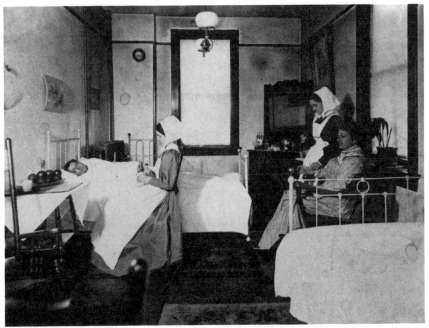

6-1. Apprentice-teaching in the School for Deaconesses. Sister Magdalene Gerhold, right, with probationer and patients.

Members of the first Deaconess Medical Staff provided personal instruction and supervision in medical procedures. When "Rights and Duties" of the medical staff were officially adopted in 1898, members of the staff agreed that "It is the duty of all staff members to participate in the educational program of the deaconesses under the leadership of the superintendent and the head deaconess."[4]

Instructions in spiritual ministry for the first deaconesses were given by the Rev. Jacob Irion, pastor of St. Paul's Evangelical Church in St. Louis and a member of the first board of directors of the Deaconess Society. He also wrote the first brief instruction manual used for those classes. When the Rev. Frederick P. Jens became pastor and superintendent of Deaconess Hospital in 1898, he taught the courses on religion.

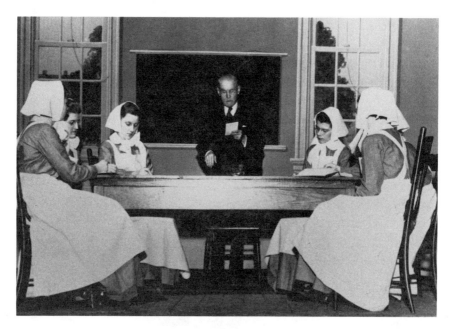

6-2. Class in Religion, School for Deaconesses. Superintendent Frederick P. Jens, instructor.

The Deaconess Society and the St. Louis community were assured of the high standards of deaconess training and patient care by Superintendent Jens, who reported in 1899:

> Our deaconesses who nurse the patients have had a thorough the-
> oretical and practical training and most of them have voluntarily
> selected nursing the sick as their life vocation; consequently they
> have a long experience and it is not necessary for us to train a new
> corps of nurses every two or three years....[5]

The Curriculum of 1901

Courses in medical and surgical nursing, German, English, Bible study, sacred hymns and the history and principles of deaconess work were all part of the instruction schedule in the School for Deaconesses from the very beginning, but the first so-called "curriculum" was published in 1901:

> For their course of instruction the probation sisters are divided into three classes:
>
> Class I has finished the course in anatomy, physiology and nursing, and is at present receiving instruction—two hours a week—in the principles of the female diaconate.
>
> Class II will soon have finished the course in anatomy, physiology and nursing [given twice a week by the house physician, Dr. H. Beedle] and then will take up the course in the history of deaconess work.
>
> Class III consists of those who entered last and receive six hours instruction weekly, four in English and German from Miss E. Bode, and two in the history of the female diaconate.... Besides all sisters have two lessons a week in Bible study, one lesson each from the Old and the New Testament, one lesson in singing, one evening of the week in reading and church history...[6]

Written and oral examinations were given at the end of each course, and in 1902, Superintendent Jens reported that in addition to the lectures of the intern, Dr. O. Th. Walser, other physicians and surgeons lectured in their respective branches of practice. By 1904 Dr. L. H. Hempelmann was teaching anatomy and physiology, Dr. H. L. Nietert lectured on surgery and Sister Marie Oehler taught the classes in required language work.[7]

Clinical Training

Outside the classroom, deaconess probationers spent their first three months in the motherhouse assisting in the general kitchen and housework. Designed to give the prospective deaconess an introduction to institutional life and the basic principles of nutrition, sanitation and group living, this three-month orientation period quickly eliminated all but the strongest and most deeply committed applicants.

After the first three months, the probationers began their clinical nurse's training and were assigned to assist in one of the patient care divisions under the supervision of a graduate deaconess. The work shifts were twelve hours per day beginning at 7 a.m. with time off for classes, study and meals.

In this strenuous and demanding environment it was understandable that "physical and emotional health and strength" were among the requirements for admission to the School for Deaconesses. Probationers were admitted for training by application to the home committee, which interviewed each applicant and evaluated her individually for approval by the board of directors.[8]

Terms of Admission

In 1908, "Terms of Admission" to the School for Deaconesses were published for the first time as part of the annual report of the Deaconess Society. The requirements then specified were: good character, affirmed by a testimonial from the applicant's pastor; good health, certified by her physician; parental approval, stated by letter; a written sketch of the applicant's life written by herself (academic ability); and an age of between 18 and 40 years. It was suggested further that a deaconess applicant "ought to cultivate a cheerful disposition," since, as recorded in Proverbs 17:22, "A cheerful heart doeth good like medicine."

Upon admission, probationers were required to live in the motherhouse and abide by its rules. They received free room and board, medical care, and after the first three months, $2.50 monthly as pocket money. In 1910 the monthly stipend was increased to $8.00 with twice that amount for the month of vacation.

There was no charge for tuition in the School for Deaconesses if the entire course of training was completed and the probationer was consecrated for service as a Deaconess Sister.

The deaconess garb was issued at the successful completion of the first year. To provide the basic wardrobe needed until that time, probationers were required to bring with them this list of articles:

> 1 plainly made black woolen dress
> 3 plain wash dresses
> Underwear, shoes and stockings to last one year
> 12 handkerchiefs
> 3 dark underskirts
> 1 box with sewing material
> Combs, tooth, nail and clothes brushes
> 1 Bible[9]

The Four-Year Course of Instruction, 1909

Beginning in 1909, the School for Deaconesses introduced a new four-year course of instruction. Deaconess students were required during their first three years to follow a weekly "Plan of Instruction and Lectures" with some classes beginning at 6:20 a.m. and others offered from 8 to 9 in the evening. Included were not only the previously required courses in languages, religion and deaconess principles but a new schedule of "Doctors' Lectures" which was adopted by the medical staff and which introduced the many new disease-oriented and diagnostic specialties developing in medical practice and patient care in the early 1900s.[10]

Curriculum of Lectures.

The following curriculum of lectures was adopted by the Medical Staff for the course of study for the deaconess nurses. Lectures begin the first Monday in October and continue to the first of May. During 1909—1910 Dr. L. B. Torrance, our house physician, gave the complete course of lectures on anatomy and physiology.

FIRST YEAR.

DR. L. H. HEMPELMANN: Anatomy and Physiology, 24 lectures.
DR. A RAVOLD: Bacteriology, 4 lectures.
NURSES' INSTRUCTION: Lectures and Demonstrations, 25 lessons.
INVALID COOKING: First three months.

SECOND YEAR.

DR. L. H. HEMPELMANN: Materia Medica and Therapeutics, 12 lectures.
DR. BRANSFORD LEWIS: Urinalysis and Catheterization, 8 lectures.
DR. W. H. STAUFFER: Dietetics, 4 lectures.
DR. A. RAVOLD: Hygiene, 4 lectures.
DR. H. L. NIETERT: Surgery, 4 lectures.
DR. E. A. BABLER: Bandaging, 8 lectures.
DR. J. R. LEMEN: General Medicine, 4 lectures.
DR. W. B. DORSETT: Obstetrics and Gynaecology, 8 lectures.

THIRD YEAR.

DR. J. J. HOUWINK: Diseases of the skin and Emptive Fevers, 6 lectures.
DR. J. F. SHOEMAKER: Diseases of the eye, 6 lectures.
DR. R. D. CARMAN: X-Ray and Electricity, 2 lectures.
DR. H. W. HERMANN: Nervous diseases, 4 lectures.
DR. J. C. SMITH: Diseases of the nose and throat, 4 lectures.
DR. H. L. NIETERT: Surgery, 4 lectures.
DR. W. B. DORSETT: Obstetrics and Gynaecology, 4 lectures.
DR. J. R. LEMEN: Diseases of Heart and Lungs, 4 lectures.
DR. W. H. STAUFFER: Diseases of the Intestinal Canal, 4 lectures.
DR. L. H. HEMPELMANN: Anaesthesia, 3 lectures.
DR. E. A. BABLER: Bandaging, 4 lectures.
DR. A. F. KOETTER: Diseases of the ear, 4 lectures.

6-3. Curriculum of Lectures, 1909.

A diploma, signed by Sister Superior Magdalene Gerhold and the officers of the Deaconess Medical Staff, was given at the successful conclusion of the first three years, but the deaconesses were then required to complete a fourth year of practical experience in private nursing in patients' homes or at different institutions outside the motherhouse.

The Deaconess Library

To keep up with all of the latest scientific medical advances being introduced so rapidly at that time, the probationers and the deaconesses could use the new Deaconess Library, described earlier as a gift in 1907 from Dr. Bransford Lewis.

Consisting of both medical and recreational books, the new library was presented to the hospital in a beautiful mahogany glass-enclosed bookcase which was placed in a library room open to convalescing patients as well as to the deaconesses and the hospital staff.

This first library grew rapidly during the next year under the donor's "fostering care and active interest." It soon included 284 volumes many of which later

6-4. The First Deaconess Library, a gift from Dr. Bransford Lewis, 1907.

became part of the hospital's professional library. The antique mahogany bookcase, now in the Deaconess Archives, remains as one of the heritage treasures from the early 1900s and it symbolizes the academic excellence for which the deaconesses were known.[11]

State Registration for Nurses, 1909

The first law on registration of nurses in Missouri was passed in 1909. As indicated earlier, the first examinations under the new law were given in 1913. Only a two-year course of training was required at that time before the examination could be taken. In addition, the law required that:

> To be qualified for registration a nurse had to be at least twenty-one years of age, of good moral character and have a general education equivalent to a grammar school course of study. Nurses who received diplomas before December, 1912, from training schools connected with a general hospital with a two-year course or those who, prior to 1895, received one year of training in a hospital could be registered upon application without examination. After 1912 applicants for registration were required to have a diploma from a training school giving a two-year course and pass an examination before the board.[12]

The governor was instructed by this new law to appoint a state board of examination and registration consisting of five nurse members who had at least five years of experience in nursing and one year of teaching in a reputable training school giving not less than a two-year course. Once registered by the board after passing the examination, a nurse was entitled to append the letters "R.N." to her name.

With their four-year training program, graduates from the School for Deaconesses were among those best prepared to qualify for state registration and they often made the highest grades. As previously recorded, Sister Sophie Hubeli was the first Deaconess Sister in Missouri to become a "Registered Nurse." Sister Anna Lenger was the first Deaconess to be licensed in both Missouri and Illinois, and she was put in charge of a training program to help prepare Deaconess probationers for state certification. Since there were few source materials available at that time, Sister Anna created her own textbooks for some of the courses she taught.[13]

St. Louis, The Primary Deaconess Training Center

With its strong emphasis on academic excellence, thorough clinical training, and spiritual growth, the School for Deaconesses in St. Louis attracted a growing number of students each year.

In 1909 there were also ten probationers from Deaconess Associations in other cities studying in St. Louis. By that time deaconess work had been established by members of the Evangelical Synod in Evansville, Indiana (1892), Marthasville, Missouri (1892), St. Charles, Missouri (1901), Lincoln, Illinois (1901), Chicago, Illinois (1907), Faribault, Minnesota (1908), Louisville, Kentucky (1909), and Milwaukee, Wisconsin (1909). Some of the Deaconess Associations in those locations began their own training programs at first, but many of them eventually sent their probationers to the School for Deaconesses in St. Louis, making it the primary training center.[14]

6-5. Deaconess Probationers and Sisters, 1905. Emmaus probationers, Julia Koch (left front) and Frieda Bettex (front right) are wearing distinctive ruffled aprons.

The Four-Year High School Prerequisite

Courses on Composition, Public Speaking, Nursing Ethics, and Chemistry were added in 1917 for first-year students in the School for Deaconesses.

In 1921, third-year students were required to take, in addition to their previously required courses, 10 hours of instruction in Massage and 10 hours in Pediatrics as "prescribed by the State Association of Trained Nurses," while the fourth year continued to be devoted to practical experience.

Applicants to the School for Deaconesses were advised in 1921 that "It is desirable that all applicants shall have taken a full high school course...." In 1928 high school credits showing completion of four years' work became a prerequisite for admission. Meanwhile, Missouri State Law required only one year of high school work for admission to schools of nursing.[15]

Added incentives toward completion of the four-year course in the School for Deaconesses were offered in 1921 in the form of an increased allowance scale at each level of achievement.

During the first three months the probationers received a stipend of $8 per month plus free room, board, and medical care; after the third month, $10; the second year, $12 per month; the third year, $14; after completion of the fourth year until consecration, $16; after consecration $20, and double that amount in their vacation month for traveling expenses.[16]

Faculty Development

The faculty in the School for Deaconesses always included, in addition to members of the medical staff and the superintendent, some of the consecrated Deaconess Sisters who taught courses in practical nursing arts and supervised the students in their clinical work.

In 1928 ten pages of the Deaconess Society's annual report were devoted to the School for Deaconesses, an indication of its growing size and importance. This report included for the first time the names of a school committee and the staff of instructors with their titles:

School Committee

Dr. Chas. Klenk ....Chairman
Prof. Frederick Pfeiffer ....Secretary
Mrs. Julia Taylor ....Board Representative
Sister Beata Schick ..............................R.N.
Sister Sophie Hubeli ..............................R.N.

School Staff and Instructors

Rev. F. P. Jens, D.D. ....Superintendent
Sister Beata Schick, R.N. ....Instructor
Sister Sophie Hubeli, R.N. ....Supt. of Nursing
Sister Hilda Mark, R.N. ....Ass't. Instructor
Sister Clara Weltge, R.N. ....Clinical Laboratory
Sister Katherine Streib, R.N. ....X-Ray and Physiotherapy
Sister Hulda Echelmeier, R.N. .....Operating Room Supervisor
Sister Theresa Kettelhut, R.N. ......Ass't.Oper.Room Supervisor
Sister Olinda Fuhr, R.N. ....Supt. of Maternity Division
Sister Mary Feutz, R.N., Ph.G. ....Pharmacist
Sister Elizabeth Schaeffer, R.N. ....Historian
Sister Bena Fuchs, R.N. ....Dietician

New subjects in the curriculum in 1928 included Physical Training, Emergency Nursing and First Aid, Dental Hygiene, Applied Psychology, and Communicable Diseases, all in the first three years.

The fourth year was no longer devoted to practical experience in private nursing or at other institutions but had a new requirement of ninety-five hours of class work covering subjects also new to the curriculum:

The Fourth Year

Nursing in Surgical Specialties. ....10 hours
Nursing in Occupational and Venereal Diseases ....10 hours
Public Sanitation. ....10 hours
Survey of Nursing Field. ....20 hours
Nursing in Mental and Nervous Diseases . ...20 hours
Modern Social Conditions . ...10 hours
Professional Problems . ...10 hours

210

Roentgenology and Physiotherapy . . . . .5 hours

With these additions, the four-year course in the School for Deaconesses required a grand total of 961 hours of class work for graduation in 1928 plus 52 hours of chorus practice. In 1929 the grand total was increased to 966 hours, much more than required for state board certification.[17]

But it was not all work and no play. In addition to educational tours one afternoon each week and recreational outings at "The Farm" in Sappington, Mo., students were informed that:

> Two pianos, a Victrola, a radio and a large seven passenger car are furnished for their use during their hours of leisure. A tennis court and a croquet ground are available. There are two libraries, the general library accessible to all members of the Home and Hospital, and the medical library where also current magazines and daily papers are to be found at all times.[18]

Sister Beata Schick, Principal of the School

In 1930 when Deaconess Hospital moved from West Belle Place to the new location at 6150 Oakland Avenue, the School for Deaconesses was assigned part of the new hospital building for dormitory, dining room and classroom space.

6-6. Sisters' Dining Room, 1930, for Deaconess Sisters and students in the School for Deaconesses.

Although, as reported earlier, Sister Beata Schick had been given responsibility for the School for Deaconesses when appointed director of nurses and nursing education in 1931, she was named as the first "principal" of the School in 1934.[19]

6-7. Sister Beata Schick Teaching Deaconess Class, 1938.

The Higher Education Emphasis

As director of nurses and nursing education, Sister Beata Schick wrote in her first annual report that "hospital work and nursing is going through a period of transition...the trend is "higher education.""

Explaining that this new trend was the result not only of the advancing standards of the Missouri State Board but also of Deaconess Hospital's desire "to render the best service possible," Sister Beata then reported that instructors in the School for Deaconesses attended an Institute for Nurses at Washington University. Five of the Deaconess Sisters were also enrolled in courses at Washington University, one to become a registered anaesthetist, one a registered X-ray technician and three to become registered clinical laboratory technicians.

She also reported that the curriculum of the School for Deaconesses was "planned according to the outline prescribed by the Missouri State Board of Nurse Examiners and the National League of Nursing Education," and that the "Methods used in teaching were: Lecture, Recitation, Project, Discussion, Demonstration, Laboratory and Excursion," with twenty conducted excursions having been made by first-year students alone to social, medical, religious and philanthropic public and private institutions in the St. Louis area.[20]

6-8. Students, School for Deaconesses, 1939.

Course "B" Offered

At the same time that higher education for the deaconesses was being emphasized, the board of directors was confronted with staff shortages in many of the non-professional areas of the new, larger hospital. To solve this problem, a "Course "B" was announced in 1930 and offered in 1931.

Planned for young women who did not meet the educational prerequisites and did not wish to take the "state boards" for registered nurses but who would be willing to become deaconesses and serve in the office, the dining room, the kitchen, or in some other non-professional capacity, Course "B" required only one year of high school to be followed by night courses completed while the student was in training.

Although references to the availability of this alternative, non-professional Course "B" appeared in announcements of the School for Deaconesses for a number of years, only one student is recorded as having entered this program (in October, 1948) and there is no record of her having completed the course. Deaconess Sisters had always been identified as professionally trained, and this alternative approach to preparation for deaconess service, though admirable in many ways, did not meet expectations and was discontinued.[21]

Scholastic Honors for Deaconess Graduates

Meanwhile, the School for Deaconesses continued to grow rapidly. Beginning in 1928 the name, "School for Deaconess Nurses," was sometimes used in hospital publications and school literature, but admissions continued to be limited to students willing to become Deaconess Sisters.[22]

In 1936 Sister Beata Schick reported that the School continued to meet all of the state board requirements and that all of the deaconess graduates passed the state board examinations. Moreover, it was announced that Norma Johanntesettel brought special honors to the School for Deaconesses that year when she achieved the distinction of making the highest grade of all contestants in the State of Missouri, the third time this honor had gone to a deaconess graduate.[23]

Eden Seminary Faculty Members Teach Religion

After the retirement of Superintendent Jens in 1940, the courses on religion in the School for Deaconesses were taught by members of the Eden Theological Seminary Faculty who were engaged part-time. Professors Herbert H. Wernecke, Samuel D. Press, and John A. Biegeleisen were the first, and in later years Professors Elmer Arndt, Allen Miller, Lionel Whiston and Richard Scheef taught the courses on religion and philosophy at Deaconess.[24]

The academic relationship of the School for Deaconesses with Eden Seminary reinforced the avowed spiritual objective of deaconess work and gave validity to Sister Beata's report that:

> We are laying more and ever greater emphasis on our religious training, since we still contend that a good nurse, above all things, must be first a good woman. The spirit in which she does her work helps much to overcome many obstacles when correlating theory and practice.[25]

214

New School Facilities, 1942

When the new, previously mentioned Sisters' Home was constructed immediately west of the hospital and dedicated in March 1942, up-to-date dormitory and classroom facilities were provided for the School. As required for state accreditation, both a chemistry and a dietetic laboratory separate from the hospital laboratories were included, and there was a well-appointed professional library. A convenient, enclosed walkway provided easy access from the new building to the hospital.[26]

The new Sisters' Home was best described by the Deaconess Sisters themselves who reported:

6-9. Deaconess Statues on Walkway.

> It is a magnificent six-story building overlooking Forest Park.... Three statues help to beautify the outside.... They signify the three groups of Sisters in our home, namely, the probationer, the student deaconess and the consecrated deaconess. (Sr. Naomi Pielemeier)

> We students certainly are thankful.... The classrooms which have the best lighting and plenty of space, the library which is an ideal place for study, also the dietetic and chemistry laboratories which are grand to work in, give us every incentive to do our best. (Sister Marie Fett)[27]

Sister Hilda Muensterman, Director of the School, 1942

Before the Sisters' Home was completed, however, changes in the administra-

215

tion of the School for Deaconesses and in the Deaconess Sisterhood were made necessary by the unexpected death of Sister Beata Schick in December 1941, and the resignation of Sister Superior Alvina Scheid early in 1942.

As principal, Sister Beata Schick had guided the School through its years of greatest growth. In limited facilities, she had maintained the high standards of intellectual, technical and spiritual training for which deaconess graduates were known. Her farsightedness in encouraging postgraduate education for the Deaconess Sisters made possible the appointment of a highly qualified successor.

Sister Hilda Muensterman, who had completed post-graduate study at St. Louis University for her B.S. degree in Nursing Education, was installed in July 1942 as the new director of nurses for Deaconess Hospital and as director of the School for Deaconesses. In 1952 she also received her M.S. in Nursing Education.[28]

6-10. Sister Hilda Muensterman, Director of Nurses and the School of Nursing, 1942.

A Lay School of Nursing in the Deaconess Tradition

Within her first year as director, Sister Hilda Muensterman was given the challenge of organizing a new Deaconess School of Nursing for lay students to run concurrently with the School for Deaconesses.

On recommendation of the Sisters' Council, as described earlier, a resolution to open a lay school had been "enthusiastically adopted" by the Deaconess Society in November 1942. Following that landmark decision, the first official *Announcement of the Deaconess School of Nursing* was published in 1942-43, and the

216

first three lay students entered in February 1943. A second group of thirty-eight were admitted the following September. At the same time there were twenty-one probationers enrolled in the School for Deaconesses.[29]

Two Schools in One

The educational requirements for admission to both the lay course and deaconess training were virtually the same. All applicants had to be graduates from an accredited four-year high school and should have completed these suggested pre-nursing subjects: English (3 or 4 years), Mathematics (2 years), Science (2-3 years), Social Studies (3 years), Foreign Language (2 years).

The faculty in 1943 included eight Deaconess Sisters, five lay nurse instructors, four part-time professors in religion, and members of the Deaconess Medical Staff.

All students were on duty for forty-eight hours weekly, six eight-hour days which included time spent in the classes.

The lay students' course was completed in three years at which time the graduates were eligible to take the state board examination leading to the registered nurse certification. The Deaconess students were also eligible to take the state board examination after completing the three-year nursing course but they were required to complete a fourth year in preparation for consecration as Deaconess Sisters.

The tuition for lay students in the School of Nursing in 1943 was $215.00 for the three-year course. The student was required to send a $10.00 registration fee upon acceptance by the school and to bring $80.00 plus the breakage fee of $5.00 at entry. This tuition covered the cost of uniforms, textbooks, use of a nurse's cape, room, board and laundry. Students provided their own regulation white shoes throughout the course.

6-11. Deaconess School of Nursing Emblem.

217

6-12. Dr. Edwin Schmidt Teaching Class in Psychiatric Nursing with Sister Elizabeth Lotz, left.

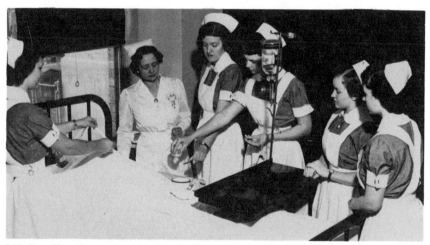

6-13. Sister Kate Nottrott Teaching Class in Clinical Nursing, 1946.

Except for a slight difference in their caps, it was impossible to distinguish the lay students from those who entered for training as deaconesses, but there were differences in costs.

The deaconess students were expected to bring with them $50.00 to cover the expense of textbooks for the four-year course. In addition, each student was expected to sign four $100.00 promissory notes, each of which was automatically cancelled by one year of service after consecration as a Deaconess Sister. All four notes were cancelled after four years of service following consecration. If the student deaconess severed her connections with the hospital before the end of four years of service, or before her four-year training course was completed, she was expected to pay $100.00 for each year of training received. A stipend (from $10 to $16 a month) was given the student deaconess while she was in training.[30]

First Graduates of Deaconess School of Nursing

The first lay graduates of the School of Nursing were some of the members of the Class of 1944 who had begun their training in the School for Deaconesses and had transferred to the School of Nursing.

6-14. Deaconess School of Nursing Class of 1944. (Left to right): Emma Barth Knight, Eunice Koehler, Helen Germeroth Koch, Sister Hulda Weise, Marie Van Gels Keller, Marie Schmidt Brown, Doris Euno Carpenter, Wilma Hoffman Kloppe, Audrey Baumgartner Marshall.

The first graduates of the Deaconess School of Nursing who entered as lay students were Maurine Nolle Hartman, Doris Drosselmeyer and Myra Welge, Class of February 1946, and thirty graduates in the Class of September 1946.

Year after year the numbers grew and, in order to accommodate the large attendance, commencement ceremonies were held at the Washington University Graham Chapel.[31]

6-15. Deaconess School of Nursing, Class of September 1946.

6-16. Deaconess School of Nursing Graduation, with student chorus at Graham Chapel, Washington University, 1971.

Gerhold Hall Dedicated

Enrollment in the Deaconess School of Nursing was already so large in November 1944 that Sister Hilda Muensterman reported, "Our school is growing so rapidly it will soon be necessary to provide additional housing facilities to take care of the increase in enrollment."

When rapid growth of the School of Nursing continued into the next year, the Deaconess Society held a special meeting on June 14, 1945, as reported earlier, and authorized the construction of a new addition to the Sisters' Home. Named Gerhold Hall in 1951 in honor of Sister Magdalene Gerhold, the new building was dedicated in September 1947 and was also soon filled to capacity.[32]

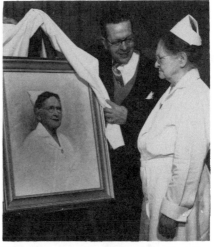

6-16b. Deaconess Hospital Board President, Rev. Dr. Elmer H. Hoefer, naming Gerhold Hall in honor of Sister Superior Emeritus Magdalene Gerhold.

School of X-ray Technology, 1947

Among those housed in Gerhold Hall were students in the new Deaconess School of X-ray Technology, established in 1947 in response to a dramatic increase in the demand for trained x-ray technicians in the 1940s. Dr. Joseph C. Peden, radiologist, was appointed director of the School and Sister Velma Kampschmidt, R.N.,R.T., director of instruction.

6-17. School of X-ray Emblem.

The two-year course in X-ray technology included anatomy, physiology and psychology, which the students took with the student nurses, and ten other subjects taught by a radiologist or a registered X-ray technician: X-ray technology I, II, III, X-ray therapy, chemistry, physics, terminology, processing, supervision and administration. Clinical as well as classroom instructions were included and students were on a forty-hour week, inclusive of classes.

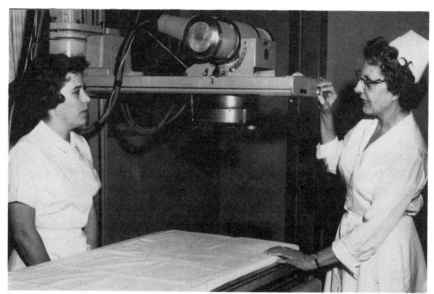

6-18. Sister Velma Kampschmidt, Director of Instruction, right, with School of X-ray student.

Tuition for the two-year course was $115 the first year and $85 the second year, payable at the beginning of each school year. Books, room, board, and laundry were provided for the two years as a working scholarship in return for x-ray service rendered by the student while learning x-ray technology.

The School of X-ray Technology was accredited by the Council of Medical Education and Hospitals of the American Medical Association, and graduates were eligible to take the examination of The American Registry of X-ray Technicians for certification (Registered Technician) after which they could affix "R.T." to their names.

Miss Marian Mahanay, who graduated from the Deaconess School of X-ray Technology in May 1949, was the first of more than 100 who completed the two-year course and have received R.T. certification. These graduates also received a gold pin designed with the distinctive emblem of the Deaconess School of X-ray Technology.

In 1968 the School was renamed The School of Radiologic Technology and an academic affiliation was arranged with Forest Park Community College. When Forest Park was accredited in 1977 to offer the complete course in x-ray technology, the school at Deaconess Hospital was phased out.[33]

School of Nursing Affiliations

In order to provide the best possible clinical experience for students in all areas of nursing service, the Deaconess School of Nursing arranged affiliations with other teaching institutions for some courses of study beginning in 1947.

Communicable disease nursing experience was at first provided at St. Louis City Hospital and pediatric nursing at Shriner's Hospital for Crippled Children.

In 1948 affiliations in pediatrics and communicable diseases were arranged at St. Louis Children's Hospital. Later, Deaconess students went to Indiana University School of Nursing, Indianapolis, Indiana, to Children's Hospital in Columbus, Ohio, and to Children's Hospital in Cincinnati, Ohio, for clinical experience in pediatrics and communicable diseases, and to the Visiting Nurse Association of St. Louis for training in home visitation.

Academic affiliations were arranged with Elmhurst College, Elmhurst, Illinois, in 1949 and with the University of Missouri and Lindenwood College from 1951 to 1960 enabling Deaconess School of Nursing students to take courses leading to the Bachelor of Science in Nursing degree.[34]

Sister Olivia Drusch, Director of the School, 1954

Sister Olivia Drusch was appointed director of the Deaconess School of Nursing in 1954 to succeed Sister Hilda Muensterman, who resigned to be married. Like Sister Hilda, Sister Olivia had earned her B.S. and M.S. degrees in Nursing Education from St. Louis University.

In a major change of administrative leadership for the School of Nursing, the hospital board of directors made the decision at this time to separate the duties of the sister superior and educational director which had been held jointly by Sister Olivia. Sister Frieda Ziegler was then appointed sis-

6-19. Sister Olivia Drusch, Director of School of Nursing and Director of Nursing, 1954.

223

ter superior of the Deaconess Sisterhood. Miss Jacqueline Boothe, a B.S. graduate of Johns Hopkins University, was appointed associate director of nursing education and Sister Hulda Weise, was appointed associate director of nursing service.

Enrollment in the School of Nursing had increased to 184 in 1954 and a quota of 80 was set for the new class in September due to limitations in housing. Meanwhile, tuition had increased to $325 for the three-year course.

As the new director, Sister Olivia Drusch declared that the goal for the 1954-55 school year was "Better nursing care...with better teaching."[35]

6-20. Faculty of the Deaconess School of Nursing, 1955. Front row: (left to right); Sister Naomi Pielemeier, R.N., B.S.; Sister Elizabeth Lotz, R.N., B.S.; Sister Hulda Weise, R.N., M.S.; Sister Olivia Drusch, R.N., B.S., M.S.; Sister Helen Schneider, R.N., B.S.; Miss Mary Ross, R.N., B.S., M.S. Second row: Sister Amanda Wulff, R.N.; Miss Audrey Brant, R.N.; Miss Lucy Hoblitzelle, R.N., M.A.; Miss Lydia Schaperkotter, R.N., B.S.; Sister Kate Nottrott, R.N., B.S.; Miss Bethena Casey, R.N., A.A.; Sister Irene Hanebutt, R.N., B.S. Top row: Mrs. Patricia Cutter, R.N., B.S.; Miss Jacqueline Boothe, R.N.,B.S.; Mrs. Florence Wintmute, R.N.; Miss Anne Baldwin, B.A.; Miss Jean McCormack, B.S.; Miss Marianne Gehlbach, R.N. Not in picture: Mrs. Ethel Helling, Librarian; Miss Louis Radloff, Student Health Nurse; Sister Frieda Ziegler, Executive Deaconess.

School for Deaconesses Phased Out

Meanwhile, although Deaconess Sisters continued to hold strong positions of leadership in hospital departments and on the faculty of the schools, enrollment in the School for Deaconesses declined steadily throughout the 1950s.

Facing the realities of the changing times, the board of directors of Deaconess Hospital and the Deaconess Sisterhood agreed in 1957, as reported earlier, to phase out the School for Deaconesses and to concentrate on providing education in the Deaconess School of Nursing, the School of X-ray Technology, and in a variety of other hospital training programs.[36]

Retraining to "Catch Up with Medicine"

Tremendous advances in medicine during the 1950s, combined with a growing shortage of professional nurses adequately trained in up-to-date procedures, led Deaconess Hospital to offer a seven-month intensive refresher course in 1957 for those wishing to return to work after an absence of a number of years. While many hospitals offered brief refresher courses, the Deaconess course was believed to be the only one so comprehensive and of such length in the country at that time. Students came from as far away as Florida and California.

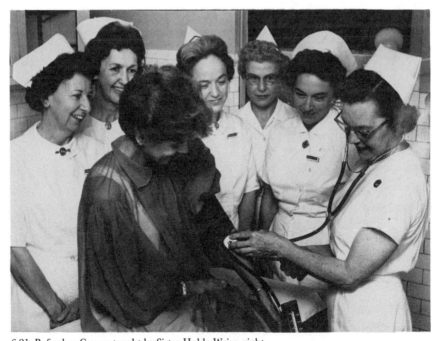

6-21. Refresher Course taught by Sister Hulda Weise, right.

Applicants had to be graduates of an accredited school of nursing, but each was judged on her merits. Character references, a health record and reasonable freedom from home responsibilities such as small children were also required. The age limit was theoretically sixty, but older applicants were accepted.

Nurses taking the refresher course received no salary but they did get a stipend of $200 per month and one meal while on duty. They had to provide their own housing and uniforms and they worked a 40-hour week which included classes and study hours.

The course included rotation through the various services of the hospital, where the trainees experienced many changes in patient care. Though classes covered every phase of nursing, most of the instruction concentrated on new developments such as drugs, electronic and cardiac monitoring equipment, intravenous feedings and psychiatric care. Medications like penicillin and streptomycin, bedside equipment such as piped-in oxygen and suction machines, and the whole field of rehabilitative nursing were new to these returning nurses, some of whom had graduated fifteen to twenty-five years earlier. They found too that there was much more paper work and less time for bedside nursing. Patients who formerly stayed in the hospital fourteen days now went home after an average of ten days, and they often required much more intensive nursing for the shorter period of time involved.[37]

In 1960 Sister Hulda Weise was appointed full-time director of the in-service training program. By 1966 there were 45 graduates, many of whom stayed on at Deaconess, some as head nurses. As a result, there was greater maturity and less turnover in the hospital's nursing staff and, at the same time, many new job opportunities were provided for older nurses.

One of the first graduates of the refresher course observed that while there were many new procedures for her to learn, some things had not changed. "Basic nursing hasn't changed," she said. "And people haven't changed. Patients are still the same —all different. That's what makes being a nurse so fascinating." An unexpected fringe benefit was that most of the graduates said, "We feel younger."[38]

The 25th Anniversary and "Change"

When the School of Nursing celebrated its 25th anniversary in 1968, so much had changed in health care and health education during the previous twenty-five years that the theme chosen by the planning committee for the anniversary program of events was "CHANGE."

Many of the School's 1500 alumnae returned to St. Louis for the two-day celebration, June 21-22, 1968, which featured one full day of educational events followed by a day of tours. They were amazed to see the 1968 work schedules, curriculum, and regulations of Deaconess students as compared to those of former years. Other changes noted in 1968 were:

> Tuition was $1,500 for the three-year course, including board and laundry.

> Male students were accepted on the same basis as female students except for special housing arrangements.

> Married students were accepted on an individual basis, and students already in the School of Nursing were allowed to marry during the last two years with permission of the faculty.

> Older students were also being accepted and two grandmothers had graduated in the Class of 1955.

6-22. New Professional Library, 1968.

There were 200 students enrolled and 23 members on the faculty.

A large, new professional library provided excellent study and reference facilities.

Deaconess Hospital had 361 beds and the patient care facilities were modernized throughout by the Decade of Development Program.

What had not changed, however, was the Deaconess commitment to academic excellence, thorough clinical training and spiritual growth, all of which helped to make the "Deaconess School of Nursing a Great School." This was the theme of the gala banquet which climaxed the anniversary celebration and was attended by 700 alumnae, faculty members, trustees and friends in the Gold Room at the Jefferson Hotel.[39]

Many Teaching Programs Benefit Students and Patients

In addition to the School of Nursing and the School of Radiologic Technology, there were many formal and informal teaching programs at Deaconess Hospital by 1968:

> Licensed practical nurse clinical training
> Nurse aide training
> Occupational therapist clinical training
> Operating room technician training
> Pharmacist clinical training
> Physical therapist clinical training
> Physician internship training
> Resident physician training in surgery
> Resident physician training in obstetrics

Designed to help caregivers throughout the hospital keep up with the many scientific advances being made in medicine, these programs were of benefit not only to the students but also to the patients who received care in this innovative teaching environment.[40]

Robert A. Falconer, Executive Director of Education

As the number of teaching programs at Deaconess continued to grow, a full-time executive director of education, Robert A. Falconer, who had a doctorate in education, was appointed in 1971 to the hospital administrative staff to coordinate the many educational opportunities being developed.

By 1975 there were nineteen separate formal educational programs at Deaconess Hospital involving nearly 300 full-time students. In addition, community outreach programs, such as seminars, audio-visual presentations, and brochures with current health information, were assuming more prominence in the hospital's educational endeavors.[41]

Sister Olivia Drusch, "Outstanding Nurse Educator"

Meanwhile, Sister Olivia Drusch's leadership as a nurse educator was acknowledged and celebrated when she received a plaque and key as "outstanding nurse educator" from the Health and Welfare Council of the United Church of Christ in 1968.

Sister Olivia had already received a number of other honors. Listed in "Who's Who of American Women" in 1961, she was the recipient of the first Gold Medal Award for "Outstanding Nurse in Missouri" that same year, and her home town, Hermann, Missouri, named her the "outstanding citizen" in 1964.

Cited in January 1970 for forty-two years as a nurse, administrator and educator and as the co-founder of the Deaconess Hospital School of Nursing, she was named a "St. Louis Woman of Achievement in Health and Health Education" at a luncheon given by the *St. Louis Globe-Democrat.* On that occasion she stated that "as long as we have hospitals, we'll need bedside nurses. Clinicians will never replace the registered nurse, who is God's answer to giving good care to the acutely ill."[42]

Sister Olivia's farsighted and progressive educational philosophy provided students with three years of excellent academic training and a working complement of clinical experience that has given Deaconess graduates an enviable reputation within the health care industry.

When she retired in June 1971 as assistant administrator and director of nursing at Deaconess Hospital, Sister Olivia Drusch was honored for her many years of outstanding leadership with a retirement tea and open house attended by many friends, co-workers and former students. She was honored again by the Deaconess Society at its annual meeting in November 1971. At that time her portrait was hung in the professional library which was designated as "The Drusch Professional Library."[43]

Olivia Collins, Director of Nursing Education, 1971

The board of trustees appointed Olivia Collins, who had a master's degree in nursing, as director of nursing education in 1971. She was the first lay person to hold this important position, and having served capably for twelve years as the assistant director, she was well-prepared for her new leadership role.

The 1970s brought many additional changes in nursing education, and Olivia Collins was confronted with a major challenge as more and more significance was placed on textbook education and theory. Unwilling to take away the personal patient contact experienced by Deaconess students, she worked with the hospital administration to upgrade the diploma educational experience by strengthening both the curriculum and the faculty.

6-23. Olivia Collins, Director of Nursing Education, 1971-1978.

In the 1970s, the conceptual framework of adaptation was developed for the curriculum of the Deaconess School of Nursing. It was based on a philosophy that places renewed emphasis on each patient's total needs as a person and teaches the student to take more initiative in working with both the patient and the physician.

Under the direction of Olivia Collins, the Deaconess School of Nursing achieved a new dimension of academic excellence during the 1970s. When she retired in 1978, the facilities of the School had also been greatly improved with air conditioned dormitories and classrooms throughout, part of the hospital's "Design for the 80s" $5 million modernization program.[44]

Ruth B. Miller, Director of Nursing Education, 1978

Academic excellence, broad clinical experience and improvement in the physical facilities of the School of Nursing continued to be major priorities when Ruth B. Miller was appointed director of nursing education at Deaconess in 1978.

A doctoral candidate in the School of Education at the University of Missouri-St. Louis, Ruth Miller served as director until November 1980, when she requested an educational leave of absence which was granted. During her tenure she helped prepare the Deaconess School of Nursing for the "Challenge of the 80's" in nursing education. Under her leadership, the offices of all instructors were located in the main building of the School.

6-24. Ruth B. Miller, Director of Nursing Education, 1978-1980.

The former Board Room on the first floor was remodelled and renamed the Oak Room, and portraits of previous directors of the School were displayed on its walls emphasizing the School's great heritage in health education.

Assistant director, Bonnie Yarger, who had a master's degree in nursing, was appointed acting director of the Deaconess School of Nursing in late 1980. She was commended "for her exceptionally fine job as acting director" when she resigned at the end of that school year in order to continue her education.[45]

Patricia Afshar, Director, Dean, Provost and CEO

A new era of nursing education began at Deaconess Hospital when Patricia Afshar, who has a master's degree in nursing, was appointed director of the Deaconess School of Nursing in June 1981. Coming from her position as director of nursing education at Lindenwood College, she brought to Deaconess not only administrative experience but a strong commitment to academic growth and excellence. Under her leadership, the strengthening of the faculty to a level equal to that of college and university based schools of nursing became a major

231

goal, and her titles changed accordingly.[46]

In 1982 the Faculty Council revised and approved a total program evaluation plan prepared by a committee with Carole Piles, assistant director of the School of Nursing, serving as co-chairperson with Marie Temmen, counselor.

Systematic evaluation of the School, a procedure which had also been used for the School for Deaconesses, verified regularly that the institution was accomplishing its purposes, provided for an in-depth study of major program areas including philosophy, objectives, curriculum, administration, faculty, students and resources. The evaluative findings were then used to identify strengths, areas of concern and future goals.[47]

The Deaconess College of Nursing, 1983

The Deaconess School of Nursing became the Deaconess College of Nursing in 1983. Patricia Afshar's title then became dean of the College, and in 1987 her title became provost and chief executive officer.

In 1983 Elizabeth Anne Krekorian, who has a doctorate in education and is a registered nurse, was brought to the College as dean of academic affairs to begin the baccalaureate program.[48]

6-25. Patricia Afshar, Director School of Nursing, 1981; Dean of the Deaconess College of Nursing, 1983; Provost and Chief Executive Officer, 1987.

6-26. Elizabeth Anne Krekorian, Dean of Academic Affairs, College of Nursing, 1983.

As one of only two hospital-based colleges in the country at that time, the Deaconess College of Nursing began offering in September 1983 a four-year baccalaureate program leading to a Bachelor of Science in Nursing degree as an option to the traditional three-year diploma program.[49]

The mission of the Deaconess College of Nursing was affirmed in October 1983 by the board of directors of the Deaconess Health Services Corporation [by then the new name of the parent organization]:

> to provide an educational program in professional nursing in an environment of mutual commitment and accountability. The College is dedicated to a holistic approach to education, incorporating Christian values, intellectual development, professional competence, and service to the community and society in which we live.[50]

This mission statement reflects continuity with the past in that it incorporates, in modern terminology, the basic concepts of the Kaiserswerth Model of nursing education which was adopted in 1889 by the founders of Deaconess Hospital and the Deaconess Sisters, who were the first instructors in nursing education in the School for Deaconesses. The threefold approach of intellectual, technical and spiritual training remains as the foundation of the curriculum, but it is offered within a conceptual framework characteristic of higher learning today.

Until the 1970s most health care education was disease oriented in response to revolutionary new medical and scientific discoveries which brought hope for healing for many hitherto incurable illnesses. A curriculum based on the conceptual framework of adaptation, on the other hand, stimulates independent thinking, promotes the development of problem-solving skills and enhances personal, intellectual and professional growth. Professional nursing's primary role, in this context, is to assist persons in adaptation to achieve the optimal level of health and well-being. To accomplish its purposes and goals in this modern learning environment, the Deaconess College of Nursing provides an academic program based upon the liberal education tradition.[51]

Although students who entered the Deaconess College of Nursing in the Fall of 1983 had a choice of the diploma or baccalaureate programs, all received the same solid academic and clinical education program for the first three years with the curriculum design for the baccalaureate option an expansion of the diploma curriculum.

The diploma program, accredited since 1911 by the Missouri State Board of Nursing and also accredited by the National League of Nursing, required 96 credit hours for graduation, 43 in nursing and 53 in general education. Upon satisfactory completion of three years, students could graduate with a diploma, take the Missouri State Board Examination and enter the work force as registered nurses.[52]

The Baccalaureate Program

The baccalaureate program in the Deaconess College of Nursing requires a total of 128 credit hours, 60 in nursing and 68 in general education. In the fourth year the students complete upper level courses to fulfill the requirements for a Bachelor of Science degree in Nursing.

From 1983 to 1986 a contractual agreement with Lindenwood College provided all non-nursing required course work taught by the Lindenwood faculty on the Deaconess campus. Since 1987 Fontbonne College, located just five minutes from the Deaconess College of Nursing, has been Deaconess' four-year liberal arts affiliate. Through a contractual arrangement, Fontbonne provides the non-nursing and some science courses essential for liberal arts education students.

The major clinical facility for students is Deaconess Hospital, a full service facility with 527 beds. In addition, the College utilizes more than 20 area agencies and health care providers for student clinical experience.

Classrooms, conference rooms and some laboratories are located on the Deaconess College campus. Students not living at home may live on either the Deaconess or Fontbonne campus. They then study and travel between both.

In 1984 the tuition for full-time students in the Deaconess College of Nursing was $3,500 per year with another $1,360 required for housing, uniforms, books and incidentals for students who lived on campus. By 1987 the tuition had gone up to $4,200 per year with the additional fees remaining about the same. The tuition in 1989 was $4,800 with additional fees of $1,575.

The Deaconess Health Services Corporation, which owns and operates the College of Nursing, subsidizes the health education programs and offers financial assistance to worthy applicants. Loans and scholarships are available to many students who qualify for them.[53]

234

In commencement exercises on May 31, 1985, eight graduates received the first degree of bachelor of science in nursing from the Deaconess College of Nursing:

Cathy Barrett   Rebecca George
Alison Cohen   Susan Greiling
Catherine Daniels   Terri Wilson
Lynn Ficker   Nancy Wujcik[54]

Once the College had graduated its first baccalaureate class, it was in the position to seek accreditation from the regional accrediting body, the North Central Association of Colleges and Schools, and from the National League of Nursing. Again, the Deaconess nursing program is setting the standard for hospital-based programs and was the first in St. Louis to qualify for such accreditation.

6-27. Deaconess College of Nursing Seal.

The Associate of Science in Nursing Program

At the same time, in response to a growing nurse shortage and the need for further education expressed by many licensed practical nurses, the Deaconess College of Nursing developed a new associate of science in nursing program. This specialized one-year program was approved by the Missouri State Board of Nursing in April 1989, and the first class was scheduled to enter in January 1990.

The associate in science program consists of a total of 68 credit hours and study is full time or part time, depending on the number of support courses that the student has completed prior to entry.

The associate of science degree provides a comprehensive foundation for further study in upper division collegiate work and the BSN program should the student decide to continue his or her education.[55]

Cathy Barrett   Allison Cohen   Cathy Daniels

Lynn Ficker   Rebecca George   Susan Greiling

Terri Wilson   Nancy Wujcik

6-28. First Baccalaureate Graduates, Class of 1985, Deaconess College of Nursing.

Alumni Honor the Deaconess Tradition

Alumni of the Deaconess Schools and of the College of Nursing have distinguished themselves around the world. Numbering more than 2,200, they are presently serving primarily throughout Missouri and Illinois, but also in forty-six other states and six foreign countries, including the Netherlands, New Guinea, India, South Korea, Ecuador and Sri Lanka.

Surveys indicate that 100 percent of the Deaconess alumni have utilized their nurses' training either in professional or volunteer positions. Many have been on the staff of Deaconess Hospital and some have served on the faculties of the Deaconess Schools and College of Nursing. Others have gone on to hold prestigious leadership roles in health care and health education elsewhere. They have often received recognition for outstanding professional achievement from local, state and national organizations.[56]

The Deaconess Sisters Alumnae and Alumnae of the School of Nursing held their first joint homecoming on June 20, 1953. Tea was served, an interesting program was presented, and booklets listing all of the graduates and their current activities were distributed. This homecoming was such a success that it was agreed by both groups to make it an annual event.

When Deaconess Hospital celebrated its 75th anniversary in 1964, a committee of alumnae was appointed to plan and direct a celebration for the School of Nursing. The homecoming program in September that year featured an original pageant, "75 Years of Progress," presented by the Deaconess students. It was followed by tours of new school and hospital facilities and a reception.

A directory, beginning with members of the Class of 1907, was also prepared and distributed in 1964. Dedicated to "the instructors, deaconesses, students, and administrative personnel who have been a part of and contributed so much to the success of the Deaconess Hospital School of Nursing," the directory concluded that "Each has left her mark."[57]

In 1968, a dream came true when the Alumni and Friends of Deaconess Hospital School of Nursing adopted a constitution and by-laws creating a new organization with 510 charter members. A publication committee was appointed to publish a news bulletin at least twice a year and the first edition of the *Deaconess Newsletter* appeared in Autumn, 1969.

Sharon Kennon, 1961.

Grace Behrendes, 1962.

Mary Litzinger, 1964.

Anne Louise Schmidt, 1965.

Mary Brooks, 1969.

6-29. Deaconess Alumnae honored by the United Church of Christ Council for Health and Human Service Ministries with "Graduate Nurse of the Year" awards.

238

6-30. First Annual Deaconess Alumnae Homecoming, 1953. Left to right: Mrs. Orville C. Schoene (Marjorie Wilke); Mrs. C. K. Brandt, Jr. (Ida Mae Simonds); Mrs. Fred Muegge (Ruth Buettner); and Mrs. Dallas Dyer (Eunice Koenig) with Sister Hilda Muensterman, Director of School of Nursing.

6-31. 75th Anniversary Alumnae Committee, 1964. Front row left to right: Jacqueline Boothe, Associate Director of School; student Carolyn Pape; Sister Kate Nottrott; Marjorie Beck; Madrean Meyer, Chairperson. Second row: Louise Radloff; Donita Oberman; Sister Olivia Drusch, Director of the School; and Freda Vollmar.

Now called The Deaconess College of Nursing Alumni Association, this organization publishes the quarterly *Alumni News*, holds annual meetings, sponsors homecoming events and presents seminars for continuing education. In 1989 it also raised $50,000 for the Centennial Building Fund, provided $10,000 in scholarships, and established an alumni of the year award to honor outstanding alumni. At the Alumni Centennial Gala in June 1989, Marian Knobloch, Class of 1954 and director of the Deaconess Employee Health Services, received the first Alumni of the Year Award "for serving as a good role model for students in a professional career devoted to caring for the whole person."[58]

6-32. Marian Knobloch, First Alumni of the Year Award, 1989.

The College of Nursing Faculty

The faculty members of the Deaconess College of Nursing, like their predecessors in the School for Deaconesses and the School of Nursing, are a vital part of institutional life.

Believing that the quality of caregiving still depends very much on the quality of education provided for the caregivers, the board of directors of Deaconess Health Services has encouraged and supported the highest quality of faculty development in the College of Nursing.

The faculty of the Deaconess College of Nursing has been described as highly-motivated, self-directed, and verbal. Most faculty members have private offices, but their doors are open and they participate actively in committees of the College and in ceremonies and activities of the students and the community. They are held in high regard by the students, as shown on course work surveys, and all belong to and are active in at least one professional organization. Their high retention rate, with 86 percent having been at Deaconess three years or more, two for more than ten years and another two for more than fifteen years, is an indication of high morale and loyalty to the Deaconess tradition of health education.[59]

6-33. College of Nursing Faculty, 1989. Back, left to right: Shirley Lindsay, Mary Ellen Brockmann, Jane Madden, Kathy Modene, Eileen Turner, Margaret Acre, Patricia Jacobs, Judith Turner. Front: Elizabeth Krekorian, Linda Erwin, Martha Spies, Julia Ann Raithel, Linda Figiel, Carmel White.

A Historic "Time to Celebrate"

Commencement for the College of Nursing, Class of 1989, was not only part of the Deaconess Centennial celebration but also an historic event.

Seventeen graduates in the three-year diploma program were the last class to receive diplomas from that Deaconess program, which was phased out in 1989 when it had become evident that most students entering the College wished to pursue studies toward a degree in nursing. The last diploma graduates at Deaconess were:

Cindy Brawley	Tracy Schaaf
Laura Courtney	Jennifer Schaefer
Cathy Ellis	Cindi Schleper
Maria Johnson	Christine Stephens
Mary Marler	Jana Vogler
Jan Novak	Mary Beth Webster

Darline Ogent	Stacy Whelan
Christine Ruff	Christy Williams
	Susan Winkelmann[60]

Nine baccalaureate graduates in the Deaconess College Class of 1989 received bachelor of science degrees in nursing. They were:

Kristen Etling	Mary Lytle
Sherill Gladhart	Susan Marshall
Kathy Keck	Melissa Perez-Mesa
Leanna Kellerman	Susan Wagner
	Jill Zeller[61]

For all of the Deaconess graduates of 1989, it was "A Time to Celebrate." This was the theme of the commencement speaker, the Rev. Dr. Carl C. Rasche, president emeritus of Deaconess Hospital, who said to the graduates,

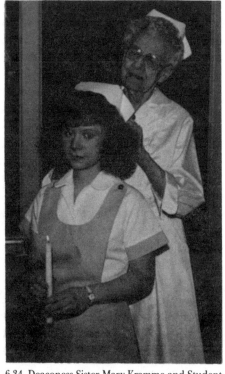

This is a time to celebrate your graduation, but it is also a time to celebrate your heritage—a nursing education based on the highest intellectual, technical and spiritual standards of the day as first developed by Frederike and Theodore Fliedner from whom Florence Nightingale received her only formal nurse's training, and which was developed further by the Deaconess Sisters in past days here at Deaconess Hospital.... It is a heritage which sees the patient as a holistic being.[62]

In the spirit of that heritage, the Class of 1989 joined more than 2,200 other alumni of the

6-34. Deaconess Sister Mary Kramme and Student Kelly Owens.

Deaconess Schools and College of Nursing, all part of a century of "educating to care." That education is based on the belief that:

Compassion may provide the motive, but knowledge is our only working power.[63]

6-34. Deaconess College of Nursing Student, Julie Marella.

Chapter Seven

THE DEACONESS AUXILIARY AND VOLUNTEER SERVICES
"Giving To Life Itself"

Volunteers have always been important at Deaconess Hospital. In 1889, when the hospital was founded in St. Louis, everyone involved in its work was a volunteer. There were no special emblems, badges or volunteer uniforms at that time except for the Deaconess Sisters, who wore a distinctive garb and contributed their professional services fulltime.

The primary mark of distinction for the first volunteers at Deaconess was known as *diakonia*, devoted service to others in need. Today, as in the past, that devoted service takes many forms, and it is the motivation for the Deaconess Auxiliary and Volunteer Services.

7-1. Deaconess Volunteer Emblem

Deaconess Society Members, a Volunteer Network

Success in the early years of deaconess work in St. Louis depended greatly on the generosity and loyalty of Deaconess Society members. As described earlier, one woman donated an eleven-room house at 2119 Eugenia Street near Union Station for use both as a place to care for the sick and as a home for the Deaconess Sisters. Other women volunteered their services to renovate, clean and furnish that first hospital building, and they spread the news of its purpose.[1]

Although all members of the Deaconess Society were required as one of the conditions of membership, "to be active for the growth and promulgation" of deaconess work, the twelve members of the board of directors carried the major responsibilities for leadership and solicitation of funds. As expected of board members in that day when personal involvement was regarded a part of one's Christian stewardship, those first board members were on the scene frequently.

244

They provided the new Deaconess Home and Hospital with everything from chicken soup to organizational advice—and anything else they thought might be needed.[2]

Members of the Deaconess Medical Staff were also volunteers. The record says that they "offered their services as the first physicians and surgeons in the treatment of patients." Moreover, as previously reported, they contributed their services for the health care needs of the Deaconess Sisters, taught classes in the School for Deaconesses, and donated equipment for the operating rooms and medical library.[3]

Grateful patients likewise became volunteers as they brought gifts to the hospital in appreciation for the care they had received. Lists of "Receipts" in the early issues of the monthly newsletter, the *Diakonissenfreund*, included "blankets, towels, ladies' night jackets, fruitcake, Quaker Oats, oranges, a tub of grapes, a barrel of apples" and cash in various amounts. One grateful patient, the aforementioned Mr. Henry Tibbe of Washington, Missouri, gave $9,000 for hospital expansion purposes in 1895 in addition to $900 which he and his wife had given earlier.[4]

By 1899, when the Deaconess Society celebrated its 10th anniversary, a significant network of volunteers had been developed to provide support of all kinds for the Deaconess Home and Hospital. The Rev. Frederick P. Jens, the new superintendent that year, wrote in the annual report:

> I want to thank all members, friends, ministers, congregations and societies most sincerely for their donations in money, household articles, and victuals, and also for the unselfish interest they have continually taken in our work.[5]

At the turn of the century, when electricity was just becoming available for use in public buildings in St. Louis, Deaconess Society members and friends, "especially many Ladies and Young Ladies Societies," contributed $1,106.29 for the purchase and installation of the first electric elevator at Deaconess Hospital.

Electric elevators were viewed by many people at that time as unnecessary, very expensive and possibly even unsafe. But as a gift, and one that could make patient care easier, the electric elevator was installed and put into use at Deaconess Hospital in 1900. An electric annunciator [patient call] system was also contributed by a donor that year. These were among the first of many

245

expensive gifts of hospital equipment donated by generous volunteers throughout the past 100 years.[6]

1500 Organized Volunteers "Give to Life Itself"

As indicated earlier, when hospital expansion was no longer possible on West Belle Place, the Deaconess Society broke with a long tradition in 1926. Instead of depending primarily on its own membership and the members of Evangelical churches for volunteer help and support, the Society decided to launch its first public fund-raising campaign throughout the City of St. Louis.

Fifteen hundred volunteers responded to the call for help and attended the kick-off dinner at the City Club, where former St. Louis Mayor Henry W. Kiel, chairman of the campaign, inspired his co-workers with this call to action:

> The Deaconess Hospital has been doing a very worthy work for the community, and we owe it to ourselves, as citizens of St. Louis, to bring success to the plan for its proposed new building at Oakland Avenue....
>
> I am counting on your help. "He who gives to a hospital gives to life itself."[7]

Among the forty-eight division leaders of this campaign were some of the prominent women of the Evangelical churches in St. Louis at that time, and they were featured in two of the city's leading newspapers.[8]

Although this first public fund-raising campaign did not reach its entire goal in the first ten-day solicitation, it did succeed, as previously described, in heightening the image of Deaconess Hospital as a civic institution. It also demonstrated the effectiveness of organized volunteer activity.[9]

The importance of organized volunteer activity was almost immediately demonstrated again when the aforementioned tornado of 1927 severely damaged the hospital buildings on West Belle Place.

Among those who assisted in the massive cleanup of tornado debris were Deaconess Society members, volunteers from the Red Cross, the Boy Scouts, the Girl Scouts, and a group of professors and students from Eden Theological Seminary.[10]

Scheduled Volunteer Service, 1930

By May 1930, when the new hospital building on Oakland Avenue was completed and dedicated, scheduled volunteer service was initiated.

Many members of the Deaconess Society were oriented and scheduled to assist in accommodating the large dedication day crowd and to lead tours of the new facilities. During the next month, many of those volunteers were also assigned to help move the Deaconess Sisters, patients and hospital equipment from West Belle Place to the new location.[11]

7-2. Dedication Day Crowd, Served by Deaconess Society Members, 1930.

"Loyal Friends" during the Great Depression

By 1933, the impact of the Great Depression was so severe that 22 percent of the patients at Deaconess Hospital were "charity" patients. Meanwhile, as reported earlier, the collection of hospital bills from many other patients had become difficult, but Superintendent Jens wrote in 1934:

> The number of patients has increased, the services of the medical and surgical staff have kept pace with the advancement of the science of medicine, the art of nursing has been improved, and we have been enabled to meet our financial obligations with the support of our loyal friends.[12]

One loyal friend, Ida Winkelmeyer, gave a $4,500 gift in 1935 so that the hospital could purchase a deep X-ray therapy machine for the non-invasive treatment of cancer patients.

Then "prompted by the finest kind of humanitarian motives" Miss Winkelmeyer gave an endowment fund of $40,000, "the interest from which is to be used exclusively for the [nonsurgical] treatment of indigent patients suffering from the dread affliction of cancer."[13]

Reported to be "profoundly happy" to have received this first endowment gift to Deaconess Hospital, the board of directors encouraged other members of the Deaconess Society to consider making such a gift.

The following year Mr. and Mrs. F. A. Sudholt took that suggestion and established another fund which would provide "approximately $120.00 per year to be applied regularly towards the maintenance and enlargement of the hospital library."[14]

300 Volunteers Present 50th Anniversary Pageant

The austerity required during the Great Depression was slowly giving way to a mood of celebration in 1939 when the Deaconess Society began preparing for the 50th anniversary of deaconess work in St. Louis. Funds were still scarce, however, so once again volunteers were recruited to assist with the celebration. As reported in the St. Louis Post-Dispatch, the response was tremendous:

> About 300 members of Evangelical and Reformed Churches will participate in a pageant, "Highlights in the Ministry of Healing," to be presented...as part of the observance of the fiftieth anniversary of Deaconess Hospital, 6150 Oakland Avenue. Students from Eden Theological Seminary, members of the Evangelical and Reformed Young Peoples' Federation and various churches will participate. A chorus of 50 from several church choirs will give the musical program.[15]

Many in the overflow audience at Kiel Auditorium for this production spoke of it as "the most outstanding event of its kind ever presented in the city." President Paul Press of the hospital board of directors reported in the annual report for 1939 that it was an achievement made possible by many volunteers who contributed "much effort, careful thinking, and concentrated planning."

New Sisters' Home Prompts New Idea

The enthusiasm generated by the 50th anniversary celebration inspired the Deaconess Society at its annual meeting in 1939 to authorize a campaign for funds and to enlist more "effort, careful thinking and concentrated planning" for a long-awaited new Sisters' Home adjacent to the hospital.

As construction of the new building neared completion, rising costs resulted in the need for more money to provide for the furnishings. To meet this need, Sister Superior Alvina Scheid suggested, with the support of the four women members of the board of directors, that women's organizations of the Evangelical and Reformed Churches in the city might be asked to help. The board agreed to this plan, and luncheons and rummage sales were held for that purpose. These fund-raising events were so successful and aroused so much enthusiasm that Sister Alvina and the women on the board came up with a landmark idea. "Why not organize a women's auxiliary to raise money and provide support on a regular basis for the special needs of the hospital and the sisterhood?"[16]

There was no model for an organized women's hospital auxiliary in St. Louis at that time, and some of the members of the hospital board of directors were apprehensive about the independent activities of such a group. Many discussions were held, but Sister Alvina and her four women advocates were persistent and persuasive. Finally, with some reluctance, the board appointed them as "THE WOMAN'S COMMITTEE of the board of directors" and gave them permission, with a number of limitations, to explore the possibility of organizing a women's auxiliary.

7-3. Sister Superior Alvina Scheid, founder, Deaconess Women's Auxiliary.

Sister Alvina was appointed temporary chairman of the Woman's Committee and Mrs. Mathilda Pfeiffer was made the acting secretary. They met with Mrs. E. Harding, Mrs. J. W. Mack, and Miss Meta Peters, the other three hospital board members on January 6, 1941 to plan their strategy. After preparing an organizational proposal which was approved by the board of directors, they sent out a 1-cent postcard to all of the women members of the Deaconess Society inviting them to a special meeting in the hospital chapel on January 30th "for the purpose of organizing a Woman's Auxiliary in the interest of the hospital and the New Home of the Sisterhood." The response exceeded all of their expectations![17]

Deaconess Women's Auxiliary Organized, 1941

The minutes of that first meeting on January 30, 1941 record the historic decision of that day with this very brief statement, "After discussion, Mrs. E. Leibner moved that we organize an auxiliary. This motion was seconded by Mrs. M. Carlstrom and carried."

Anticipating that development and acting as a nominating committee, the board-appointed Woman's Committee was ready with a slate of officers who were presented and elected:

Mrs. Frederick A. Keck . . . . .president
Mrs. John E. Mack . . . . .first vice-president
Mrs. William Geyer . . . . .second vice-president
Mrs. Frederick A. Goetsch . . . . .third vice-president
Mrs. Edward Harding . . . . .fourth vice-president
Mrs. Frederick Pfeiffer . . . . .secretary
Mrs. Erich E. Leibner . . . . .treasurer[18]

It was a wisely chosen slate. Each of these officers was a well-known, highly regarded woman leader in the Evangelical and Reformed Church of St. Louis at that time, and together they represented a wide geographical area of the city.

Mrs. Keck, the president, gave the new "Women's Auxiliary of the Evangelical Deaconess Society," as it was named, immediate status and credibility. A gifted speaker and tireless worker, Mrs. Keck had served as the first president of the Evangelical Women's Union, the national organization of women in the Evangelical Church; as a member of the Deaconess Society board of directors; and as a leader in the previously mentioned public campaign for funds in 1926. Moreover, her husband, Mr. Frederick A. Keck, was the treasurer of the denomination, then known as the Evangelical and Reformed Church.

Mrs. Mack, Mrs. Harding and Mrs. Pfeiffer were members of the Deaconess Society board of directors in 1941, and Mrs. Leibner was the wife of the Rev. Erich Leibner, vice-president of the board. Mrs. Goetsch was well known as a former missionary to India and the wife of the executive secretary of the Board of International Missions of the Evangelical and Reformed Church. All together, these first officers of the Women's Auxiliary of the Evangelical Deaconess Society were an impressive and very able group of leaders.[19]

7-4. Clara Huning Keck (Mrs. F. A.), First President, Deaconess Women's Auxiliary, 1941.

Auxiliary Constitution and Bylaws Adopted

After electing officers, the Auxiliary (as it soon came to be called) adopted a motion empowering the executive committee to prepare a constitution and bylaws for presentation at the next meeting. Conferring frequently, sometimes downtown for lunch, and using their experience in national women's organizations of the church as a guide, the Auxiliary officers were able to prepare a document which was approved by the hospital board of directors and adopted by the Auxiliary on March 25, 1941.

As the name of the new organization implied, membership was at first limited to the women members of the Deaconess Society without payment of additional dues. Later revisions of the constitution and bylaws changed the name to "The Deaconess Auxiliary," and extended membership to all interested persons, both men and women. Annual dues and life memberships were also eventually adopted.

The executive board met monthly, and quarterly meetings were held for the whole membership on the fourth Tuesdays of January, March, May and October. Business was conducted at the four membership meetings, and educational programs were presented by the Deaconess Sisters and members of the medical staff.

The purpose of the Auxiliary was "To interest the women of the Evangelical Deaconess Society in the Hospital, in the Deaconess Sisterhood, and in the Sisters' Home, and to be of service whenever and wherever possible." That purpose has been expanded to include promotion of the highest quality of patient care and advancement of educational programs in ways approved by the hospital board of directors.[20]

The First Auxiliary Project

The first project presented to the Auxiliary in 1941 was a request for help in sewing draperies under the leadership of Mrs. Frederick P. Jens for all of the rooms on the six floors of the new Sisters' Home. Another committee was responsible for purchasing linens, china, silverware and some furniture. More luncheons and rummage sales at churches throughout the city were given in order to raise funds.[21]

Soon after beginning their first project, however, the Auxiliary members were confronted with a tremendous loss and great sorrow. Their first president, Mrs. Keck, died suddenly in September 1941 after a very brief illness. This was a serious setback for the new organization, but the constitution provided for such a possibility and the first vice-president, Mrs. John Mack, became president. Like her predecessor, she was an able leader and she inspired the membership to work harder than ever in tribute to Mrs. Keck.[22]

By the end of 1941, the Auxiliary had 337 members and a total income of $954.89, out of which $800 was paid for 240 place settings of china, glassware and silverware for the Sisters' Home; $50 for a chair in the Sisters' living room; and $100 to the building fund.

Obviously pleased, the president of the hospital board of directors commended the Auxiliary in his annual report for that year with these words of appreciation,

> At this time I should like to indicate that the recently organized Woman's Auxiliary to the Evangelical Deaconess Society is making very fine strides in the right direction. By various legitimate methods the members of this group have raised sufficient funds to furnish the new building with dishes, silverware, glassware, and are being responsible for the making of window drapes. We, of the Board of Directors and the hospital family, are very grateful to these ladies for their splendid efforts.[23]

When the Sisters' Home was dedicated on March 15, 1942, the Auxiliary members could point with pride to the beautiful furnishings throughout the six-floor building as evidence of their "splendid efforts," and they served a luncheon for all of the guests that day, using the lovely new china, silverware and glassware which they had purchased. With a profit of $100.30 received from a freewill offering at the luncheon, the Auxiliary promptly purchased tablecloths for the tables in the dining room and some additional equipment for the kitchen. In the meantime, an electric stove had already been purchased with gifts from individual members.

Having accomplished their first projects so successfully and having won the commendation of the hospital board of directors, the Auxiliary members voted at their regular meeting on March 24, 1942 to print their own stationery, letterheads and envelopes![24]

Wartime Shortages and More "Splendid Efforts"

By September 1942, wartime shortages were making some hospital supplies hard to get. So it was that the Deaconess sewing department asked the Auxiliary for help with the growing number of articles in need of mending. The membership voted to set aside regular workdays for this purpose, and 25 women volunteered immediately to rotate twice a week in the sewing room. Within the first three months they completed 1,746 articles.[25]

Sister Olivia Drusch, who succeeded Sister Alvina Scheid as sister superior in 1942, also recognized the Auxiliary's ability to provide good help when needed. She suggested that with the wartime rationing of food, the hospital dietary department could use some home-canned vegetables and fruits from the many victory gardens growing in the city. Once again, Auxiliary members took the hint, and by the end of the next summer they had canned 936 quarts of food for the hospital pantry.[26]

Patterns of Giving Established

Meanwhile, the profits from a luncheon, book review and rummage sale made it possible in October, 1942, for the Auxiliary to present a $100 scholarship to the Sisterhood for college courses and $363 for a resuscitating machine in the obstetrical department.

In addition to the many hours of volunteer service given by Auxiliary members, these gifts were the beginning of a pattern of giving which, in keeping with the Auxiliary's purpose, has promoted the highest quality of patient care and advanced the educational programs of the hospital for five decades.[27]

Red Cross Volunteers, 1942

During 1942 the need for trained volunteers in the patient care areas of the hospital also became apparent as a result of wartime personnel shortages. To meet this need, classes in Red Cross work were conducted daily in the Sisters' Home.

Under the supervision of Sister Loretta Wohlschlaeger, the Red Cross volunteers were the first volunteers to serve in patient care areas. They wore special volunteer uniforms not only to give the program authenticity but to assure patients that those who served them had been properly trained.[28]

Among the first volunteers in nursing service in 1942 was Mr. Frederick Saborosch, the first male volunteer in a regularly scheduled program at Deaconess Hospital. After completing his training, Mr. Saborosch worked every Friday night for more than ten years as a male nurse's aide in the hospital from 7:00 to 10:30 P.M. Frequently he served as many as two or three nights in a single week when the need for his services became urgent, and he missed only two nights at his post in ten years, these because of illness.

When he retired in 1951, Mr. Saborosch was invited as a special guest to the employees' recognition dinner where he was honored for his many years of extraordinary volunteer service to patients in the hospital.[29]

In 1944, with wartime personnel shortages greater than ever, Red Cross volunteers were working four-hour weekly shifts on a regular schedule in many departments of the hospital. Margaret Graebner, head of the hospital dietary department, reported:

> Since April of 1944 our hospital has been receiving aid from the American Red Cross through its Dieticians' Aid Corps. The members making up our group represent an interdenominational interest in our hospital. However, 75% of these ladies are members of the Evangelical Church.... About 25 women are active in this effort and most of them furnish us with four hours of their time every week.[30]

These Red Cross volunteers served at Deaconess Hospital throughout World War II. They were the forerunners of the first volunteers who began four-hour regularly scheduled assignments under the Director of Volunteer Services a few years later.

Auxiliary's Accomplishments Acknowledged

During the 1940s the Auxiliary became a strong and acknowledged presence in the hospital. Its members contributed thousands of hours of devoted service every year for a multitude of otherwise unmet needs, including the serving of tea and refreshments on Hospital Day.

7-5. Auxilians Serving Tea on Hospital Day, 1944. Mrs. Frederick P. Jens, serving at left; Augusta Mack, president, center right wearing corsage; Mathilda Pfeiffer, president-elect, holding tray.

In 1949 the Auxiliary officers and the accomplishments of the organization were listed for the first time in the hospital's annual report. Included, in addition to $2,850 for a new organ and chimes in the chapel in Gerhold Hall, were a $100 scholarship, a $193.93 final payment on a mimeograph machine, $423.42 for new dishes and silver, and the purchase of six new tables.

In 1952 the Auxiliary executive committee was pictured in the hospital's annual report for the first time with a report on volunteer activities. Luella Erhardt, the president at that time, explained in her published report a year earlier that, "The effectiveness of our service is in direct proportion to the faithfulness and willingness of our members."[31]

255

7-6. Luella Ehrhardt, Auxiliary President and Executive Board, 1952. Left to right; Lydia Weisser, Jeanette Ehlhardt, Evelyn Cotner, Janet Curry, Elsie Leibner and Amanda Stockhoff.

"Twigs" Organized and Uniforms Adopted

The 1950s brought many more opportunities for volunteer service, and there were many willing auxilians who organized themselves into "Twigs," groups who functioned as service committees to carry out the Auxiliary's projects.

Each Twig had a specific area of responsibility, and in 1953 there were eight: Sewing, Typing, Tour, Library, Hostess, Gift Cart, Feeding and Tray Favors. The Favor Twig has made thousands of patient tray favors each year since it began and in 1961 received a first-place award from the Missouri Hospital Association for its original ideas.

Some Deaconess Auxiliary members began wearing the official hospital auxiliary uniform in the early 1950s. It consisted of a pink and white cap, white blouse, and pink jumper with the auxiliary emblem on the front and chevrons (indicating hours of volunteer service) on the sleeve. [32]

Membership in the Missouri Hospital Association

As auxiliaries were organized in other hospitals in Missouri during the 1940s and early 1950s, the Missouri Hospital Association recruited members for participation in its programs.

7-7. Favor Twig, 1953. Elizabeth Klotz, Auxiliary president, second from left, and Alice Metz, center right, wearing the volunteer uniform and cap.

The Deaconess Auxiliary sent delegates to the Missouri Hospital Association's annual meetings and became a dues-paying member of the state-wide organization. In 1954 a large copy of the auxiliary emblem, which is based on the emblem of the American Hospital Association, was displayed in the Deaconess board room.

Alice Metz gave an interpretation of that emblem at the Auxiliary's 20th Anniversary Dinner, and the membership voted to use the emblem and a prayer for auxiliaries on its printed programs and official publications.

The Lorraine Cross in the center of the shield has been the symbol of relief to the unfortunate since medieval times. The Wand of Mercury and the Serpent in the upper left corner represent the healing arts. The Maltese Cross in the upper right corner was used by the Knights Hospitalers during the Crusades and symbolizes healing institutions. In the

7-8. The Deaconess Auxiliary Emblem.

lower left corner, the Geneva or Greek Cross is the international sign of relief for the sick and the wounded. The urn in the lower right corner represents the nursing profession. The classic Latin motto, "Nisi Dominus Frustra," declares "Without God we can do nothing."[33]

New Projects and a $10,000 Gift

The need to raise more and more money led the Auxiliary to a great new venture, a smorgasbord dinner that served 1200 people on one evening in 1952. Almost every member, and there were more than 400 by then, along with as many friends and relatives as each could recruit, helped on that project. The food was beautifully presented, abundant and delicious, and the smorgasbord was so successful that it was repeated in 1953 and 1954. By then, the kitchen in the Sister's Home had seen so much hard use that a $10,000 renovation was necessary. Profits from the big smorgasbord dinners made that possible, and the Auxiliary wrote its first five-digit check to pay for it.[34]

Even though the profits from the smorgasbords were impressive and the renovated kitchen made food preparation easier, the Auxiliary adopted an alternative money-making project in 1956, a bazaar called a Santa Claus Village.

The Santa Claus Village with its colorful decorations, festive food, and handmade gifts was also very successful as a source of income, and it was renamed the Anniversary Fair a few years later. Then it became the annual Fall Festival and included the sale of antiques, jewelry, plants and many choice secondhand items

7-9. Auxiliary Leaders with Santa Claus Village Handmade Gifts, 1956.

donated by the Auxiliary members and their friends. Whatever the name, this money-making event grew larger, was extended to two days, and became more profitable each year.[35]

First Gift and Coffee Shop Opened, 1957

In the meantime, the South Memorial Building of the hospital had been built, increasing the total number of patient beds to 358 and bringing a similar increase in hospital visitors. Since Deaconess did not have a place for visitors to get food or personal necessities if they had to stay any length of time at the hospital, many requests came for a gift-coffee shop on the premises.

7-10. First Deaconess Gift Shop, 1957. Evelyn Cotner, Auxiliary President, left.

Once again, the Deaconess Auxiliary rose to the occasion, and in March 1957 the first Deaconess Gift and Coffee Shop was opened. The gift section was staffed by auxilians while employees managed the coffee counter. Visitors expressed great appreciation for the reasonable prices and the convenient location on the first floor east corridor of the main hospital building.

The Auxiliary appreciated the profits from the Gift Shop and Coffee Shop, and they quickly put this new income to use by purchasing twenty-nine new bassinets

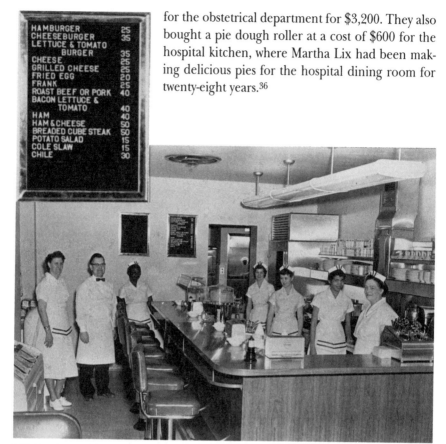

for the obstetrical department for $3,200. They also bought a pie dough roller at a cost of $600 for the hospital kitchen, where Martha Lix had been making delicious pies for the hospital dining room for twenty-eight years.[36]

7-11. First Deaconess Coffee Shop, 1957. Mr. Otto Lange, Manager, with employees.

Gertrude Miketta, Director of Volunteer Services, 1959

The 1950s ended with so much volunteer activity at Deaconess Hospital that Gertrude Miketta, a former deaconess, was appointed full-time director of volunteer services in 1959. With Sister Amanda Wulff, who assisted her as clinical instructor for volunteers, the director of volunteer services was made responsible for "planning, organizing, coordinating and directing all volunteer activities in the hospital," including those of the Deaconess Auxiliary.[37]

Under Gertrude Miketta's leadership, the Auxiliary scheduled bi-weekly workshops throughout the year in 1959 to facilitate the completion of handmade gifts, puppets and tray favors for its many projects.

Doctors' Day was a new activity celebrated by the Auxiliary in 1959, and that event has become an annual observance on March 30. Members of the Deaconess Medical Staff are greeted as they arrive in the Doctor's Lounge and they are honored with boutonnieres and refreshments as expressions of appreciation from the Auxiliary.

7-12. Gertrude Miketta, first Director of Volunteer Services, 1959.

In 1961 the Auxiliary added two new money-making projects, the Photo-Ident Program and the Stay-at-Home Night, to its schedule of events, and a new Puppet Twig was begun. More than 500 hand puppets were created for all of the pediatric patients during that first year and almost twice that many each year after that. This project, which continues to serve young patients at Deaconess today, became so popular that other hospital auxiliaries asked for the pattern and one puppet travelled half around the world to India.[38]

7-13. Sister Amanda Wulff, Clinical Instructor for Volunteer Services.

New volunteers and auxilians at Deaconess began wearing the distinctive pink volunteer smock as a uniform in 1961. More comfortable and easier to maintain than the older jumper uniform, the smock was being adopted by volunteers in many other hospital auxiliaries at that time, thus it easily identified those who wore it.

7-14. Auxiliary Celebrates Doctors' Day, 1967. Esther Tibbles, Auxiliary president, pins a carnation on Dr. Harold A. Goodrich, with (left to right): Amanda Offerjost, Berta Lippert and Dr. John Roth.

7-15. Puppet Twig Chairpersons, Myrtle Wegehoft and Amanda Offerjost, with Gertrude Miketta, center, 1961.

New Gift and Coffee Shop, Largest Money-maker

In 1965 the Auxiliary assumed full responsibility for the Gift and Coffee Shop, which was relocated and enlarged in 1967 in space made possible by the hospital's Decade of Development expansion program. A pledge of $100,000 to that program was paid off in 1969 after only four years, making this the Auxiliary's first six-digit gift to the hospital.

7-16. New Gift Shop-Coffee Shop, 1967.

In its new location, the Gift Shop generated a larger and larger income each year under the capable leadership of Esther Tibbles, who served as its first manager until she retired in 1980. A loyal gift shop committee assisted her throughout those years, and more than sixty volunteers contributed their services to keep the shop open seven days per week, soon making it the Auxiliary's largest money-maker.[39]

With its increasing income, the Auxiliary was able to pledge $80,000 in the early 1970s to install a cobalt unit in the hospital. This was followed by a pledge of $165,000 for air conditioning the Sisters' Home and School of Nursing. In 1975 the Auxiliary gave $85,000 for new cardiac equipment, wheelchairs and bed tables. In 1976 it gave $86,000 for closed circuit T.V., ultrasound equipment and 30 new tables. This was followed by a pledge of $250,000 (to be paid in five years) to the hospital's "Design for the 80s" Building Program. In 1979 that pledge was doubled to $500,000 in celebration of the 90th Anniversary of Deaconess Hospital and the Deaconess Sisterhood. It was paid off within three years.[40]

7-17. $500,000 Auxiliary Gift to "Decade of Development." Dorothy DeDoyard, Auxiliary president, presenting $500,000 Auxiliary check to President Richard P. Ellerbrake. Looking on, left to right, Auxiliary past presidents Marguerite Oelze, Gladys Feldmeier, Esther Tibbles, and Marcella Soutiea with Esther Blacksher, gift shop chairperson.

Life Memberships Established, 1978

Dues of $1.00 per year had been adopted for the first time by the Auxiliary in 1959, but in 1977 five longtime members of the Auxiliary each paid $25.00 and requested that life memberships be established with the payment of this amount. These first five life members were: Lee Wandel, Olga Gieselmann, Paula Madlinger, Dorothy Hermann and Edna Wetterau.

A constitutional revision was therefore adopted by the Auxiliary in 1978 to include life memberships for a onetime payment of $25.00, with annual dues for regular memberships to be increased first to $2.00 and later to $4,00.

Life memberships proved to be a popular alternative, and by 1989, the hospital's centennial year, there were 166 life members in the Auxiliary.[41]

264

Sponsorship of the Deaconess Archives

With a strong sense of heritage, the Auxiliary has given annual gifts of $1,000 for many years to sponsor the Deaconess Archives, which are staffed by an archival-ly-trained volunteer.

The Auxiliary's minutes, records, publications, pictures and chronology of historic events are preserved in the Archives, where they are part of the Deaconess heritage and are also a valuable resource for women's history in St. Louis and in the United Church of Christ.

The antique Deaconess Dolls, on display in the hospital front lobby, were rejuvenated by the Auxiliary in 1984 as a special project in honor of the Deaconess Sisters' 95th Anniversary. Representative of the many artifacts preserved in the Archives, the Deaconess Dolls continue to tell an important story and create interest in Deaconess history.[42]

Jeanette Weber, Director of Volunteers, 1981

After directing volunteer activities at Deaconess Hospital for twenty-two years, Gertrude Miketta retired in 1981 and her assistant, Jeanette Weber, was appointed as the new director of volunteer services.

Under the leadership of Director Jen Weber and her assistant, Volunteer Coordinator Clare Pilla, the activities of the Volunteer Services and the Auxiliary continued to grow and expand to keep up with growth and expansion of the hospital.[43]

Some Auxiliary and volunteer activities of today rest on past traditions. The beautiful quilts and handmade gifts created for the Fall Festival and

7-19. Jeanette Weber, Director of Volunteer Services, 1981.

Gift Shop are made by modern counterparts to the original sewing group organized in the 1940s. Lobby sales and the annual Second Time Around Sales bring memories of the first Auxiliary members who spent long hours preparing and conducting Rummage Sales. The Book Fair is not only an important annual fund-raiser but is symbolic of the Auxiliary's strong commitment to health education and the educational programs of the institution.[44]

7-19. Auxiliary Quilters. Left to right: Lorene Betz, Helen Springmeyer, Eleanor Laubengayer, Judy Reis (quilt owner), Ruth Woltemath, Marie Deuschle, Frieda Abele, Dorothy Fuist, Esther Kuergeleis, Ruth Dauster.

7-20. Auxiliary Fall Festival.

Past Presidents Honored on 45th Anniversary

In gratitude for the dedicated leadership of its officers, and with appreciation for its heritage, the Auxiliary celebrated its 45th Anniversary in 1986. A tea and reception for members and friends honored all who have contributed as volunteers to health care and health education at Deaconess throughout its history.

7-21. Edna Mumm, longtime member and past chairperson of Auxiliary's ways and means committee, with Kay Templeton and Dorothy Ziegler in the Fall Festival Christmas booth.

The past presidents of the Auxiliary, many of whom were present for this occasion, were recognized for outstanding and devoted leadership. Portraits of all of the Auxiliary's presidents and of Sister Alvina Scheid, the founder, were featured in a heritage display, which inspired many fond memories and appreciation for volunteer activities and achievements at Deaconess in past years.[45]

7-22. Auxiliary Past Presidents at 45th Anniversary Tea. Standing, left to right: Elizabeth Klotz, Gladys Feldmeier, Dorothy DeDoyard, Marcella Soutiea, Gertrude McKenney, President Richard P. Ellerbrake. Seated: Margaret Oelze and Esther Tibbles, 1986.

267

Gift Shop Renamed "Park Place Gift Shop"

The Gift Shop continues to be the Auxiliary's primary source of revenue, and in 1988 it was remodeled and renamed the "Park Place Gift Shop."

More than sixty volunteers work to keep the Park Place Gift Shop open seven days a week. Their contributed services provide important necessities for patients, visitors and hospital employees and, at the same time, they have helped increase the Auxiliary's income to an all-time high.[46]

7-23. Park Place Gift Shop.

The Diakonian

To keep the more than 400 members of the Auxiliary better informed about the many events of interest and concern to them, a quarterly newsletter, *The Diakonian*, has been published since 1988.

Clare Pilla, volunteer coordinator, has served as editor of the newsletter and Jean Sprung has been the roving reporter. Many auxilians contribute information and ideas.

Each issue of the *The Diakonian* includes a message from the director of volunteer services, information about meetings, events and activities from the Auxiliary president and the executive board, which meets monthly. Interesting health news as well as news about members' birthdays and special celebrations are also included.[47]

Awards Honor All Volunteers

Each year since 1962, when the first Volunteer Awards Luncheon was held at Deaconess Hospital, an annual Volunteer Awards Dinner in September is the special celebration honoring all volunteers and auxilians.

Award pins and chevrons are presented annually at the Volunteer Dinner to those who have reached landmark levels of service. The pins, with their precious stones, are highly-prized

7-24. Clare Pilla, Volunteer Coordinator and Editor, *The Diakonian.*

symbols of faithfulness. Each represents a significant contribution of volunteer hours, from three rubies for 1,000 hours to two emeralds and one diamond for 6,000 or more.

7-25. 1989 Auxiliary Officers and Board Members. Front: Marguerite Oelze, Mildred Grimm, President Gertrude McKenny, Mildred Hood, Lillian Bennett. Back: Virginia Leone, Gladys Feldmeier, Lucile Sheldon, Grace Bennett, Frieda Abele, Jen Weber. Not pictured: Eleanor Laubengayer, Chris Dutton, May Marts, Jean Sprung, Leona Mauthe.

In 1966 ten volunteers reached a level of more than 1,000 hours each. Since then the levels continue to go higher and higher, with some auxilians having contributed more than 10,000 hours. In 1989 those honored in this group were: Elvira Alewel, Marie Brandt, Sister Mary Kramme, Alvera Leicht, Ruth Rasche, Maxine Short, and Laura Zimmer. Each of them has received an inscribed plaque for this level of volunteer service.

7-26. 10,000 Hours Plus Volunteers. With Executive Vice President Jerry W. Paul, Top: Laura Zimmer, Maxine Short, Sister Mary Kramme, Marie Brandt, and Ruth Rasche. Bottom: Alvera Leicht and Elvira Alewel.

The all-time record of 18,208 hours was set, however, in 1986 by Mr. Carl Riesinger, who served as a Deaconess volunteer for twenty-one years!

Since 1979, the total number of contributed hours at Deaconess has increased annually each year for more than ten years. In 1985 more than 70,000 volunteer hours were contributed. At the prevailing minimum wage rate of $3.25 per hour, it amounted to a contribution of $234,500 from volunteers in that one year alone.

In 1989 volunteers at Deaconess contributed 74,756 hours, 2,000 hours more than in the previous year, with candystripers (youth volunteers) contributing 2,525 of those total hours.[48]

7-27. Carl Riesinger, 18,200+ Hour Volunteer.

The Auxiliary, Major Donor to Deaconess

In addition to contributing almost 75,000 volunteer hours to Deaconess annually, the Auxiliary has provided funds during the past ten years alone for an impressive number of very costly hospital services and equipment:

A YAG Laser $60,000
Cardiac rehabilitation equipment $32,100
Deaconess South Dialysis Center $10,000
Deaconess Child Care Center $65,000
Surgi Waiting Room $80,000
Chesterfield Med Center $100,000
Infant life support $15,000
Kitchen remodeling $8,000
SurgiCenter expansion $500,000
Zeiss universal microscope $40,000
Cancer Screening Center $70,000
East parking pavilion canopy $75,000
Centennial Fund (5 year pledge) $1,000,000

With these gifts, in addition to annual scholarships to the College of Nursing, special love gifts to the Deaconess Sisters, and support for the Deaconess Archives, the Auxiliary's cash contributions thus far total more than $4 million, making it the major donor to Deaconess.[49]

7-28. Deaconess Child Care Center, a $65,000 Auxiliary gift. Denise Cunningham, right, director and Sheree Thompson, left, preschool instructor, 1984.

7-29. Surgi Waiting Room, an $80,000 Auxiliary Gift. Left to right: Jen Weber, Director, Volunteer Services; and Jerry Paul, Executive Vice President; with Auxiliary Volunteers Leona Mauthe and Margaret Oelze (standing); Audrey Leibundgut (seated); and Betty Faust, Assistant Director of Nursing Service, right.

A Century of "Giving to Life Itself"

Deaconess volunteers and auxilians have responded enthusiastically for 100 years to new opportunities for service "whenever and wherever possible." Throughout these years they have demonstrated again and again that:

"Whoever gives to a hospital, gives to life itself."[50]

7-30. $100,000 Auxiliary Gift toward $1 Million Centennial Pledge, Gertrude McKenney, Auxiliary President, and Deaconess President Richard P. Ellerbrake, 1989.

Chapter Eight

THE SPIRITUAL MINISTRY
"In a Christian Setting"

The Deaconess name has always been associated with a Christian community. In Biblical times it was used to identify those engaged in a ministry of loving service to others in need of care, particularly the sick, the poor and the persecuted. Since then, persons and institutions named Deaconess have declared by their name alone that they propose to function in a Christian setting.

Theodore and Frederike Fliedner, the founders of modern deaconess work in Kaiserswerth, Germany, taught that "a deaconess is first of all a disciple of the Lord." Mrs. Fliedner is reported to have said to the Deaconess Sisters again and again, "The soul of service must never be sacrificed to the technique." She also declared, "Prayer and work are the watchwords of our institution."[1]

8-1: The Kaiserswerth Chapel at the Deaconess Motherhouse and Hospital in Germany, where modern deaconess work began and where Florence Nightingale studied nursing.

Florence Nightingale was so impressed with the atmosphere in the Kaiserswerth hospital that after studying there in 1851 with the Fliedners she wrote:

274

...go to Kaiserswerth, and see the delicacy, the cheerfulness, the grace of Christian kindness, the moral atmosphere, in short, which may be diffused through a hospital, by making it one of God's schools, where both patients and nurses come to learn of Him.[2]

Other visitors to Kaiserswerth such as Dr. Jane Bancroft, a prominent Methodist educator from the United States, called attention to the Deaconess Sisters "who assist the clergyman... in ministering to spiritual needs."[3]

Based on the Kaiserswerth model, The Evangelical Deaconess Society of St. Louis, Mo., began its work in 1889, as described earlier, by declaring that its purpose was "to nurse the sick... by deaconesses, i.e. theoretically and practically trained Christian nurses...." Moreover, the Society's Articles of Association provided that "Every meeting shall be opened and dismissed with prayer and conducted in a manner corresponding to the Christian charity work of this association."[4]

Throughout the 100 years since that time, the Christian environment at Deaconess Hospital has been reaffirmed many times and in many ways. Mission statements adopted by the board of directors have emphasized the "Christian setting" and health care and health education provided in the "compassionate spirit of Jesus Christ."[5]

This emphasis on the spiritual dimension of healing and teaching is an important part of the deaconess heritage. It is recognized today as an element in modern medicine as well.[6]

The Spiritual Framework

Sister Katherine Haack and Sister Lydia Daries, the first Evangelical Deaconess Sisters, began their work in St. Louis on the premise that it was a spiritual as well as a healing and educational ministry. Trained in deaconess methods, they engaged in worship, prayer, and Bible study to provide a spiritual framework for their daily activities and to create an atmosphere in which compassionate service to others could be nurtured.

Further religious instructions were provided for the first deaconesses and their probationers by Pastor Jacob Irion, a member of the board of directors, who wrote the first short deaconess manual for the Deaconess Society. Other pastors in the Society provided leadership for worship services and administered the sacraments at the first Deaconess Home and Hospital.[7]

Qualifications and Means of Spiritual Ministry

The spiritual ministry of the deaconesses was of such importance that a later book of instruction, *Principles of Deaconess Work*, was published by the Federation of Evangelical Deaconess Associations and used as the primary study manual for Deaconess Sisters in Evangelical institutions throughout the land. The longest chapter (twenty-five pages) was devoted to "The Spiritual Ministry." Included in it are specific instructions for approaching and carrying out the many variations of that ministry.

But even before a deaconess could be accepted for training in the School for Deaconesses she had to have a letter of recommendation from her local church pastor attesting to her good reputation and to her basic spiritual qualifications for deaconess work. As outlined near the beginning of the guidebook, these were: "1. *Conversion...*, 2. *Obedience* to the word of God, to the regulations of the Church and to the mother-house..., and 3. ...a large measure of *Love* for the Lord and our fellowmen."[8]

8-2: Deaconess Sister at Bedside.

Once admitted to the sisterhood for deaconess training, the probationers were taught that the means of spiritual ministry are the "Word of God, prayer and sacred hymns." Classes in the School for Deaconesses included Bible study, the History and Principles of Deaconess Work, Christian Doctrine and Sacred Hymns.

With the patients' permission, deaconesses were to read the Word of God daily to their charges, to sing sacred hymns and to pray with them. But they were to observe the rule: "do not use many pious words at the sick-bed, for they very easily prove to be meaningless, vain talk devoid of spirit and power." The Deaconess Sister was further admonished that whatever she read to her patients, or when she prayed with them, "let it be brief." Spiritual ministry included respect for the patient as a person.

Since bedside nursing did not always provide a Bible or hymnbook within easy reach, the Deaconess Sisters were encouraged to memorize helpful Scripture passages and the verses of entire hymns in order to bolster their own strength in difficult situations and to share with patients who requested encouragement. After years of such spiritual ministry, some of the Deaconess Sisters could quote many favorite long passages of the Bible from memory and they knew a score or more of the great hymns of the church by memory as well.[9]

Deaconess Chapel, 1893

At first, when Deaconess Hospital was located on Eugenia Street, there was no room for a chapel. Worship was held at that time in the patients' rooms or wherever it could be arranged.

In 1893 the first Deaconess Chapel was dedicated as part of the new hospital on West Belle Place. Located in the center of the new facilities, this chapel was simple in design and accessible to everyone. Moreover, the House Rules of the Deaconess Home and Hospital stated that "All deaconesses are expected to attend regular chapel services and devotions...." Patients, visitors and the hospital staff were also all encouraged to attend.[10]

The Rev. J. D. Illg, First Deaconess Pastor

In order "to provide better for the spiritual ministry of deaconesses and patients," as explained to Deaconess Society members in their monthly publication, *The Diakonissenfreund*, the Rev. J.D. Illg was called in 1896 to serve as the first full-time pastor of the Deaconess Home and Hospital. Soon after Rev. Illg began his work, however, he became seriously ill and had to submit to surgery. Unfortunately, poor health made it necessary for him to give up his position within the year. Though short-lived, his presence as the pastor in the Deaconess Home and Hospital convinced the Deaconess Society board of directors of the need to appoint a full-time superintendent and pastor to serve the hospital.[11]

The Rev. Frederick P. Jens, Pastor and Superintendent, 1898

In 1898 the Rev. Frederick P. Jens was called to be the first superintendent and pastor of the Deaconess Home and Hospital. Working closely with Sister Magdalene Gerhold, who had been appointed sister superior, Superintendent Jens soon assumed the responsibilities not only of serving as pastor to the deaconesses and patients but also as business manager and public relations director of the hospital, as instructor in the School for Deaconesses, and as editor of *The Diakonissenfreund*.[12]

The spiritual ministry in the Deaconess Home and Hospital was a high priority for the superintendent, however, and he devoted much of his time to that ministry, declaring,

> Without the thorough training of the sisters ...by means of the Word of God and of prayer, the calling has no foundation; it then loses its interesting feature and its noble aim, and cannot continue to exist.[13]

Response to the new leadership revitalized deaconess work and within a year there were twenty deaconesses in the St. Louis Sisterhood.[14]

"A Christian Household"

Almost 700 patients were admitted to Deaconess Hospital in 1899, a large increase over the previous year. Many came from out of the city and from other church denominations. Since most patients had never been in a hospital before, "Terms for Admission," as recorded in the chapter on "Patient Care," were published for the first time that year.

> Persons of all creeds, and of no creed are admitted, and receive the same quality of nursing care, but the hospital is a Christian household, and the services held in the chapel are those of the German

278

Evangelical Church. Every patient, however, is privileged to receive the ministrations of whatever form or faith he may profess or prefer.[15]

By 1908 the number of patients had increased to almost 1400 annually, and the atmosphere of the hospital as a Christian household was becoming more difficult to maintain. A document, "Rules for Patients," was then published. As previously listed, it included specific guidelines which were not considered an infringement on patients' rights in that day but necessities for providing an environment conducive to health and healing:

> Smoking within the Hospital is prohibited; also the use of wines or spiritous liquors, unless prescribed by the physician.
>
> Profane or indecent language, or the expression of immoral or infidel sentiments, will not be tolerated.
>
> Convalescents are desired, as far as possible, to be present at the services in the Chapel.[16]

To accommodate a continuing growth in the number of patients and the size of the staff, a new chapel, built in 1906 as part of the fireproof hospital facilities, was completed that year.

8-3: Deaconess Chapel, 1908.

The Ministry of Parish Deaconesses

As indicated earlier, all Deaconess Sisters were trained first as nurses. After their basic training in the School for Deaconesses, they could then complete additional studies for assignments in teaching, parish work or as missionaries.[17]

Deaconesses in the first century are said to have been parish deaconesses because they were part of the local church congregation and had among their duties the responsibility for taking care of the suffering martyrs in prison.

> Persecution of the Christians was severe in those early days of the church and it is observed that the deaconesses were particularly suited to taking care of the suffering martyrs since they could find access to them when others could not.[18]

The Fliedners, who developed the Kaiserswerth model of deaconess work, designated the parish deaconess as "the crown of the female diaconate, i.e., the highest development or most perfect form of it."[19]

Usually responsible for Christian education, social work and home visitation in a large congregation or institution, the parish deaconess combined teaching and nursing with her spiritual training and was, in reality, an assistant pastor. Sisters Alvina Scheid and Anna Meyer were among the first Deaconess Sisters from St. Louis to be assigned as parish deaconesses. They were sent to Louisville, Kentucky, in 1910 to assist the Evangelical Deaconess Association of that city, which concentrated its efforts at that time on parish work. Sisters Alvina and Anna are reported to have done "much parish work until 1912, when they returned to their motherhouse."[20]

Sister Adele Hosto, a parish deaconess in a large congregation in Chicago described her work in this way:

> It is evident that in no other branch of the work can a deaconess serve the Lord in such manifold ways as are opened to her within the confines of a large city parish which affords an abundance and variety of work. The deaconess in going from house to house comes in contact and keeps in touch with all the people, and by getting acquainted with the situation and circumstances of the individual, has occasion to serve all, the sick and the well, the rich and poor, and the senior as well as the junior members of the church.[21]

But there were pitfalls as well as special opportunities for service in parish work. The Deaconess Sisters were cautioned that:

> The dangers which accompany parish work are:
>
> (1) To become superficial in character. Coming into contact with so many people has a tendency to distract your thoughts, to make you superficial, fickle and given to gossip....
>
> (2) To become a restless busy-body that cannot stay at home, and believes that service consists only in running from place to place....
>
> (3) To become conformed to the world... By this is meant eye-service to please men, and to seek favoritism with families and superiors....[22]

When the The Good Shepherd Center, forerunner of Caroline Mission and the present United Church Neighborhood Houses, was opened in St. Louis in 1913, Sister Bena Fuchs was assigned as the first parish deaconess in that institution and its inner city congregation. She ministered to the families of the neighborhood and twice a month a group of women met under her leadership for social fellowship and for making garments for those in need of assistance. In 1915 it

8-5. Sister Anna Goetze, Parish Deaconess at Caroline Mission, 1921.

281

was reported that the parish deaconess had made 346 visits during the previous year.

Sister Anna Goetze succeeded Sister Bena as the parish deaconess at Caroline Mission in 1916, and sometimes she seemed to perform miracles. One year she reported that she was granted an extra allowance of $2.50 with which she held a picnic for more than 100 children attending Vacation Bible School.[23]

Former Sister Alma Jungerman was the parish deaconess at Caroline Mission from 1925 until 1932, when she became a missionary to India. In 1930 she reported that she conducted a Teacher Training Class, gave leadership to a Daily Vacation Bible School for 286 children, was responsible for the Sunday School with an average attendance of 220, worked with the Mother's Club and the Sewing circle, and made 425 home visits.[24]

Meanwhile, parish deaconesses from the St. Louis Sisterhood served congregations at St. James and St. Peter's Evangelical Churches in St. Louis, Bethlehem Evangelical Church in Chicago, a church in Kansas City, Missouri, and another in Rochester, New York. The minutes of the board of directors of the Evangelical Deaconess Society from 1924 to 1930 record many other requests for parish deaconesses from congregations near and far, but the demand far exceeded the number available for such assignments. During the 1930s, the need for nurses and teachers in the new, larger hospital on Oakland Avenue in St. Louis became so great that parish deaconess work eventually had to be discontinued. Sister Marie Sprick, the last parish deaconess in St. Louis, served at Kingdom House, a Methodist agency in the inner city, from 1928 to 1930 and at Caroline Mission from 1933 to 1935.[25]

Deaconess Missionaries

Foreign missionary service remained an important option for the St. Louis Deaconess Sisters, however, and they served in India, Honduras and Ecuador.

Missionary work was a combination of all three types of deaconess service—nursing, teaching and parish work. The missionary deaconess had to be particularly skilled and devoted to the spiritual ministry in order to carry on her work in a distant land. Foreign language study and long periods of isolation from the deaconess motherhouse and the sisterhood were additional challenges.

First among the deaconesses to enter foreign mission service was former Sister

Marie Nottrott, who had been a parish deaconess at St. Peter's Evangelical Church in St. Louis and was married in 1921 and commissioned with her husband, the Rev. H. A. Feierabend, to serve in India.

Sister Minnie Gadt was commissioned as a missionary by the Evangelical Synod in 1926, and she devoted her entire professional life of forty-two years to service in India. She began her work as the nurse in charge of the large hospital for 750 leprosy patients in Bisrampur. Then she established the School of Nursing at the nearby Evangelical Hospital in Tilda and served there as director of nurses until she became a supervisor for the Indian government's program for accreditation of nurses, a position she held until her retirement in 1968. In 1978 she was honored for her many years of service as a deaconess missionary by the St. Louis Task Force of the United Church Board for World Ministries.

Also commissioned as missionaries from the St. Louis Deaconess Sisterhood were: Sister Hulda Sturm, in Honduras from 1926 to 1928; Sister Alma Jungerman, in India as a deaconess from 1932 to 1942 and then as Mrs. Alma Tauscher until her retirement; Sister Rosadel Albert, in Honduras from 1947 to 1956; and Sister Marilou Mitchell, in Ecuador from 1952 until 1954.[26]

Typical of all of the missionary deaconesses was the experience of Sister Rosadel Albert, who described her work in Honduras while home on furlough. She said that the last lap of her journey to assignment at a rural clinic in the mountains was made on muleback, the only means of transportation. Once there, she said,

8-6. Sister Minnie Gadt, Missionary Deaconess with nursing students at Evangelical Mission Hospital, Tilda, India.

I realized that there was a tremendous need for medical help.... My principal fight is with poor nutrition.... A doctor, his wife and I were the only Americans in a village of 600 Spanish-speaking people... miles from nowhere.... But already I am lonesome for my mission post... they're my people, and I want to go back to help them.[27]

"The Chapel with a View"

While missionary deaconesses carried on their ministry in distant places and parish deaconesses served as pastoral assistants, most of the Deaconess Sisters in St. Louis cared for patients in the hospital or taught in the School for Deaconesses. In

8-7. Sister Rosadel Albert, Missionary Deaconess with patients at rural clinic in Honduras, 1947-1956.

1930, as previously described, they moved from West Belle Place into the new hospital on Oakland Avenue.

The chapel in the new hospital was on the seventh (top) floor of the east wing, a temporary location until a separate chapel could be built. Accessible to everyone by elevator, this new chapel was starkly simple in design, but it had a magnificent rooftop view of the city and its skyline—a dramatic reminder of the rapidly increasing medical needs of people right at the doorstep and as far away as one could see.

In this new setting, the Rev. Dr. Frederick P. Jens was asked to continue "as General Superintendent and with the special task of assuming the duties of Pastor in the hospital, to offer comfort, cheer and spiritual administrations to the sick and to the suffering," while Assistant Superintendent Paul R. Zwilling was assigned special responsibility for business management.[28]

As mentioned previously, Superintendent Jens had been honored in 1925 with a Doctor of Divinity degree from Eden Theological Seminary for his leadership in the ministry of the Evangelical Synod. This new opportunity to devote more time to the spiritual ministry of deaconess work was a welcome change for him. He not only visited patients and conducted Sunday worship in the chapel, but

284

8-8. Sister Hulda Sturm, Missionary Deaconess in Honduras, 1926-1928.

8-9. Sister Alma Jungerman, Missionary Deaconess in India, 1932-1942.

he arrived at the hospital daily at 6:30 a.m. to conduct morning devotions with the Deaconess Sisters and he returned each evening for vespers with them at 7 p.m. after dinner, maintaining this schedule until ill health forced his retirement in 1940.[29]

The Rev. Paul R. Zwilling, Superintendent and Pastor

The spiritual ministry of Deaconess Hospital continued to receive strong emphasis from the Rev. Paul R. Zwilling when he was appointed superintendent and pastor in 1940 to succeed Superintendent Jens.

8-10. Sister Marilou Mitchell, Missionary Deaconess in Ecuador, 1952-1954.

Because all of the floor space in the hospital was by that time urgently needed for patient care services, the chapel was relocated temporarily in 1942 to the lower level of the new Sisters' Home. A beautiful new chapel was built as part of Gerhold Hall in 1946 under Superintendent Zwilling's leadership, and he was

8-11. Rev. Paul R. Zwilling, Superintendent and Pastor, Deaconess Chapel in Gerhold Hall, 1946.

the first to serve there as pastor to the hospital family.[30]

Committed to a close relationship between the hospital and the church, Superintendent Zwilling served as the President of the Commission on Benevolent Institutions of the Evangelical and Reformed Church, forerunner of the Council for Health and Human Service Ministries of the United Church of Christ. He was also President of the American Protestant Hospital Association when the first Commission on Religious Work in Hospitals was appointed in 1939.[31]

Standards for Chaplain Certification Adopted

During the 1930s, clinical pastoral education began to be developed as an innovative approach to preparing pastors for spiritual ministry to patients in hospitals and institutions.

The Rev. Julius W. Varwig, an Evangelical pastor in St. Louis had begun in 1926 to devote his ministry to the spiritual needs of patients in public institutions where there was no on-going pastoral care. For twelve years he is said to have "literally spent himself in ministering to the destitute and forsaken, the erring and wayward, the suffering and dying, regardless of creed or color." As the first pastor on record to provide a full-time ministry in public institutions, he was a pioneer "hospital chaplain."[32]

Other pioneers in this field were the Rev. Anton Boisen, regarded by many as "the father of clinical pastoral training," and the Rev. Dr. Russell L. Dicks, who gave strong leadership to the effort to set standards for the work of chaplains in general hospitals.

It took years of discussion and a number of fact-finding surveys, but in 1939 the American Protestant Hospital Association appointed the aforementioned Commission on Religious Work in Hospitals to study the field. The Rev. Dr. Dicks, the Rev. Dr. Seward Hiltner and the Rev. Dr. Harold P. Schultz were given the responsibility to formulate a set of standards. As a result of their work, a comprehensive statement, *Standards for the Work of Chaplains in the General Hospital,* was adopted by the American Protestant Hospital Association in 1940. These standards finally led to the certification for chaplains in hospitals belonging to the American Protestant Hospital Association.[33]

The Rev. Carl C. Rasche, Administrator and Chaplain

The Rev. Carl C. Rasche was appointed administrator and chaplain of Deaconess Hospital in 1948 following Rev. Zwilling's retirement. An ordained clergyman like his predecessors (as required by the 1945 revised constitution of the Deaconess Society), Administrator Rasche also had special training and experience in administration. He was the first chief executive officer of Deaconess Hospital to be appointed "Administrator and Chaplain," new terminology at that time. Committed to the spiritual ministry of the hospital as a top priority, as well as to his duties as the chief executive officer, he conducted the Sunday chapel worship services, ministered to the Deaconess Sisters and served as chaplain to the patients in the hospital.

In 1949 Administrator Rasche became a member of the Committee on Accreditation of the Chaplains' Association of the American Protestant Hospital Association. Serving on that committee from 1949-1969 and as its chairman from 1961-1969, he gave strong leadership to accreditation for chaplains in health and welfare institutions. Speaking at a session on religion and patient care at the American Hospital Association Convention in 1967, he said,

> The chaplain is one of the few persons in the hospital setting who has the training, the skills and the time to come to know patients as persons.... It is imperative to select professionally trained, mature pastors as hospital chaplains and that they not be loaded down with unrelated tasks.[34]

In recognition of his contribution to the accreditation process in professional chaplaincy services, Rev. Rasche was made an honorary fellow of the Chaplains' Association in 1958.

Committed to the importance of a continuing strong relationship between the hospital and the church, Rev. Rasche served in 1951-52 as president of the Council for Health and Welfare Services of the Evangelical and Reformed Church, now known as the Council for Health and Human Service Ministries of the United Church of Christ. In 1955-56 he was president of the American Protestant Hospital Association and he also served during those years on the Executive Committee of the Department of Social Welfare of the National Council of Churches, New York City.[35]

Deaconess United Church of Christ

The spiritual ministry of Deaconess Hospital was reaffirmed in yet another way in 1952 when Deaconess Evangelical and Reformed Church, now the Deaconess United Church of Christ, was founded.

As described earlier, the sisterhood had always functioned much like a local congregation in the Kaiserswerth tradition. In 1952, however, it became evident that as a result of denominational mergers and the writing of new constitutions and bylaws, the Deaconess Sisters no longer had legal standing in the denomination. The founding of the Deaconess congregation, under the leadership of Rev.

8-12. Rev. Carl C. Rasche, Administrator and Chaplain, with Deaconess Consistory, 1954. Around table from center front: Sisters Frieda Ziegler, Frieda Hoffmeister, Naomi Pielemeier, Velma Kampschmidt, Edna Stoenner, Clara Weltge and Matilda Matthes.

8-13. The Deaconess Sisters' Choir. Left to right front: Sisters Helen Scheider, Elsa Weiss, Emma Fruechte, Hulda Weise, Clara Weltge, Elizabeth Schaefer, Naomi Pielemeier, Velma Kampschmidt, Christine Schwarz. Back: Frieda Hoffmeister, Edna Stoenner, Frieda Eckoff, Flora Pletz.

Rasche with the help of denominational leaders, strengthened the relationship of the Deaconess Sisters and their spiritual ministry to the wider Christian community.[36]

8-14. Deaconess Student Choir, following the tradition of the Deaconess Sisters, 1959.

The Rev. Paul E. Irion, First Accredited Chaplain

In keeping with his philosophy of accreditation for hospital chaplains and in trying to provide a more effective spiritual ministry for a growing number of patients, Administrator Rasche advised the board of directors in 1956 to call a full-time chaplain and pastor to Deaconess Hospital as a new member of the staff. This suggestion met with the ready agreement of the board and the Rev. Dr. Erwin H. Bode, president of the board, announced in 1956:

8-15. Chaplain Paul E. Irion, first accredited Deaconess Chaplain, with students in the new Deaconess Memorial Chapel, 1956.

One of our finest advances has been the hiring of the Rev. Paul E. Irion as full-time hospital chaplain. After 11 years of service in the Church, and equipped with specialized preparation for his work as chaplain, for which he has received accreditation by the Association of Hospital Chaplains, he began his work September 1.[37]

Chaplain Irion was the first full-time accredited chaplain at Deaconess Hospital. He was also the first chaplain to serve in the new Deaconess Memorial Chapel, where he ministered not only to the Deaconess sisters and patients but also to staff members and to students in the School of Nursing.

Deaconess Memorial Chapel, 1956

The beautiful Deaconess Memorial Chapel, dedicated on October 21, 1956 in honor of the Deaconess Sisters, stands today as the center for worship in the hospital complex. Located between the main hospital building and the South Memorial Building, it accommodates 150 persons and is open daily for private prayer and meditation.

290

Replacing the chapel in Gerhold Hall, which was very attractive but not accessible to most patients, the new Memorial Chapel was the fulfillment of the dreams of the Deaconess Sisters and has been their place of regular worship since 1956. It has also been the scene of baccalaureate services, baptisms, weddings, anniversary celebrations, funerals and memorial services.[38]

8-16. The Deaconess Memorial Chapel, 1956.

Chaplain Ernest W. Luehrman Installed, 1959

The Rev. Ernest W. Luehrman was installed as the chaplain of Deaconess Hospital and pastor to the Deaconess Sisters on October 25, 1959, succeeding Chaplain Irion, who accepted a position on the faculty at Lancaster Theological Seminary.

Chaplain Luehrman began his new ministry after completing special studies in Boston for accreditation in chaplaincy services. Administrator Carl C. Rasche reported to the annual meeting of the Deaconess Society in 1959,

> In the relatively short time that Chaplain Ernest W. Luehrman has been a member of our staff, he has made his mark with patients and the hospital staff as well. His patient visitation, his counselling with many who seek him out, and his preaching in Sunday morning worship services will be a strong force toward keeping all of us true to our calling to serve others in response to our Lord's claim upon us.[39]

8-17. Chaplain Ernest W. Luehrman greeting Sister Elizabeth Schaefer.

Affiliation with Eden Theological Seminary

The spiritual ministry of the hospital was enlarged further when the Deaconess Chaplaincy Program became affiliated with Eden Theological Seminary.

Continuing a chaplaincy training program begun by Chaplain Irion in 1958, Chaplain Luehrman taught the course at the seminary on the Ministry to the Sick beginning in 1960.[40]

The Clinical Pastoral Education Program

As part of the Deaconess Chaplaincy Services, the Clinical Pastoral Education Program was instituted in 1972 under the direction of the Rev. Dr. Leon R. Robison Jr., who was accredited as a clinical pastoral education supervisor. This program used depth psychology with theology, and students were required to complete four quarters of training in order to be accredited as hospital chaplains. The Rev. Dr. Robison also assisted Chaplain Luehrman with the spiritual ministry to patients in the hospital.

In 1974 when Chaplain Robison retired, the Rev. Claude Alan Campbell was appointed clinical pastoral education supervisor at Deaconess Hospital, a position he held until 1989, when Chaplain Nancy Dietsch succeeded him in that position.[41]

Executive Chaplain Luehrman Honored

The Association of Hospital Chaplains became the College of Chaplains of the American Protestant Hospital Association in 1968 as qualifications for the spiritual ministry of accredited chaplains became standardized on a level commensurate with other professional groups in the hospital setting.

In 1968 Chaplain Luehrman's title was changed to Executive Chaplain at Deaconess Hospital. He served as the President of the College of Chaplains in 1976 and he was honored for his leadership in this specialized ministry by Eden Theological Seminary, which awarded him a Doctor of Divinity degree in 1981.

The College of Chaplains is now an international, interfaith certifying organization related to the American Protestant Health Association, successor to the American Protestant Hospital Association. The College has certified more than 2,000 chaplains in four decades. Its members are chaplains, pastoral counselors, and pastoral educators. In 1989, the College admitted 124 new members and fellows, the largest number ever admitted in any one year.[42]

Close Denominational Ties under President Richard P. Ellerbrake

The Rev. Richard P. Ellerbrake was appointed president and chief executive officer of Deaconess Hospital in 1982 following the retirement of President Carl C. Rasche. As previously described, President Ellerbrake was an ordained clergyman with a master's degree in health administration. He had served for twenty years, first as assistant and associate administrator, and then as executive vice president and chief operating officer.

Like his predecessors, President Ellerbrake supported the strong spiritual ministry of the hospital and a close relationship to the church. In 1987-88 he served as president of the Council for Health and Human Service Ministries of the United Church of Christ and in 1989-90, as chairman of the board of directors of the American Protestant Health Association.[43]

With the appointment of the Rev. Jerry W. Paul as vice president of Deaconess Hospital in 1984, and subsequently as executive vice president and chief operating officer, the board of trustees reaffirmed the commitment to a close church relationship. Also an ordained clergyman with a master's degree in health administration, Rev. Paul serves in the tradition of a strong spiritual ministry within the growing complexity of modern health care.[44]

An Ecumenical Ministry

Although the caring, healing and teaching ministry of Deaconess Hospital was established within the Evangelical tradition 100 years ago and is today a part of the health and human service ministry of the United Church of Christ, the spiritual ministry and chaplaincy program have always been ecumenical.

From the beginning in 1889, as noted previously, it was the policy of the hospital that every patient was privileged to receive the administrations of whatever form of faith he or she professed. That policy continues to this day.

In addition to Executive Chaplain Luehrman and Chaplain Supervisor Nancy Dietsch, there is a full-time Roman Catholic chaplain, Fr. James Gummersbach, on the Deaconess chaplaincy staff, and Catholic Mass is held in the chapel on a regular schedule.

As part of the St. Louis Cluster of the Association for Clinical Pastoral Education, the Chaplaincy Program of Deaconess Hospital trains students for spiritual ministry in health care from a variety of institutions and denominations.[45]

The Language And Effects of Spiritual Ministry

Beginning with the Deaconess Sisters in 1889, it has been taught at Deaconess Hospital that healing has its strong, necessary spiritual component and that "In all cases it [spiritual ministry] will try to effect three things in the person: cheerful hope, strong faith in God and an earnest desire to live."[46]

The hospital chaplain assists the healing process by bringing the special language and effects of spiritual ministry to patients. As one chaplain described it,

> Each day [we] are called to be present in silence between words where no verbal vocabulary is adequate to convey life's most troubled moments. Sickness is most often borne in silence. So [we] learn to listen and speak through the vowels of touch and tone, to hear the adjectives of tears, the adverbs of laughter and to evoke the nouns and pronouns of God's presence.... In those times, [our] job is to speak for others in medicine whose language has failed.[47]

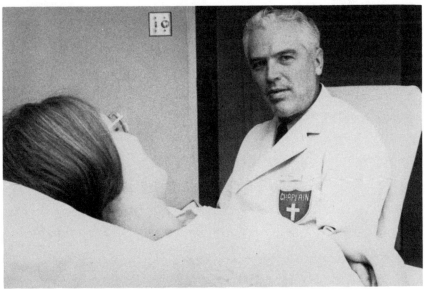

8-18. Executive Chaplain Ernest W. Luehrman visiting Deaconess patient.

For 100 years, the Deaconess Sisters, the Deaconess Chaplaincy Program and many faithful Deaconess employees have worked together "in a Christian setting." Though modern medical breakthroughs enhance and hasten healing as never before, the spiritual ministry is an important part of the Deaconess mission which seeks to provide health care and health education "in the compassionate spirit of Jesus Christ."[48]

8-19. Jesus, the Great Physician, Babler Memorial Window in Deaconess Chapel lobby.

Chapter Nine

THE CENTENNIAL
"Tradition With Vision"

The Deaconess Centennial in 1989 celebrated 100 years of caring, healing and teaching as a rich heritage of devoted service, known as *diakonia*. That heritage inspired the centennial symbol and theme, "Tradition with Vision."[1]

To highlight the many forms of devoted service offered throughout Deaconess history in St. Louis, and to honor all who have been part of it, the centennial celebration included numerous special events.

The Deaconess Medical Staff and the alumni of the Deaconess Schools and College of Nursing held previously described galas to celebrate a century of professional and academic excellence. The Deaconess Sisters were honored as pioneer professional women with the publication of a Centennial Commemorative, and they received national recognition from the United Church of Christ for their "dedication to the ideas of *diakonia.*"[2]

9-1. The Deaconess Centennial Symbol.

A Time of Praise and Thanksgiving

Since the founders of the Deaconess Society held their first meeting on March 18, 1889, in a church environment, Deaconess Chapel became the setting for a symbolic 100th anniversary worship service on Sunday, March 19, 1989.

Executive Chaplain Ernest W. Luehrman led the Deaconess Sisters, hospital patients, and visitors in a time of praise and thanksgiving for a century of Deaconess ministry which has always placed a strong emphasis on the spiritual dimension of care for the whole person.

297

9-2. Deaconess Chapel Centennial Celebration.

This centennial event honored the members of the Deaconess Society and all who worked with them to establish and support the Deaconess heritage in health care and health education throughout the past 100 years. In the spirit of earlier anniversary celebrations, however, it was acknowledged that, "we owe the success of our work to the help of the Lord, our God."[3]

Heritage Displays Honor the Past

To illustrate some of the changes, growth and development of Deaconess Hospital, and the role of the Deaconess Sisters in health care and health education since 1889, a visual history was created for the Centennial in two large display cases in the hospital front lobby.

Pictures and artifacts from the Deaconess Archives, and some on loan from the St. Louis Science Center, tell a graphic story of people and events related to Deaconess history.

9-3. Deaconess Sisterhood Heritage Display in Hospital Front Lobby.

9-4. Deaconess Hospital Heritage Display in Hospital Front Lobby.

"Living Pictures" Enliven the Heritage

"Living pictures" from Deaconess history came to life on stage in an original pageant, written by historian Ruth Rasche, and presented by members of the Deaconess Auxiliary to honor the Deaconess Sisters at a Centennial dinner in April 1989.

9-5. "Living Pictures" on Stage.

Dressed in authentic deaconess garbs and costumes dating back 100 years, members of the cast walked through a large picture frame on center-stage to tell the Deaconess story. From the first volunteers, women board members, and deaconesses in 1889 to present-day auxilians in modern pink smocks, a rich heritage of faithful services was enacted and applauded.[4]

A Centennial Tribute

A record crowd of nearly 700 in attendance at the Centennial Employees' Recognition Dinner on June 2 at the Hyatt Regency Hotel heard a message from President George Bush who congratulated them for their "professionalism, compassion and dedicated service" during the past 100 years. Special honors in 1989 for longtime service to Deaconess were award-

9-6. Honored Employees, 1989, Ray McAnnar (left) and Walter Major (right) for 41 years, with President Richard P. Ellerbrake (center).

ed to Walter Major and Ray McAnnar for 41 years; Lois Schatzmann and Charles Schmidt, Sr. for 39 years; Bernice Glover for 36 years and Joan Ware for 35 years. There were also 26 employees honored for 25 to 34 years; 44 employees for 20 to 24 years and 407 employees for 10 to 14 years.

President Richard P. Ellerbrake paid tribute to all dedicated Deaconess employees saying,

> Without you and your predecessors our achievements would not have been possible; the rich heritage of service would not have graced St. Louis...Thank you very, very, much.[5]

The Centennial Fund to "Build the Future"

The Centennial Fund, established in 1989 "to build the future," received many gifts for a new Deaconess Centennial Center. The Auxiliary pledged $1 million to the Fund, to be paid in five years. As described earlier, this pledge heightened the Auxiliary's leadership as the major donor to the hospital and it stimulated many other significant gifts to the Centennial Fund.

Remarking that the Deaconess tradition has been sustained and enhanced by the gifts of generous donors who have helped Deaconess meet the challenges of the past, President Richard P. Ellerbrake spoke at the Foundation's Donor Gala on the theme, "Making Dreams a Reality—The Deaconess Vision."[6]

The Deaconess Second Century Club was also promoted by The Deaconess Foundation in 1989 to help make more dreams a reality for future generations. The members of this club, of which there were more than fifty the first year, have designated The Deaconess Foundation as a beneficiary through their wills, life insurance or living trusts, or they have established life income gifts, such as a charitable gift annuity, unitrust or pooled income fund.[7]

9-6a. Deaconess Second Century Club Emblem.

Diaconal Ministry Program, a Centennial Gift

A Centennial gift of yet another kind, from the Deaconess Health Services to the church and the community, was inaugurated on Sunday, September 10, 1989, with the affirmation of four full-time volunteers in a new Diaconal Ministry Program.

Volunteering to serve in this new program for one year or more were: Maryann Bruening, Charlotte Ferguson, Monica Kekulah and Natalie Keys.

After an orientation period which included study of the theology of service and Biblical foundations of Diaconal ministry as well as tours of facilities in many United Church of Christ health and human service ministries, these first Diaconal ministers served as a tutor and classroom assistant at Evangelical Children's Home, as a "friendly visitor" at Hitz Memorial Home, as an assistant in patient care areas at Deaconess and as a helper in the Deaconess Child Care Center.

Patterned after the Deaconess tradition of loving service, the Diaconal Ministry Program was coordinated by Susan Sanders and is directed by the department of religion and health.[8]

9-7. Service of Affirmation for Diaconal Ministers, from the left: Executive Deaconess Sister Frieda Ziegler with the first Diaconal ministers, Maryann Bruening, Charlotte Ferguson, Monica Kekula and Natalie Keys.

The Deaconess-United Church of Christ Family Celebration

The grand finale of the Centennial was a Deaconess-UCC Family Celebration held on Sunday afternoon, October 29, at the Adam's Mark Hotel in St. Louis. Members of the Deaconess Society and of United Church of Christ congregations in Missouri and South Illinois were invited to participate, and more than 2,000 attended!

In addition to the Deaconess Health Services family, there were more than 30 representatives present from partner institutions and organizations in education, health and human service ministries. Also in attendance were the clergy, zone leaders and parish representatives with many members of almost 200 UCC congregations in Missouri and Illinois, making this one of the largest gatherings in UCC history for a centennial event.

This celebration began with a buffet luncheon at noon, followed by the opening of a "marketplace" consisting of many health-centered information booths and activities for all ages.

A Deaconess-United Church of Christ Family Worship Service in the grand ballroom at 2:30 p.m. was the major event of the day, with the United Church of Christ and Deaconess emblems prominently displayed as a background for the worship center.

9-8. Deaconess College of Nursing at the Centennial Marketplace. Faculty members and students took blood pressures and gave away "Future Nurse" caps.

Great festive music was provided by organist Paul Laubengayer, The Encore Brass Quintet, percussionist Robert Cohlmeyer, the Bell Choir of St. Lucas UCC, the Youth Choir of St. John UCC, St. Charles, and a combined 337-voice Adult Choir from 23 United Church of Christ churches.

9-9. Deaconess - UCC Family Worship, with Centennial Symbols and Bell Choir.

Sister Velma Kampschmidt led the invocation prayer, and Executive Deaconess Frieda Ziegler spoke for Deaconess Sisters of the St. Louis Sisterhood who were also present: Sisters Bertha Grollmus, Elsie Jungerman, Mary Kramme, Marie Lee, Elizabeth Lotz, Kate Nottrott, Naomi Pielemeier, Flora Pletz, and Gertrude Poth.

The Rev. Dr. Paul H. Sherry, president of the United Church of Christ, brought greetings from the national church and gave thanks for the health and human service ministries related to the UCC, which provide health care and health education for millions of people every year.

9-10. The Rev. Dr. Paul Sherry, President of the United Church of Christ, (center) with the Rev. Dr. Walter A. Brueggemann, (left), Student Nurse Susan Ashwell, Executive Chaplain Earnest W. Luehrman, and Deaconess Board Member, the Rev. Dr. Dwayne Dollginer, at Deaconess - UCC Family Worship.

Deaconess President Emeritus Carl C. Rasche spoke of "Heritage Highlights" as he honored the members of the Deaconess Society, who founded and have given leadership to Deaconess work in St. Louis; Superintendent Frederick P. Jens and Administrator Paul R. Zwilling, who led the administration through decades of significant hospital growth; members of the Deaconess Medical Staff, who have served with distinction and dedication; and the faculties of the School for Deaconesses and the School and College of Nursing, who have nurtured academic excellence with technical training and spiritual values, thus maintaining the standards of health education and care begun by the Deaconess Sisters, whose requirements for admission and graduation were always among the highest of their times.

Deaconess President Richard P. Ellerbrake honored all of the Deaconess Sisters and gave thanks for their ministry throughout the past 100 years which has been offered with "obedience, willingness, and faithfulness" to God and the Deaconess community. In a "Challenge to the Future," he envisioned Deaconess on the forward edge of health care and health education, and he concluded with the prayer that "as we enter this second century full of promise and hope, our commitment is unwavering."[9]

"New Possibilities" for the Future

The Rev. Dr. Walter A. Brueggemann, well-known Biblical scholar formerly of Eden Theological Seminary and now of Columbia Seminary, Decatur, Georgia, was the featured speaker of the day. His message, "What the Church Has Always Known," reminded the Deaconess-UCC Family celebrants that,

> We are discovering once again that healing is the courageous act of caring, presence, and compassion. This is not to demean or denigrate the best in medical technology, but it is to say that healing is an odd mystery that technique will never explain or comprehend or administer....
>
> What we [the church] have known, and continue to know with passion, is that healing is the the strange act of the power of life being present in the midst of the power of death, or more simply and directly, healing consists in human life making contact with human life, and finding together the gift of new possibility strangely given.[10]

Inspired by this challenge to hope and rejoice in new possibilities for healing in the years to come, the participants in the festival of worship concluded the centennial festivities with these significant words from the benediction, led by the Rev. John Trnka, chairman of the program committee, who said,

> May you catch a vision of greatness according to God's standard of true worth. May you find genuine fulfillment as you invest yourselves in serving others.[11]

Centennial Flags Continue to Honor the Deaconess Heritage

To share the festive spirit of the Deaconess Centennial with the City of St. Louis, three large flags were presented on Flag Day to the hospital as gifts from the Deaconess Auxiliary.

The Deaconess corporate flag, the St. Louis flag and the American flag now fly on 50-foot flagpoles erected above the visitor's parking pavilion at the busy intersection of Oakland and Hampton Avenues. There they continue to honor our city, our nation and the Deaconess heritage as we begin a second century of caring, healing and teaching.[12]

9-11. The Deaconess Centennial Flags.

Appendix A

Albert, Rosadel - 1946
Alexander, Catherine - 1935
Artus, Martha - 1946
Baird, Mildene - 1935
Baker, Esther - 1945
Barth, Emma - 1944
Baumgarten, Audrey - 1944
Becker, Pauline - 1930
Beek, Ruth - 1938
Benning, Hazel - 1935
Berg, Mathilda - 1899
Bergesch, Catherine - 1938
Bergstrasser, Frieda - 1922
Bergstrasser, Pauline - 1920
Biekert, Lydia - 1911
Bieri, Ida - 1929
Bischel, Anna - 1911
Bischoff, Melba - 1939
Boekhaus, Charlotte - 1899
Borcherding, Florence - 1941
Borgman, Olga - 1920
Brunner, Sophie - 1892
Buchn, Philippine - 1892
Burgener, Kathryn - 1940
Buschmann, Lydia - 1911
Childers, Beatrice - 1937
Conzelman, Louise - 1934
Crusius, Irene - 1922
Dallmer, Helene - 1938
Daries, Lydia - 1889
Demey, Dorothy - 1938
Demey, Helen - 1941
Dexheimer, Frieda - 1904
Dickmann, Adelia - 1925
Diestelkamp, Nelda - 1938
Drusch, Olivia - 1931
Eckelmeier, Hulda - 1904
Eckoff, Frieda - 1921
Ehrle, Anna - 1932
Eich, Emilie - 1905
Engelke, Elsie - 1937

Ernst, Lina - 1907
Euno, Doris - 1944
Euno, Thelma - 1940
Faris, Alma - 1936
Feucht, Lareda - 1940
Feutz, Mary - 1901
Fischer, Roma - 1938
Flottmann, Minna - 1914
Frederick, Bertha - 1905
Frick, Mildred - 1935
Fruechte, Emma - 1911
Fuchs, Bena - 1913
Fuerst, Ella - 1940
Fuhr, Olinda - 1919
Gadt, Minnie - 1923
Geiger, Elizabeth - 1940
Gerdeman, Selma - 1935
Gerding, Ella - 1936
Gerhold, Magdalene - 1893
Goetze, Anna - 1911
Grollmus, Bertha - 1923
Haack, Katherine - 1889
Habbe, Ferol - 1935
Hahn, Wilhelmina - 1918
Hampel, Anna - 1934
Hanebutt, Irene - 1945
Hess, Selma - 1927
Hesterberg, Arlou - 1937
High, Ellen - 1936
Hildebrand, Ella - 1918
Hirschler, Elise - 1911
Hoffmeister, Frieda - 1932
Hohlt, Gertrude - 1936
Holderle, Florence - 1921
Hummerich, Erlinde - 1906
Hubeli, Sophie - 1907
Huntmann, Bertha - 1925
Hupp, Doris - 1946
Johanntosettal, Norma - 1936
Johnson, Lena - 1922
Jung, Johanna - 1938

Jungerman, Alma - 1926
Jungerman, Elsie - 1934
Kaiser, Pearl - 1938
Kampschmidt, Velma - 1928
Katterjohn, Thelma - 1937
Keck, Katherine - 1905
Keller, Marie - 1929
Kelm, Selma - 1940
Kettelhut, Theresa - 1904
Kettman, Kathryn - 1940
Kiser, Velma - 1937
Knaup, Emilie - 1919
Koberstein, Erna - 1933
Koehler, Eunice - 1944
Kopp, Gretchen - 1937
Korte, Irma - 1941
Korte, Marie - 1933
Kramme, Elma - 1938
Kramme, Florentine - 1928
Kramme, Mary - 1927
Kuhlenhoelter, Clara - 1907
Kunze, Elizabeth - 1920
Lactrup, Verna - 1940
Lee, Marie - 1932
Lenger, Anna - 1914
Lix, Louise - 1893
Loew, Ella - 1914
Lotz, Elizabeth - 1928
Luker, Norma - 1939
Lutten, Henrietta - 1928
Mall, Hilda - 1908
Marcus, Alma - 1933
Mark, Hilda - 1925
Maroske, Charlotte - 1936
Marzahn, Emma - 1918
Martzke, Emma - 1919
Matthes, Amalie - 1905
Matthes, Mathilde - 1915
Mayer, Louise - 1929
Mehrtens, Eugenia - 1934
Meier, Anna - 1909
Meyer, Cleola - 1938
Michel, Edna - 1934
Mitchell, Marilou - 1939
Muensterman, Frieda - 1924
Muensterman, Hilda - 1931
Niewoehner, Johanna - 1902

Nissel, Anna - 1908
Nollau, Hulda - 1921
Nollau, Johanna - 1920
Nottrott, Kate - 1929
Nottrott, Maria - 1919
Nullmeyer, Theodora - 1945
Oehler, Marie - 1902
Pahmeier, Lydia - 1929
Pepmeier, Caroline - 1904
Petzoldt, Frieda - 1939
Pielemeier, Naomi - 1939
Pletz, Flora - 1927
Pohlmann, Anna - 1903
Poth, Gertrude - 1934
Raabe, Mildred - 1936
Rabius, Emilie - 1927
Roglin, Martha - 1919
Rompf, Katherine - 1935
Saeger, Irene - 1946
Sawade, Dolores - 1939
Schaefer, Clara - 1933
Schaefer, Elizabeth - 1924
Scheid, Alvina - 1909
Scheid, Katharine - 1903
Scherrer, Dorothy - 1941
Schick, Beata -1904
Schlottach, Irma - 1932
Schmidt, Florence - 1936
Schmidt, Marie - 1944
Schneider, Helen - 1938
Scholze, Erna - 1924
Schwarz, Christine - 1903
Senger, Ruth - 1935
Shih, Teh Chen - 1929
Shipp, Dorothy - 1937
Sieveking, Cornelia - 1925
Sievert, Frieda - 1904
Smith, Mida - 1940
Soechting, Isabel - 1938
Soehlig, Caroline - 1908
Sprick, Marie - 1927
Stoenner, Clara - 1922
Stoenner, Edna - 1917
Stoll, Edna - 1939
Streib, Katherine - 1902
Stremme, Mildred - 1938
Stuecken, Elvira - 1933

Sturm, Hulda - 1920
Timens, Georgia - 1940
Ullrich, Anna - 1922
Uthlaut, Erna - 1940
Van Dyck, Margaret - 1933
Vogel, Wilma - 1937
Wedel, Marie - 1911
Weise, Hulda - 1944
Weiss, Elsa - 1928
Wellpot, Charlotte - 1892
Weltge, Clara - 1922

Williamson, Irma - 1950
Wohlfeil, Agnes - 1937
Wohlschlaeger, Loretta - 1924
Wohlwend, Anna - 1935
Wolf, Anna - 1903
Woltemath, Verlia - 1917
Wood, Kathryn - 1940
Wulff, Amanda - 1929
Zeiser, Edna - 1936
Ziegler, Frieda - 1928

LOCATIONS OF LEADERSHIP BY ST. LOUIS DEACONESS SISTERS

Hospitals
Evansville, Indiana
Lincoln, Illinois
Faribault, Minnesota
Milwaukee, Wisconsin
Chicago, Illinois
Marshalltown, Iowa
East St. Louis, Illinois
Detroit, Michigan
Cleveland, Ohio
Indianapolis, Indiana
St. Louis, Missouri

Homes for the Aged
Rochester, New York
Belleville, Illinois
Bensenville, Illinois
Dorseyville, Pennsylvania
St. Louis, Missouri

Children's Homes
Hoyleton, Illinois
St. Louis, Missouri

Neighborhood Houses
St. Louis, Missouri

Home for the Developmentally Disabled
Marthasville, Missouri

Parish Work
Louisville, Kentucky
Chicago, Illinois
Kansas City, Missouri
St. Louis, Missouri

Foreign Missions
India
Honduras
Ecuador

Appendix B

PRESIDENTS AND CHAIRMEN OF DEACONESS BOARDS

Presidents of the Deaconess Society Board of Directors
1889-1898—Rev. John F. Klick
1899-1903—Rev. Henry H. Walser
1904-1909—Rev. John F. Klick
1910-1911—Rev. Fred Klemme
1912-1917—Rev. Jacob P. Irion
1918-1919—Rev. Fred Klemme
1920-1921—Rev. Henry Bode
1922-1924—Rev. Henry H. Walser
1925-1929—Rev. Dr. Paul Press
1930-1932—Rev. Dr. August C. Rasche
1933-1937—Rev. Dr. J. P. Meyer
1938-1939—Rev. Dr. Paul Press
1940-1942—Rev. Arno H. Franke
1943-1946—Rev. Erich E. Leibner
1947-1948—Rev. Richard A. Miller
1948-1950—Rev. Carl Sturm
1951-1955—Rev. Dr. Elmer H. Hoefer
1956-1958—Rev. Dr, Erwin H. Bode
1959-1960—Rev. Dr. Oscar C. Nussmann

Presidents of the Deaconess Hospital Board of Trustees:
1960-1961—Rev. Paul Prell
1961-1963—Rev. Paul Press Jr.
1964-1967—Rev. Dr. Herbert H.Wintermeyer
1968-1969—Rev. Dr. Fred C. Allrich
1970-1970—Mr. Monte E. Shomaker

Chairmen of the Deaconess Hospital Board of Trustees:
1971-1972—Mr. Monte E. Shomaker
1972-1974—Mr. Edward J. Bock
1975-1976—Mr. Wayne D. Nusbaum
1976-1977—Mr. H. E. Wuertenbaecher Jr.
1978-1981—Mr. Larry A. Swaney
1982-1984—Mr. William E. Winter
1985-1986—Mr. Robert O. Piening

Chairmen of the Deaconess Health Services Corporation:
1983-1986—Mr. Kenneth A. Marshall
1987-1989—Mr. A. Jack Reimers

MEMBERS OF DEACONESS HOSPITAL BOARDS
1889-1989

Acker, Dr. Harry L.
Babbitt, Mr. Edward
Bailey, Mr. Louis C.
Baltzer, Rev. John
Bangert, Mr. Emil
Baumer, Rev. Martha Ann
Beeh, Miss Mildreta
Bhattacharya, Dr. Arjun
Biekert, Mrs. Elizabeth
Bittner, Mr. John R.
Bleibtreu, Rev. E.
Bleikamp, Mr. Chester E.
Bloom, Judge Lackland

Bode, Rev. J.G.
Boesch, Rev. T. L.
Bosemann, Mr. J.
Bolte, Mr. Fred S.
Bontjes, Mrs. Pauline
Brauss, Mrs. Bertha
Brinner, Mr. Harold A.
Brown, Mr. James E.
Brueggemann, Rev. Mary Miller
Burkhalter, Rev. Don J.W.
Burkle, Rev. Carl
Busse, Mr. Frederick E.
Carlstrom. Mr. Dewey

Carlstrom, Mr. S.C.
Carpenter, Rev. Anthony H.
Chapman, Mr. William A.
Chapman, Mrs. William A.
Chapman, Mr. William J.
Chipps, Mr. Roy R.
Clement, Mr. Richard F.
Comens, Dr. Ruth C.
Convery, Dr. Paul V.
Cotner, Mrs. Evelyn
Crecelius, Mr. Edgar P.
Crecelius, Mrs. Edgar P.
Cummings, Rev. Alfred D.
Davis, William L. Jr,
Decker, Mr. Henry Jr.
Deters, Rev. H.F.
Deuser, Mr. Phil G.
Dieckmann, Mr. Edward
Dielmann, Mr. Harold L.
Dill, Mr. Jacob
Dollgener, Rev. Dr. C. Dwayne
Dorton, Dr. Robert K.
Drese, Mr. W.H.
Dressel, Mr. John H.S.
Dressel, Mr. Roy R.
Drusch, Sister Olivia
Ebert, Rev. Laverne E.
Ehlhardt, Mrs. B.B.
Ehrhardt, Mr. Willis G.
Eichenlaub, Rev. Dr. Lorenz L.
Ellersieck, Rev. Arthur P., Jr.
Elsesser, Mr. James R.
Emerson, Dr. Reynolds L.
Ervin, Mr. John B.
Esser, Rev. F. W.
Esser, Mrs. Louise
Fehl, Mrs. G.
Feutz, Mrs. Calvin F.
Fischer, Rev. A.
Fogarty, Dr. Wm. M. Jr
Francis, Mr. Darryl R.
Frankenfeld, Rev. Raymond
Friend, Mr. William
Fritsch, Rev. C.F.
Gable, Mr. L. John
Geyer, Mr. William
Goedecke, Mr. Vernon L.

Grant, Mr. William P.
Graubner, Mrs. F.I.
Green, Dr. William R.
Gruenewald, Rev. Dr. Harold C.
Grueninger, Mr. Oscar
Haas, Rev. C. G.
Haldeman, Mr. Arthur
Hammacher, Miss Adele
Hammerstein, Mr. Robert W.
Hamsher, Mr. Elwood C.
Hannemann, Mr. F.
Hanpeter, Mrs. F. W.
Hansen, Mrs. Alvin G.
Harding, Mrs. Edward
Hart, Mr. Russell J.
Hartmann, Mrs. Charles
Helmkamp, Mr. F. W.
Hengelsberg, Mrs. E.
Hess, Mr. W. E.
Heutel, Dr. Lee B.
Hilmer, Mr. E. C.
Hoelscher, Mr. Wilfred F.
Holekamp, Mr. Carl H. Jr.
Horn, Rev. Daniel V.
Horstmann, Rev. J. H.
Huntington, Mr. F. Wendell
Kaechelen, Miss Emma
Kaiser, Mr. Frederick A.
Kampmeinert, Mr. F. W.
Kasper, Rev. Robert E.
Keck, Mr. F. A.
Keck, Mrs. F. A.
Kienker, Rev. Otto
King, Mr. Walter W.
Klasing, Mrs. August
Klein, Rev. Dr. Carl W.
Klick, Mr. Emil
Knickmeyer, Mr. Henry
Koenig, Mr. O. G.
Kopf, Mrs. J. M.
Korte, Mr. Ralph
Krafft, Rev. Dr. F. H.
Krieger, Mr. E. A.
Kroening, Rev. Robert W.
Kronsbein, Mr. Henry
Lehman, Mr. Edward C.
Leidner, Mr. H.

Leidner, Mrs. Matilda
Lewin, Dr. Howard
Lishen, Mr. Albert C.
Mack, Mrs. John
Madigan, Mrs. Frank
Maisch, Rev. Robert S.
Mangels, Mrs. Henry
Maull, Mr. Louis, Sr.
McCool, Dr. James F.
McKenney, Mrs. Gertrude J.
Meckfessel, Mr. Charles
Meckfessel, Mr. Chris
Mellish, Rev. Dr. Stanley
Mesle, Rev. Dr. O. Kenneth
Metz, Mrs. L. K.
Meyer, Mr. Fred W.
Mistry, Dr. Tehmton S.
Mocker, Mr. J. F.
Moellenhoff, Dr. Robert W.
Moeller, Mrs. Emma
Morgan, Dr. Stephan S.
Mueller, Mr. Conrad G.
Mueller, Rev. Th. L.
Murphy, Dr. James P.
Naumer, Mr. Ronald M.
Neilson, Dr. Arthur W.
Nicolai, Dr. Charles H.
Niestrath, Mr. Edward C.
Norton, Rev. Carlton E.
Nourse, Rev. John
O'Neill, Mr. E. Dennis
Oberhellmann, Rev. Theo.
Oelze, Mrs. Marguerite
Oertli, Mr. Charles W.
Pauley, Mrs. G.
Pauley, Mrs. Ida
Peters, Miss Meta
Peters, Mr. John F.
Peters, Mr. Charles
Peterson, Mr. William E.
Pfeiffer, Mrs. Matilda
Pfeiffer, Rev. P.
Pinckert, Mrs. Nell
Planting, Mr. Charles O.
Pleger, Rev. K.
Poelker, Mayor John H.
Poser, Mr. H.

Press, Rev. Dr. S. D.
Puchta, Judge Randolph E.
Rahmeier, Rev. Dr. Paul H.
Rieke, Mr. Franz
Roesch, Mr. Anton
Roesch, Mr. Walter W.
Sabbert, Rev. Donald S.
Samel, Mr. William
Savage, Mr. Russell L.
Scheer, Rev. Dr. Walter A.
Schenler, Mr. Henry
Schmidt, Dr. Edwin H.
Schmidt, Rev. Dr. John L.
Schneider, Rev. K. L.
Schoen, Rev. Victor H.
Schultz, Mr. E. H., Jr.
Schultz, Mr. H. E.
Schwarz, Mr. Arthur
Senseman, Mr. Donald E.
Shaver, Miss Marie
Shiell, Mr. John A.
Shockley, Mr. R. Ray
Sickbert, Rev. Donald
Simonson, Rev. Richard E.
Sincox, Dr. Charles H.
Smith, Mrs. Edythe
Smith, Ms. Robin
Sodemann, Mr. William
Sommerich, Mrs. J. H.
Spross, Mrs. Katherine A.
Stifel, Mrs. Emma
Stock, Rev. Paul R.
Stockhoff, Mrs. Amanda
Stocksieck, Mr. H. G.
Straub, Mr. Ralph H.
Stumborg, Mrs. Margaret
Sudholt, Mr. F. A.
Sudmeyer, Rev. L.
Taylor, Mrs. Julia
Taylor, Mrs. William A.
Theiss, Mr. John J.
Tibbles, Mrs. George
Toelle, Rev. Henry C.
Toennies, Mr. A. G.
Tremayne, Mr. Bertram W. Jr.
Trnka, Rev. John
Utheil, Mr. John L.

Vogel, Mr. Clarence H.
Wandel, Miss Lee
Wehrenberg, Rev. Dr. Fred W.
Weigel, Mr. Howard H.
Weis, Mr. Carl J.
Welker, Mrs. H.
Weltge, Rev. Wm. B.
Wetterau, Mr. G. H.
Wetterau. Mr. Oliver G.
Wetterau, Mr. Theodore C.
Wetterau, Mrs. Otto

Wiegand, Mrs. L.
Wiese, Mr. Edw. W.
Wilton, Mr. William E.
Wolford, Mr. Robert C.
Woods, Mrs. Howard B.
Wrieden, Mr. Wm.
Ziercher, Mr. Herbert W.
Zimmer, Mr. Phillip
Zimmermann, Mrs. F.
Zipf, Mrs. Dorothea
Zulauf, Rev. Dr. Norman C.

Appendix C

PRESIDENTS OF THE DEACONESS AUXILIARY

Clara Huning Keck 1941
Augusta Mack .... 1942 - 1944
Mathilda Pfeiffer .... 1945 - 1948
Luella Ehrhardt .... 1949 - 1952
Elizabeth Klotz .... 1953 - 1954
Evelyn Cotner .... 1955 - 1956
Jeanette Ehlhardt .... 1957 - 1958
Esther Tibbles .... 1959 - 1961
Dorothca Docrr .... 1902 - 1964
Esther Tibbles .... 1965 - 1967

Alma Schaefer .... 1968 - 1969
Donna Pollmann .... 1970 - 1971
Ruth Taylor .... 1972 - 1973
Evelyn Droke .... 1974 - 1975
Gladys Feldmeier .... 1976 - 1977
Marguerite Oelze .... 1978 - 1979
Marcella Soutiea .... 1980 - 1981
Dorothy DeDoyard .... 1982 - 1985
Gertrude McKenney .... 1986 - 1989

Appendix D

PRESIDENTS OF THE DEACONESS MEDICAL STAFF

1889-1904	A. F. Bock, M.D.	1958-1959	Bert H. Klein, M.D.
1904-1913	J. R. Lemen, M.D.	1959-1960	Guerdan Hardy, M.D.
1913-1915	Walter P. Dorsett, M.D.	1960-1961	George E. Scheer, M.D.
1915-1919	W. A. Shoemaker, M.D.	1961-1962	John J. Roth, M.D.
1919-1922	H. L. Nietert, M.D.	1962-1963	William L. Macon, Jr. M.D.
1922-1925	C. H. Shutt, M.D.	1963-1964	James Y. Griggs, M.D.
1925-1934	L. H. Hempelman, M.D.	1964-1965	William G. Arney, M.D.
1934-1935	Fred W. Bailey, M.D.	1965-1966	Frederick Martin, M.D.
1935-1936	Edwin J. Schisler, M.D.	1966-1967	Robert K. Kurth, M.D.
1936-1937	John C. Morfit, M.D.	1967-1968	Robert N. Tindall, M.D.
1937-1938	John P. Altheide, M.D.	1968-1969	James P. Murphy, M.D.
1938-1939	William H. Norton, M.D.	1969-1970	Charles H. Nicolai, M.D.
1939-1940	John W. Hotz, M.D.	1970-1972	Arthur W. Neilson, M.D.
1940-1941	Henry J. Ringo, M.D.	1972-1973	Ernest W. Schaper, M.D.
1941-1942	Claude D. Pickrell, M.D.	1973-1974	Clarence E. Mueller, M.D.
1942-1943	E. Lee Dorsett, M.D.	1974-1975	W. Howard Lewin, M.D.
1943-1944	William H. Norton, M.D.	1975-1976	Ruth C. Comens, M.D.
1944-1945	Otto W. Koch, M.D.	1976-1977	Lee B. Heutel, M.D.
1945-1946	Henry P. Thym, M.D.	1977-1978	Harry L. Acker, M.D.
1946-1947	John P. Altheide, M.D.	1978-1979	William R. Green, M.D.
1947-1948	Roy E. Mason, M.D.	1979-1980	Robert K. Dorton, M.D.
1948-1949	Ellsworth Kneal, M.D.	1980-1981	Reynolds L. Emerson, M.D.
1949-1950	Stanley S. Burns, M.D.	1981-1982	James F. McCool, M.D.
1950-1951	Franz Arzt, M.D.	1982-1983	Edwin H. Schmidt, M.D.
1951-1952	Allen B. Potter, M.D.	1983-1984	Stephen S. Morgan, M.D.
1952-1953	Harold A. Goodrich, M.D.	1984-1985	William M. Fogarty, Jr. M.D.
1953-1954	Arthur W. Neilson, M.D.	1985-1986	Arjun Bhattacharya, M.D.
1954-1955	L. M. Webb, M.D.	1986-1987	Tehmton S. Mistry, M.D.
1955-1956	Clarence E. Mueller, M.D.	1987-1988	Paul B. Convery, M.D.
1956-1957	Edward M. Canon, M.D.	1988-1989	James O. Boedeker, M.D.
1957-1958	Birkle Eck, M.D.		

BOARD APPOINTED CHIEFS OF SERVICE AND DEPARTMENT HEADS
Deaconess Hospital Medical Staff

Radiology
J. D. Carmen, M.D. . . . . .1907 - 1913
F. B. Hall, M.D. . . . . .1913 - 1920
Joseph C. Peden, M.D. . . . . . .1920 - 1967
Francis O. Trotter, M.D. . . . . .1967 - 1978
Julian N. Verde, M.D. . . . . . . .1978 -

Pathology
Armand Ravold, M.D. . . . . .1899 - 1921
Charles L. Klenk, M.D. . . . . .1921 - 1947
Henry C. Allen, M.D. . . . . .1947 - 1974
Robert W. Brangle, M.D. . . . . .1974 -

Surgery

Arthur R. Dalton, M.D..............1958 - 1963
Vincent T. Houston, M.D. ....1963 - 1967
James Y. Griggs, M.D. ....1967 - 1968
William R. Cole, M.D...............1968 - 1970
Raymond O. Frederick, M.D....1970 - 1980
Arthur R. Dalton, M.D..............1981 - 1986
Philip J. Schmidt, M.D..............1987 -

Medicine

James P. Murphy, M.D. ....1958 - 1962
Herbert C. Wiegand, M.D. ....1962 - 1968
John H. Woodbridge, M.D. ......1968 - 1969
Robert C. Kingsland, M.D. ....1969 - 1979
James P. O'Regan, M.D. ....1979 - 1981
M. Robert Hill, M.D. ....1981 -

Obstetrics - Gynecology

William D. Hawker, M.D...........1958 - 1961
Benjamin F. Smith, M.D. ....1961 - 1964
Seth D. Wissner, M.D................1964 - 1967
Lee A. Hall, M.D. ....1967 - 1970

William D. Hawker, M.D...........1970 - 1973
A. M. Yazdi, M.D. ....1973 - 1974
John W. Durkin, Jr., M.D. ....1974 - 1977
A. M. Yazdi, M.D. ....1977 - 1982
Paul J. Ritter, M.D. ....1982 -

Neuro - Pychiatry

George A. Ulett, M.D................1974 -

Anesthesiology

John P. Eberle, M.D. 1954-1975
Ruth C. Comens........................1975-1987
Frederick E. Youngblood, M.D. 1987-

Family Practice

David C. Campbell, M.D...........1988 -

Note: Prior to 1958 all Department Heads were elected by members of the medical staff with the exception of Radiology, Pathology and Anesthesiology which involved compensatory contracts.

Notes

GUIDE TO FREQUENTLY USED ABBREVIATIONS

AA . . . . .Articles of Association
AR . . . . .Annual Report
CCR . . . . .Carl C. Rasche
DA . . . . .Deaconess Archives
DCN . . . . .Deaconess College of Nursing
DF . . . . .Deaconess Foundation
DH . . . . .Deaconess Hospital
DHS . . . . .Deaconess Health Services
DMS . . . . .Deaconess Medical Staff
DSN . . . . .Deaconess School of Nursing
EDS . . . . .Evangelical Deaconess Society
RPE . . . . .Richard P. Ellerbrake
SD . . . . .School for Deaconesses

Chapter 1.
THE EVANGELICAL DEACONESS SOCIETY

1. *St. Louis Post-Dispatch*, Weather Report, March 18, 1889; EDS, *1st AR, 1890*, 3; *11th AR, 1899*, 9; *15th AR*, 1903, 11; "Pastor H. Walser," *Evangelical Benevolent Institutions*, v. 18, n. 10, October, 1926, 3.
2. C. Golder, *History of the Deaconess Movement in the Christian Church*, (Cincinnati: Jennings and Pye, 1903), 69, 604-605; Carl E. Schneider, *The German Church on the American Frontier*, (Eden Publishing House, St.Louis, Missouri, 1939), 340; Dr. Robert M. Schlueter," Some Medical History of St. Louis," *St. Louis Medical Society, Centennial Volume*, (St. Louis, Missouri, 1939), 44,46, records that "...the Good Samaritan Hospital was served by physicians who followed the Homeopathic System of medical practice" and that in 1904 "...its staff was completely reorganized by the appointment of physicians and surgeons of the regular medical profession. This arrangement lasted for five or six years until the adherents of the Evangelical Faith realized that their needs were better served by the fast-growing Evangelical Deaconess Home and Hospital. So the Good Samaritan Hospital became the Good Samaritan Altenheim...."
3. "Immigration to the United States," *Encyclopedia Britannica*, (1958), 15:467; Dena Lange and Merlin M. Ames, *St. Louis, Parent of the West* (St. Louis: Webster Publishing Company, 1939), 256; Harry M. Hagan, *This is Our... St. Louis* (St. Louis: Knight Publishing Company, 1970), 354.
4. Edwin A. Christ, *Missouri's Nurses* (The Missouri State Nurses' Association, Jefferson City, 1957), 58, 286-287.
5. Schneider, 226.
6. EDS, *Articles of Association*, (State of Missouri, 1891), typed copy of original with names of charter members filed in the Deaconess Archives.
7. Ibid. Article IV-1, Management; Article VII, Amendments.
8. Ibid.
9. EDS, *The Evangelical Deaconess Home and Hospital, St. Louis, 1889-1914*, a commemorative 25th Anniversary Booklet including *24th and 25th AR*, 1914, 30.

10. EDS, *Evangelical Deaconess Home and Hospital,* 15th Anniversary Booklet, 1904, 9.

11. EDS, *Evangelical Deaconess Home and Hospital,* 25th Anniversary Booklet, 1914, 30.

12. Charles E. Rosenberg, "What It Was Like To Be Sick in 1884," *American Heritage,* v. 35, n. 6. October/November, 1984, 23.

13. EDS, *11th AR,* 1899, 3.

14. Ibid., 10.

15. Carl E. Schneider, *The Genius of the Evangelical Synod of North America,* (Eden Publishing House: St. Louis, 1940), 5, 11.

16. EDS, *AA,* Article III, Membership.

17. Hagan, 317.

18. EDS, *Dues and Gifts,* 1889, in Deaconess Archives.

19. EDS, *25th AR,* 1914, 30. Records obtained from St. Louis Medical Society for individual members are on file in Deaconess Archives.

20. EDS, *AA,* Article V, Duties of Officers.

21. EDS, *11th AR,* 1899, 10.

22. *Der Friedensbote,* v. 40, n. 7, 134; v. 40, n. 21, 166.

23. EDS, *25th AR,* 1914, 30.

24. Federation of Evangelical Deaconess Associations, *Principles of Deaconess Work,* (St. Louis: Eden Publishing House, 1918), 88.

Chapter 2.
THE DEACONESS SISTERS

1. Elizabeth Schussler Fiorenza, "Word, Spirit and Power: Women in Early Christian Communities" in Rosemary Ruether and Eleanor McLaughlin, eds. *Women of Spirit, Female Leadership in the Jewish and Christian Traditions* (New York: Simon and Schuster, 1979), 36; Jane M. Bancroft, *Deaconesses in Europe and Their Lessons for America* (New York: Hunt and Eaton, 1890), 23.

2. Carl J. Scherzer, *The Church and Healing* (Philadelphia: The Westminster Press, 1950), 43-45.

3. Henry Wheeler, *Deaconesses Ancient and Modern* (New York: Hunt and Eaton, 1889), 87; EDS, *The School for Deaconesses Bulletin,* 1951-52, St. Louis, Mo., 7.

4. Sister Julie Mergner, *The Deaconess and Her Work,* trans. by Mrs. Adolph Spaeth (Philadelphia: United Lutheran Publishing House, 1911), 40-49.

5. Anne L. Austin, *History of Nursing Source Book,* (New York: G. B. Putnam's Sons, 1957), 196. This quotation is from Florence Nightingale in a letter to the British Museum in 1897.

6. C. Golder, *History of the Deaconess Movement in the Christian Church,* (Cincinnati: Jennings and Pye, 1903), 69, 604-605; Scherzer, 121-128; EDS, *25th AR,* 1914, 24.

7. Mergner, 94; Wheeler, 183; Emil Wacker, *The Deaconess Calling,* trans. by E. A. Endlich, (Philadelphia: The Mary J. Drexel Home, 1893), 87; Sister Katherine Haack's Obituary, *Der Friedensbote,* v. 70, n. 8, Feb. 23, 1919, 119.

8. Rosemary Reuther, "Mother of the Church: Ascetic Women in the Late Patristic Age," Reuther and McLaughlin, 72-73.

9. Christian Golder, *The Deaconess Motherhouse in Its Relation to the Deaconess Work* (Pittsburgh: Pittsburgh Printing Company, 1907), 54-55.

10. Ibid., 102.

11. Wacker, 85.

12. Golder, *Deaconess Motherhouse,* 49, 109.

13. *Principles of Deaconess Work,* 38.

14. Ibid., 37.

15. Wheeler, 289.

16. Bancroft, 91; Wheeler, 281; Golder, *History*, title page.

17. Golder, *Deaconess Motherhouse*, 42-43; Wheeler, 287.

18. Florence Nightingale, *The Institution of Kaiserswerth on the Rhine*, (London: Ragged Colonial Training School, 1851), 19. Copy on file in the Deaconess Archives.

19. Bancroft, 83.

20. The Evangelical Synod of North America, *The Evangelical Book of Worship*, (St. Louis and Chicago: Eden Publishing House, 1916), 228-31; Bancroft, 85. Wacker, 95.

21. Mergner, 192; *Principles of Deaconess Work*, 28-33.

22. Golder, *The Deaconess Motherhouse*, 84-85. Also see chapter on "The Spiritual Ministry."

23. Marguerite Martyn, "Nurse for Nearly Fifty Years," *St. Louis Post-Dispatch*, Oct. 11, 1940, Everyday Magazine Section.

24. DA, Sister Katherine Haack, *Income and Expenditures*, 1891.

25. *Principles of Deaconess Work*, 88.

26. *Evang. Diakonissenfreund*, v. 6, n. 1, Jan. 1898.

27. EDS, *25th AR*, 1914, 30.

28. Ibid.

29. *Evang. Diakonissenfreund*, v. 5, n. 6, Nov. 1897; Robert D. Haack, *The Haack Family*, A Family History, 1988, 17-19; EDS, *25th AR*, 1914, 30.

30. Ibid.

31. *Evangelical and Reformed Monthly*, v. 12, n. 8, Apr., 1941, 4.

32. EDS, *11th AR*, 1899, 12. The term "ordained" was first used to describe Deaconess Sisters who completed their training and were inducted into the sisterhood for lifetime service. Later, the term "consecrated" was used.

33. Ibid., 17-18.

34. EDS, *20th and 21st AR*, 1908-09, 7.

35. Lange and Ames, 226.

36. EDS, *15th AR*, 1903, 15; *16th AR*, 1904, 12, 32.

37. EDS, *Evangelical Deaconess Home and Hospital*, 1904, 11.

38. EDS, *20th and 21st AR*, 1908-09, 11. See Appendix for complete list of twenty-five locations of deaconess work by St. Louis Deaconess Sisters.

39. *Principles of Deaconess Work*, 87.

40. EDS, *20th and 21st AR*, 1908-09, 9.

41. Ibid.

42. *Sears Roebuck and Co. Consumers Guide*, Fall 1909 (Chicago), 926.

43. EDS, *20th and 21st AR*, 1908-09, 5.

44. Louise Irby Trenholme, *History of Nursing in Missouri* (Columbia, Mo.: Missouri State Nurses Association, 1926), pp. 83-84; EDS, *48th AR*, 1937, 5. Information about Sister Sophie Hubeli and Sister Anna Lenger in files of Deaconess Archives.

45. EDS, *25th AR*, 1914, 23-32.

46. *Evangelical Wohltatigskeitfreund*, v. 10. n. 8, May, 1918, 3; *Information Please Almanac*, 41st ed. (Boston: Houghton Mifflin Company, 1988), 120; Mary Kimbrough, "New Uniforms for Deaconess Society," *St. Louis Post-Dispatch*, May 8, 1952, quotes interviews with deaconesses on duty in 1918.

47. *Evangelical Wohltatigskeitfreund*, v. 13, n. 4, Apr., 1921, 3.

48. EDS, *33rd AR*, 1921, 27.

49. Ibid., 8, 14, 20.
50. EDS, *13th AR,* 1901, 17.
51. EDS, *38th AR,* 1928, 16-17.
52. EDS, *60th AR,* 1949, 4; DA, Files on individual Deaconess Sisters.
53. EDS, *41st AR,* 1930, 29.
54. Ibid., 11.
55. *St. Louis Globe-Democrat,* Dec. 2, 1951, 3.
56. EDS, *48th AR,* 1937, 4,9.
57. EDS, *49th AR,* 1938, 7-10,12; 50th AR, 1939, 6;
58. Ibid. 3; *St. Louis Post-Dispatch,* March 26, 1939.
59. EDS, *Fourteen Hundred Years,* 1939, 50th anniversary brochure.
60. EDS, *50th AR,* 1939, 9.
61. EDS, *For Greater Service,* 1940, capital campaign booklet, Deaconess Archives.
62. DA, *The Pulse,* April, 1942, a small news publication "edited by the Sisterhood every month or two."
63. DA, Deaconess Women's Auxiliary, *Minutes,* Jan. 30, 1941. Also see chapter on Deaconess Auxiliary.
64. EDS, *53rd AR,* 1942, 5.
65. Ibid., 6, 30; *E. and R. Monthly,* v. 14, Dec. 1942, 16.
66. EDS, *53rd AR,* 1942, 10.
67. EDS, *54th AR,* 1943-44, 16; DA, Sister Bena Fuchs' File.
68. EDS, *62nd AR,* 1951, 5; *65th AR,* 1954, 7; EDS, *71st AR,* 1960. When no new applications for admission to the School for Deaconesses were received, the school was no longer listed in the annual report.
69. DA, Filed Reports on DIAKONIA, World Federation of Sisterhoods and Deaconess Associations and DOTA, the Diakonia of the Americas.
70. EDS, *63rd AR,* 1952, 6; also see chapter on "Spiritual Ministry."
71. EDS, *65th AR,* 1954, 6; *66th AR,* 1955, 7.
72. See Appendix for List of Consecrated Deaconess Sisters; DA, Oral Tapes of Deaconess Sisters and Volunteer Services files.
73. Ruether and McLaughlin, 24; Ruth W. Rasche, *The Deaconess Sisters, Pioneer Professional Women,* A Centennial Commemorative, 1989 (St. Louis: Deaconess Health Services Corporation), 5.
74. United Church of Christ, Minutes, Seventeenth General Synod, Fort Worth, Texas, 1989, 61.
75. DA, Citations and plaques in Sisterhood file.

Chapter 3.
THE MANAGEMENT

1. EDS, AA, 1891 (State of Missouri), Article IV, Management. Typed copy of original in Deaconess Archives.
2. Ibid., Art. V, Officers, 2f.
3. Charles E. Rosenberg, *The Care of Strangers,* (New York: Basic Books, Inc., 1987), 48-49; Malcolm T. MacEachern, *Hospital Organization and Management,* 2nd ed, (Chicago: Physicians Research Co., 1947), 79.
4. Robert M. Cunningham, Jr., *Governing Hospitals: Trustees and the New Accountabilities,* (Chicago, The American Hospital Association, 1976), 50.

5. DA, Sister Katherine Haack, *Household Income and Expenses*, 1889; Joseph M. Schuster, "Centennial," Missouri Botanical Garden Bulletin, v.77, n.2, March-April, 1989, 4. Stories of Rev. Henry Walser's plea to his wife to make chicken soup for the Deaconess Sisters were reported to author by Mrs. Loretta Schoenberg of the Walser family. EDS, Dues and Gifts, 1889.

6. EDS, *1st AR*, 1890; *Dues and Gifts*, 1891; *25th AR*, 30.

7. DA, Haack, *Household Income and Expenses*, 1891.

8. *Principles of Deaconess Work*, 88-89.

9. DA, *Evangelical Diakonissenfreund*, v.1, n.1, January, 1893.

10. EDS, *25th AR*, 1914, 30. Mr. Tibbe is pictured in the Dedication Bulletin for the new building on Oakland, May 25, 1930. His role as a prominent business leader in Washington, Mo., is described in an article by Virginia Fries, "Washington Celebrates Its 150th Birthday," *Midwest Motorist*, May/June, 1989, p.49; *Principles of Deaconess Work*, 89.

11. EDS, *25th AR*, 1914, 30.

12. *Diakonissenfreund*, v.6, n.1, Jan. 1898.

13. DA, Original letter from Deaconess Medical Staff signed by the six members of the staff.

14. *Diakonissenfreund*, v.5, n.6, Nov. 1897, 5; *Evangelical and Reformed Monthly*, v.12, n.8, Apr. 1941, 4; EDS, *11th AR*, 1899, 19.

15. Ibid., 11.

16. Lange and Ames, 226.

17. EDS, *15th AR*, 1903, 12.

18. EDS, 15th Anniversary Booklet, 1904.

19. EDS, *16th AR*, 1904, 32.

20. Ibid., 14.

21. EDS, *19th AR*, 1907-08, 5, 27.

22. EDS, *20th and 21st AR*, 1908-09, 6.

23. Editorial, "The Superintendent," *Hospital World I*, April, 1912, 228, quoted in Rosenberg, *Care of Strangers*, 279.

24. Golder, *History*, 353; EDS, *20th and 21st AR*, 1908-09, 6.

25. DA, Reports of Federation of Evangelical Deaconess Associations; Evangelical and Reformed and UCC Yearbooks.

26. EDS. *24th and 25th AR*, 1914, 32.

27. William B. Flaherty, S.J., *The St. Louis Portrait*, (Tulsa: Continental Heritage, Inc., 1978), 123; DA, Publications files.

28. EDS, *33rd AR*, 1921, 8,13,21,23; Rosenberg, *Care of Strangers*, 9, 10.

29. Malcolm T. MacEachern, *Hospital Organization and Management*, 2nd ed., (Chicago: Physicians Record Co., 1947), 22.

30. Ibid., 23,24. *Evang. Wohltatigskeitfreund*, v.13, n.3, March 1921, 4.

31. EDS, *33rd AR*, 1921, 27.

32. Eden Archives, Eden Theological Seminary, Alumni Records.

33. *Evangelical Benevolent Institutions*, v.17, n.11, Dec. 1925; v.18, n.2, Feb., 1926.

34. *St. Louis Globe-Democrat*, Sept. 12, 1926.

35. Ibid., Sept. 25, 1926.

36. *St. Louis Times*, Sept. 24, 1926. *St. Louis Star*, Sept. 24, 1926.

37. *St. Louis Globe-Democrat*, Oct. 7, 1926.

38. EDS, *38th AR*, 1927, 6; *Evangelical Benevolent Institutions*, v.19, n.10, Oct. 1927.

39. EDS, *38th AR*, 1927, 4, and *40th AR*, 1929, 5,6.

40. *Evangelical Benevolent Institutions*, v.22, n.5, May, 1930; v.23, n.6, June, 1930; v.23, n.7, July, 1930.

41. EDS, *41st AR*, 1930, 13.

42. Ibid., 10, 11; *Evangelical Benevolent Institutions*, v.23, n.7, July, 1930 and v.24, n.11, Nov. 1931.

43. EDS, *42nd AR*, 1931, 7

44. *Evangelical Benevolent Institutions*, v.24, n.6, June, 1931.

45. EDS, *Minutes*, Board of Directors, July 17, 1930. EDS, *42nd AR*, 1931, 15.

46. Carroll C. Calkins, Ed., "1929: The Economy Falls Apart," *The Story of America*, The Readers' Digest Assoc., (New York: Pleasantville, 1975), p. 289; *Evangelical Benevolent Institutions*, v.16, n.7, July, 1933.

47. EDS, *44th AR*, 1933, 3.

48. EDS, *47th AR*, 1936, 5.

49. From the records in the office of Dennis Kruse, vice president for finance, Deaconess Hospital, 1989; MacEachern, *Hospital Organization and Management*, pp. 736, 787-788.

50. EDS, *49th AR*, 1938, 8; *50th AR*, 1939, 23; Evangelical and Reformed Monthly, v.10, n.7, March, 1939, 3; *50th AR*, 1939, 3.

51. Alumni Class List, 1925, Office of the President, Eden Theological Seminary; EDS, *51st AR*, 1940, 23.

52. Ibid., 22; *50th AR*, 1939, 9. See chapter on Deaconess Auxiliary for full account; EDS, "Service of Dedication" for the Sisters' Home, March 15, 1942; DA, *The Pulse*, 1942.

53. EDS, *53rd AR*, 1942, 5,10,30; *49th AR*, 1938, 1. Sister Ella Loew served as "night administrator" until her retirment in 1971; EDS, *52nd AR*, 1941, 5,8.

54. EDS, *55th AR*, 1944-45, 18.

55. E. and R. *Monthly*, v.14, n.10, June, 1943, p.7; v.15, n.1, Sept. 1943, 4.

56. EDS, *54th AR*, 1944, 8; *56th AR*, 1945-1946, 12.

57. EDS, *53rd AR*, 1942, 6; E. and R. *Monthly*, v.14. n.6, Feb. 1943, 12.

58. E. and R. *Monthly*, v.19. n.3, Nov. 1947, 2; June, 1949, 10; EDS, *62nd AR*, 1951, 4.

59. EDS, *56th AR*, 1945-46, 30-36; E. and R. *Monthly*, Sept. 1948, v.20. n.6, 10.

60. EDS, *59th AR*, 1947-48, 10.

61. E. and R. *Monthly*, Feb. 1949, 10, 14.

62. Sister Olivia Drusch, "The Cost of Hospital Care," F. and R. *Monthly*, v.20, n.4, Dec. 1948, 7,8, E. and R. *Monthly*, v.20, n.1, Sept. 1948, 5; EDS, *60th AR*, 1949, 2; *61st AR*, 1950, 2; *64th AR*, 1953, 12; Drusch, E. and R. *Monthly*, v.20, n.4, 7,8; Carl C. Rasche, "The Administrator's Report to the Board of Directors," Dec. 30, 1948.

63. Ibid., Feb. 24, 1949.

64. EDS, *60th AR*, 1949, 4.

65. Ibid., 10; E. and R. *Monthly*, v.21, n.5, Jan. 1950, 3.

66. EDS, *60th AR*, 1949, 3,6,12.

67. EDS, *63rd AR*, 1952, 11-12.

68. DA, Records from the office of Dennis Kruse, vice president for finance, Deaconess Hospital; EDS, *67th AR*, 1956, 4.

69. EDS, *65th AR*, 1954, 3,6,7,9.

70. EDS, Dedication Service Bulletin, October 21, 1956, 4. EDS, *67th AR*, 1956, 3.

71. Ibid., 7-12; EDS, *68th AR*, 1957, 7-10.

72. The Joint Commission, *Guide to Quality Assurance*, (Chicago: Joint Commission on Accreditation of Healthcare Organizations, 1988), 9-11.

73. EDS, *69th AR*, 1958, 4,5,12,13.

74. EDS, *70th AR*, 1959, 6. Also see chapter on "Spiritual Ministry."

75. CCR, Administrator's Report to the Board, Dec. 28, 1950; Jan. 24, 1963; Dec. 9, 1963.

76. DA, Carl C. Rasche Curriculum Vitae.

77. DA, Elmhurst College Citation to CCR, June, 1961; EDS, *73rd AR*, 1962, 5; *74th AR*, 1963, 3,5; *75th AR*, 1964, 11.

78. Sue Ann Wood, "Deaconess Looks Back and Forward," *St. Louis Globe-Democrat*, Nov. 14-15, 1964, 9; *74th AR*, 1963, 2; *75th AR*, 1964, 9; *76th AR*, 1965, 3.

79. CCR, Administrator's Report to the Board, June 23, 1966 and Sept. 27, 1966; EDS, *77th AR*, 1966, 3.

80. EDS, *76th AR*, 1976,2; *79th AR*, 1968, 5; *81st AR*, 1970, 4; Andrew Wilson, "Deaconess Hospital...A Look at the Future," *St. Louis Globe-Democrat*, Sept. 19, 1968; *NCR-ALPHA*, v.2, n. 4, 1982, 9; Interview with Homer Schmitz, Ph.D., July 26, 1989.

81. CCR, Administrator's Reports to the Board, Mar. 26, 1968, and June 25, 1968; EDS, *79th AR*, 1968, 5.

82. Ibid.

83. EDS, *80th AR*, 1969, 4; Dedication Program, May 24, 1970.

84. EDS, *82nd AR*, 1971, 7.

85. EDS, Constitution and By-Laws, October 14, 1971; *Deaconess Reports*, Spring/Summer, 1987, 11; Fall/Winter, 1988, 18; "Program," Centennial Donor Recognition Gala, Oct. 6. 1989.

86. EDS, *85th AR*, 1974, 2,4; 85th Anniversary Brochure.

87. DA, "Recognition of Mr. Herbert Ziercher," Dec. 4, 1975.

88. DH, *89th AR*, 1; DA, Ann E. Yarnell, Executive Assistant, *MPLIA Report*, Oct. 15, 1985, and *Update Report*, May 19, 1989.

89. EDS, *87th AR*, 1976, 1; James A. Hamilton Associates, Inc., *A Development Program, Deaconess Hospital, St. Louis, Missouri*, (Minneapolis, 1972); *Design for the 80s*, Campaign Booklet, 1977, 2,6.

90. CCR, Report of the President to the Board, Oct. 16, 1979; EDS, 90th Anniversary Dedication Program; EDS, *90th AR*, 1979, 2,3.

91. EDS, "Objectives for Deaconess Hospital," Fiscal Year, 1979-80.

92. DA, Letter in "Archives Development" file acknowledging gift of $1,500 in memory of the Rev. and Mrs. Wm. B. Weltge to establish Deaconess Archives.

93. EDS, *89th AR*, 1978, 3.

94. EDS, *92nd AR*, 1981; DH, *Report to the Community*, 1982, 5, 10, 16; *Deaconess Reports*, Fall, 1989, 21.

95. DA, "A Salute to Carl C. Rasche," Luncheon Program, January 22, 1982.

96. *St. Louis Globe-Democrat*, Jan. 23-24, 1982, 12A.

97. *The United Courier*, Missouri Conference of the United Church of Christ, v.53, n.7, March, 1982, 1.

98. Ibid.

99. DH, *Report to the Community*, 1983. 3.

100. Ibid.

101. Mary Little, "Survival, Specialized Programs Boost Hospital Revenue," *St. Louis Post-Dispatch*, June 5, 1989, 15BP.

102. Ibid. Also see chapter on "Patient Care."

103. DH, *Report to the Community*, 1983, 3.

104. Ibid., 12; *Focus*, June 1985. Also see chapter on "The Deaconess Schools and College."

105. RPE, Curriculum Vitae, Deaconess Archives.

106. DHSC, *Tradition with Vision*, Report to the Community, 1986, 1.

107. *Focus*, Sept. 1986, 6.

108. RPE, Letter to Members of Deaconess Health Services and the Evangelical Deaconess Society of St. Louis, Missouri, November 3, 1986.

109. DHSC, *Focus,* June, 1983, 2; *Tempo,* Spring, 1984, 4.

110. DHSC, *Annual Reports,* 1984-1989; *St. Louis Magazine,* February, 1985. Also see detailed list of patient services in chapter on "Patient Care."

111. DHSC, Board of Directors Minutes, March 28, 1989.

Chapter 4.
THE MEDICAL STAFF AND MEDICAL EDUCATION

1. Ludmerer, Kenneth M., *Learning to Heal,* (New York: Basic Books Inc., 1985), 3.

2. St. Louis Medical Society, *The St. Louis Society's Medical Museum,* (St. Louis: 1964), 7, gives a chronological list of the founding of St. Louis medical schools; Ludmerer, 94, states that "In the 1890s, the long-standing archrival of medicine, homeopathy (a system of therapeutics in which patients are treated with minute doses of drugs capable of producing in healthy persons symptoms like those of the disease to be treated), began to lose popularity, and within twenty years it vanished as a significant competitor to regular medicine."

3. Ibid., 31-33.

4. St. Louis Medical Society, "The Evolution of the St. Louis Medical Society," *Centennial Volume* (St. Louis: 1939), 15.

5. Ludmerer, 19; Charles E. Rosenberg, "What It Was Like to be Sick in 1884," *American Heritage,* v. 35, n. 6, Oct./Nov., 1984, 25.

6. Ibid.; George Hickenlooper, "Remembering the Streetcar," *St. Louis Home,* Feb. 1988, 7-11.

7. Rosenberg, *American Heritage,* 27.

8. Tracy Kidder, "Wry Recollections by a Giant of Modern Medicine," (Review of book by Dr. Lewis Thomas), *Science Digest,* May, 1983, 97.

9. See Chapter on Deaconess Sisters.

10. EDS, *Articles of Association;* St. Louis Medical Society Archives, File on Dr. Henry Summa.

11. Ibid., File on Dr. A. F. Bock; Records from St. Paul's United Church of Christ, Waterloo, Ill. and at Monroe County, Illinois, Courthouse, provided by Helen Osterhage.

12. EDS, *First AR,* 1890, 3; *16th AR* 1904, 3 *24th and 25th AR,* 1914, 30.

13. Ibid.; St. Louis Medical Society Archives, File on Dr. Arthur E. Ewing.

14. EDS, *24th and 25th AR,* 1914, 30; St. Louis Medical Society Archives, File on Dr. John Green, Sr.; DA, *Patient Admissions and Discharges,* Handwritten Record Book, October, 1889.

15. Marguerite Martyn, "Nurse for Nearly 50 Years," *St. Louis Post-Dispatch,* Everyday Magazine, Oct. 11, 1940.

16. EDS, *24th and 25th AR,* 1914, 30; *Evangelical Diakonissenfreund,* v.2, n.2, March, 1894, 3; St. Louis Medical Society Archives, Membership Roster.

17. DA, Letter from the Deaconess Medical Staff to the board of directors of the Deaconess Society, dated Dec. 14, 1898, signed by Doctors Bock, Ewing, Hermann, Dorsett, Lemen and Shapleigh.

18. EDS, *24th and 25th AR,* 1914, 11.

19. DA, Medical Staff File, "Rules and Regulations of the Medical Staff," 1898, Document in German script translated by Sister Elizabeth Lotz.

20. EDS, *11th AR,* 1899, 2.

21. Ludmerer, 17-18.

22. EDS, *11th AR,* 1899, 3.

23. EDS, *12th AR*, 1900, 12.
24. Ludmerer, 18.
25. Ibid.
26. EDS, *11th AR*, 1899, 3 and yearly to *16th AR*, 1904, 5; *21st AR*, 1908-09, 18.
27. Ibid.
28. See Chapter on "Patient Care" for references to increase in patients and charity patients served in 1904.
29. DA, Minutes of the Meetings of the Medical Staff of the Evangelical Deaconess Hospital, 1904-22.
30. Ludmerer, 184-190.
31. DA, *Constitution and Bylaws, Medical Staff of Evangelical Deaconess Hospital*, adopted Feb. 17, 1911.
32. EDS, *11th AR*, 1911, 2.
33. DMS, *Constitution and Bylaws*, Revised 1914, Art. I, Bylaws.
34. DMS, Minutes, May 7, 1912; Sept. 29, 1913.
35. Ludmerer, 257.
36. *Evangelical Wohltatigskeitfreund*, v.13. n.3, March, 1921.
37. EDS, *38th AR* 1928, Report of the Superintendent, 11.
38. Ibid., President's Report, 4.
39. EDS, Dedication Program, May 25, 1930.
40. EDS, *41st AR*, 1930, 8,9.
41. Ludmerer, 234, 247.
42. EDH. *42nd AR*, 1931, 7.
43. Ibid., 4-6; *Evang. Benevolent Institutions*, v.24, n.6, June, 1931.
44. Ibid., v. 26, n.7, July, 1933, p.3; Dr. Henry Scott's senior resident's key was given as a gift to the Deaconess Archives in 1989 in memory of Dr. Scott by his wife, Mrs. Irma Schlottach Scott, who was a Deaconess Sister before her marriage.
45. EDS, *47th AR*, 1936, 11; *48th AR*, 1937, p. 13; *56th AR*, 1945-46, 25.
46. DMS, *Constitution and Bylaws*, Revised 1940, p. 7.
47. EDS, *45th AR*, 1934, 12; *48th AR*, 1937, 14; *56th AR*, 1945-46, 25.
48. Medical staff members serving in the armed forces were listed with the medical staff in EDS annual reports beginning with the *52nd AR*, 1941, until the *55th AR*, 1944-45.
49. CCR, Administrator's Report to the Board, Dec. 9, 1948.
50. DA, Medical Education File, 1948.
51. DMS, *Bylaws, Rules and Regulations*, 1949, Art. III, 1.
52. EDS, *61st AR*, 1950, 10.
53. EDS, *60th AR*, 1949, 4; *61st AR*, 1950. 11; *62nd AR*, 1951, 6.
54. Ibid.
55. EDS, *63rd AR*, 1952, 7.
56. EDS, *64th AR*, 1953, 10; DA, The Joint Commission, *Guide to Quality Assurance*, 9-11.
57. EDS, *66th AR*, 1955, 12; DMS, Medical Staff Bylaws, Revised 1955; EDS, *67th AR*, 1956, 5; DH, *Opportunities for Rotating Internships and General Practice Residencies*, 1957, 8.
58. EDS, *67th AR*, 1956, 13.
59. EDS, *68th AR*, 1957, 12.
60. EDS, *69th AR*, 1958, 5, 12.
61. EDS, *70th AR*, 1959, 5, 12.
62. CCR, Administrator's Report to the Board, Oct. 23, 1958.
63. EDS, *71st AR*, 1960, 5.

64. *St.Louis Post Dispatch*, Sept. 30, 1964.

65. CCR, Administrator's Report to the Board, Mar. 19, 1964. EDS, *75th AR*, 1964, 12; *76th AR*, 1965, 3; *78th AR*, 1967, 1; DH, *Medical Education*, 1964, 8.

66. EDS, *79th AR*, 1968, 5. Under this contractual agreement, "full-time chiefs of service" were allowed to serve some private patients.

67. Ibid., 1.

68. CCR, Administrator's Report to the Board, Sept. 1969.

69. EDS. *80th AR.* 1969, 1,2; *90th AR,* 1979, 1.

70. EDS. *81st AR,* 1970, 7.

71. EDS, *82nd AR,* 1971, 2,4; CCR, President's Report to the Board, Sept. 26, 1972.

72. DMS, *Bylaws*, Rev. 1973, 10, 12; CCR, President's Report to the Board, June 26, 1973.

73. RPE, *The Direct Line*, v. 2, n. 24, Sept. 7, 1989.

74. EDS, *14th AR*, 1902, 17; *15th AR*, 1903, 15, 16; Martha R. Clevenger, "From Lay Practitioners to Doctors of Medicine: Women Physicians in St. Louis 1860-1920," *Gateway Heritage*, v.8, n.3, Winter, 1987-1988, 12.

75. Ibid.; EDS, Dedication Bulletin, 1930; DA, Medical Education File, House Staff Roster for 1989-90

76. EDS, *69th AR*, 1958, 15; *77th AR*, 1; *79th AR*, 1968, 1.

77. EDS, *86th AR*, 1975, 2; *64th AR*, 1953, 15.

78. EDS, *91st AR*, 1980, 2; DHS, "1989 Report to the Community," *Deaconess Reports*, Spring, 1990, 16.

79. DH, "1983 Report to the Community," 7.

80. *St. Louis Post Dispatch*, "Health Care," June 5, 1989, 1.

81. Interview by author with Dr. M. Robert Hill, Director, Deaconess Medical Education, and Chief of Medicine.

82. Ibid.

83. Ibid.

84. DHS, "Deaconess A Learning Hospital, "*Deaconess Reports*, Summer/Fall, 1988, 11.

85. DHS, *Medical and Dental Staffs Bylaws, Rules & Regulations*, Revised Dec. 8, 1987, Art. VIII, Medical Staff Committees, Sec. 2n, 20, 21.

86. Dr. Tehmton S. Mistry, President, DMS, 1986-87, Annual Report to Medical Staff/Board of Directors Dinner, 1986.

87. DMS, "Program," Deaconess Centennial Celebration, April 22, 1989; Jerry Berger, *St. Louis Post-Dispatch*, Apr. 23, 1989.

88. Susan Schiefelbein, "The Incredible Machine," *100 Years of Adventure and Discovery*, (New York: Nat. Geographic Society, 1987), 469.

89. DHS, *Medical and Dental Staffs Bylaws, Rules & Regulations*, Revised June 26, 1990, Article II-1, Purpose.

Chapter 5.
PATIENT CARE

1. MacEachern, 29.

2. See Chapter 1, "The Evangelical Deaconess Society."

3. Sister Hulda C. Weise, "The History of the Development of the Nursing Department of Deaconess Hospital, St. Louis, Missouri, 1940-1953" (unpublished M.S.N.E. thesis, St. Louis University, 1954), 38.

4. Rosenberg, *American Heritage*, 23,24,27.

5. Hart, Larry, *Hospital on the Hill*, (Schenectady, N.Y., Ellis Hospital, 1985), vii.

6. T. J. Ritter, M.D., *Mothers' Remedies*, (Detroit: G. H. Foote Publishing Co., 1910), iv.

7. Rosenberg, *American Heritage*, 23,24,27.

8. *St. Louis Post-Dispatch*, May 8, 1952, Everyday Magazine.

9. Florence Nightingale, *Notes on Nursing*, 134, quoted in Rosenberg, *Care of Strangers*, 396.

10. *Principles of Deaconess Work*, 78-82.

11. DA, *Patient Admitting Record*, Evangelical Deaconess Home, 1889; EDS, *25th AR*, 1914, 30.

12. Rosenberg, *American Heritage*, 23,27.

13. EDS, *11th AR*, 1899, 3.

14. Ibid.

15. EDS, *Evang. Diakonissenfreund*, v. 1, n. 2, March, 1893, 2-4; v.3, n.2, March, 1895, 3.

16. Bennett, *American Heritage*, 46; MacEachern, 19-20; Ludmerer, 75-76.

17. Martyn, *St. Louis Post-Dispatch*, October 11, 1940.

18. DA, Medical Staff Documents, Letter from Medical Staff to Board of Directors, Dec. 14, 1898.

19. EDS, *12th AR*, 1900, 5; Rosenberg, *Care of Strangers*, 149; Bennett, *American Heritage*, 49.

20. Martyn, *St. Louis Post-Dispatch*, October 11, 1940.

21. EDS, *11th AR*, 1899, 12.

22. Ibid., 13; Rosenberg, *Care of Strangers*, 288-289; Also see Chapter on "Spiritual Ministry."

23. EDS, *11th AR*, 1899, 17.

24. Ibid., 21.

25. EDS, *14th AR*, 1902, 38.

26. Ibid., 31.

27. EDS, *19th AR*, 1907-08, 21.

28. Rosenberg, *Care of Strangers*, 342.

29. EDS, *13th AR*, 1901, 29; *Messenger of Peace*, June, 1902.

30. EDS, *13th AR*, 1901, 19-20.

31. Martyn, *St. Louis Post-Dispatch*, October 11, 1940.

32. EDS, *Annual Reports, 1899 to 1904*, 27. Author's interviews with Sister Velma Kampschmidt.

33. *St. Louis Globe-Democrat*, April 18, 1904.

34. L. Joseph Butterfield, M.D., *The Incubator Doctor in Denver*, 356, Missouri Historical Society Library.

35. Linda A. Fisher, M.D., "Is There A Doctor On The Grounds? Health Issues at the 1904 World's Fair," Lecture, October 4, 1990, Missouri Historical Society; Butterfield, 354.

36. EDS, *19th AR*, 1907-09, 16; *Information Please Almanac, 1988*, (Boston: Houghton Mifflin Co.) 117; MacEachern, 20; Bennett, 49.

37. EDS, *11th AR*, 1899, 1; Rosenberg, *Care of Strangers*, 157; EDS, *19th AR*, 1907-08, 16.

38. Ibid., 14.

39. Ibid., 18.

40. EDS, *20th & 21st AR*, 1908-09, 7.

41. EDS, *19th AR*, 1907-08, 12.

42. DA, Letter from Mr. Joe Ponder, Patient Care File.

43. EDS, *11th AR*, 1899, 1; *25th AR*, 1914, 39.

44. EDS, 33rd AR, 1921, 21,19,15,17-18; DA, Oral Tapes, The Deaconess Sisters; "The History of Medicine," *Encyclopedia Britannica*, Home Reading Guide, (U.S.A., 1955), 14-15; Rosenberg, *Care of Strangers*, 150, 341.

45. *Evang. Wohltatigskeitfreund*, v.13, n.3, March, 1921, 4; MacEachern, 24.

46. DA, Sister Elizabeth Schaefer, "Description of Dr. MacEachern's Inspection for the Amer. Med. Assoc.," Medical Records File; EDS, *Annual Reports,* 1927 to present.

47. EDS, *33rd AR,* 1921, 26; John P. Winkelmann, History of the *St. Louis College of Pharmacy,* 1964, 87.

48. DA, Sister Sophie Hubeli, Deaconess Sisters File.

49. *Ev. Benevolent Institutions,* v.19, n.10, Oct. 1927.

50. Ibid., June 1930 and July 1930; EDS, *41st AR,* 1930, 19; *47th AR,* 1936,5.

51. EDS, *42nd AR,* 1931, 19,14,15,28.

52. EDS, Minutes of the Board of Directors, Oct. 17, 1933.

53. From the records in the office of Dennis Kruse, Vice President for Finance, Deaconess Hospital, 1988; MacEachern, 736, 787-788; EDS, *44th AR,* 1933, 5; *48th AR,* 1937, 4.

54. EDS, "50 Years of Deaconess Ministry," 2; *50th AR,* 1939, 8; *Information Please Almanac, 1988,* 793, 795-796.

55. EDS, *53rd AR,* 1942, 5,9; *E. and R. Monthly,* v.14,n.10, June, 1943, 7; Sister Hulda Weise, "History," 25-26.

56. "Military Medicine," *American Heritage,* v.35, n.6, Oct./Nov. 1984, 72.

57. EDS, *58th AR,* 1947-48, 5-6.

58. EDS, *55th AR,* 1944-45, 20.

59. Sister Hulda Weise, 41-42.

60. EDS, *60th AR,* 1949, 6; 61st AR, 1950, 2.

61. EDS, *63rd AR,* 1952, 5; *E. and R. Monthly,* v.24, n. 1, Sept. 1952, 6.

62. EDS, *65th AR,* 1954, 10,4,5; *64th AR,* 1953, 7; *Voice of the Valley,* January, 1954.

63. EDS, *67th AR,* 1956, 4,6,7-11.

64. EDS, *68th AR,* 1957, 5,12; *St. Louis Globe-Democrat,* Sunday Magazine, March 27, 1960.

65. EDS, *69th AR,* 1958, 4,5,12; *70th AR,* 1959, 4.

66. EDS, *72nd AR,* 1961, 5.

67. EDS, *77th AR,* 1966, 3; Richard P. Ellerbrake, "Memo to Members, EDS, Nov. 30, 1984; John Smith, M.D., 226.

68. EDS, *77th AR,* 1966, 4; *79th AR,* 1968, 4.

69. EDS, *82nd AR,* 1971, 2,7,9.

70. EDS, *75th AR,* 1974, 2; *81st AR,* 1970, 8; EDS, *89th AR,* 1978, 2; EDS, *87th AR,* 1976, 1; *88th AR,* 1977, 2.

71. DA, "Design for the 80s," Campaign booklet, 1977, 2,15.

72. DA, "90th Anniversary Dedication Program," 1979; EDS, *90th AR,* 1979, 2,3.

73. DA, "Objectives for Deaconess Hospital, Fiscal Year, 1979-80."

74. EDS, *Annual Reports,* 1980-1989; DA, "Chronology of Historical Events," 1889-1989.

75. DA, Hospital Service Report, September 1989, 2.

76. DA, Dennis Kruse, Treasurer's Report, Deaconess Health Services Annual Meeting, November 16, 1989, 2. RPE, "Message from the President," *Deaconess Reports,* v. 4, n. 1, Spring, 1990, 14.

77. *Information Please Almanac, 1988,* 796.

78. DHS, *Focus,* Sept. 1987, 4.

79. DA, "Philosophy and Objectives of the Patient Care Services Department," Deaconess Hospital, St. Louis, Missouri, May, 1988, 1,2.

Chapter 6.
THE DEACONESS SCHOOLS AND COLLEGE OF NURSING

1. M. Patricia Donohue, Ph.D. R.N., *Nursing, the Finest Art*, (St. Louis: C.V. Mosby Co., 1985) 469.
2. EDS, "Objectives for Deaconess Hospital," Fiscal Year, 1979-80; DCN, *Educating to Care: 100 Years*, A Selt Study Report submitted to the Commission on Institutions of Higher Education, North Central Assoc. of Colleges and Schools, Dec. 1989, 2; EDS, *Articles of Association*, Article II.
3. DA, Letter from Deaconess Medical Staff to board of directors, December 14, 1898.
4. EDS, *Rules and Regulations of the Medical Staff, 1898*.
5. EDS, *11th AR*, 1899, 3.
6. EDS, *13th AR*, 1901, 17.
7. EDS, *14th AR*, 1902, 16; *16th AR*, 1904, 15.
8. DA, Memoirs of Sister Anna Lenger; EDS, *Evangelical Deaconess Home and Hospital*, 15th Anniversary Commemorative Booklet, 1904, 16.
9. EDS, *19th AR*, 1907-1908, 8, 9, 18, 19, 28-30.
10. Trenholme, 84; EDS, *20th and 21st AR*, 1908-1909, 12, 13, 15, 24.
11. Ibid., 7; *19th AR*, 1907-08, 18.
12. Trenholme, 84.
13. Ann Doyle, "Nursing by Religious Orders in the U.S.," Part V, *American Journal of Nursing*, v. 29, n. 11, Nov., 1929, 1339; DA, Files on Sister Sophie Hubeli and Sister Anna Lenger.
14. EDS, *20th and 21st AR*, 1908-1909, 11; *24th and 25th AR*, 1914, 32, 33; *Minutes*, The First Evangelical Deaconess Conference, St. Louis, Mo., 1909, 10.
15. Sister Olivia Drusch, *The Pulse*, 7; EDS, *33rd AR*, 1921, 23, 33; *38th AR*, 1928, 19.
16. EDS, *33rd AR*, 1921, 33.
17. EDS, *38th AR*, 1928, 16-17, 24; *40th AR*, 1929, 24.
18. Ibid., 21.
19. EDS, *41st AR*, 1930, 11; *42nd AR*, 1931, 17, 18; *45th AR*, 1934, 7.
20. EDS, *42nd AR*, 1931, 17-18..
21. EDS, *41st AR*, 1930, 21-22; *42nd AR*, 1931, 22; *E. and R. Monthly*, v.20, n.2, Oct. 1948, 5, 16; v. 20, n.6, Feb. 1949, 9.
22. EDS, *50th AR*, 1939, 5.
23. EDS, *51st AR*, 1940, 7; 47th AR, 1936, 5.
24. EDS, *51st AR*, 1940, 7, 12; *58th AR*, 1947-48, 14; DSN, *Bulletin*, 1966-67, 31.
25. EDS, *49th AR*, 1938, 6.
26. EDS. *54th AR*, 1944, 6, 19, 23.
27. *The Pulse*, 1942, 3, 10, 13.
28. EDS, *52nd AR*, 1941, 30; *53rd AR*, 1942, 5, 10; DSN, *Announcement of the School of Nursing*, 1951-52, 6.
29. Ibid., 6; *E. and R. Monthly*, v. 14, Dec. 1942, 16.
30. EDS, *53rd AR*, 1942, 13-15; *Announcement of the School of Nursing*, 1942-43, 8-15.
31. EDS, *56th AR*, 1945-1946, 8, 22; *57th AR*, 1946-1947, 8.
32. EDS, *58th AR*, 1947-1948, 5.
33. *E. and R. Monthly*, Sept. 1948, v. 20, n. 1; v. 20, n. 10, June, 1949; *United Courier*, Sept. 1968, v. 39, n.1.
34. EDS, *Announcement of the School of Nursing*, 1947-48, 17; 1948-49, 19; DSN, *35th Anniversary*, June 24, 1978.
35. EDS, *65th AR*, 1954, 11, 12; DSN, *Bulletin*, 1955-1956, 6.

36. EDS, *62nd AR*, 1951, 4; DSN, *Bulletin*, 1956-1957, 13, lists the School for Deaconesses for the last time.

37. *St. Louis Post-Dispatch*, Feb. 23, 1962; *St. Louis Globe-Democrat*, July 26, 1966.

38. Ibid.; EDS, *71st AR*, 1960, 4.

39. DSN, *Bulletin*, 1968, 6; *The 25th Anniversary*, 1943-68, 6; EDS, *79th AR*, 1968, 5.

40. *United Courier*, Insert, Nov. 1968.

41. EDS, *82nd AR*, 1971, 7; *87th AR*, 1975, 3.

42. *St. Louis Globe-Democrat*, Dec. 27-28, 1969 and Jan. 20, 1970.

43. EDS, Minutes, Annual Meeting, 1971.

44. DSN, Minutes, School of Nursing Advisory Committee, May 19, 1971, 2; "Conceptual Framework for Curriculum Development," *35th Anniversary*, June 24, 1978. See Chapter on Management and Administration for description of "Design for the 80s."

45. DSN, *Alumnae News*, V. 12, n. 1, Spring, 1980; Minutes, School of Nursing Advisory Committee, Jan. 6, 1981, 3; May 12, 1981, 3, 6.

46. Ibid.

47. DCN, *Catalog*, 1984-86, ii; *Catalog*,1987-1989, 67, 83; *Continuing a Proud Tradition*, A Self-Study Report, Mar. 1985, 3; and *Educating to Care: 100 Years*, A Self-Study Report Dec. 1989, 2, submitted to the Commission on Institutions of Higher Education, North Central Assoc. of Colleges and Schools.

48. DCN, *Catalog*, 1984-86, iii.

49. DCN, *Catalog*, 1987-1989, 7.

50. Ibid., 1984-1986, ii, 2, 12, 18; 1987-1989, 13, 39, 32-41; 1989-1991, 34.

51. Interview with Provost Patricia Afshar.

52. DSN, Correspondence File; DCN, *Catalog*, 1984-1986, 13-18.

53. DCN, *Catalog*, 1984-1986, 18-20.

54. *Focus*, June, 1985.

55. DCN, *Catalog*, 1989-1991, 79-85.

56. DCN, *Educating to Care, 100 Years*, 121-123; Deaconess College of Nursing Alumni Association, *Alumni News*, v. 5, n. 1, Summer 1989, l.

57. EDS, *64th AR*, 1953, 11, 12; DSN, *75th Anniversary*, Sept. 19, 1964.

58. Alumni and Friends of Deaconess Hospital School of Nursing, *Deaconess Newsletter*, v. 1, n. 1, Autumn, 1969, 1.

59. DCN, *Educating to Care*, 121-123.

60. DCN, *Yearbook*, 1989, 12-13.

61. Ibid., 10.

62. DHC, *Focus*, June 1989, 4, 5.

63. M. Adelaide Nutting, Teacher's College, Columbia University, New York City, "Greetings," *Souvenir Programme*, Annual Convention, New York State Nurses' Assoc., Albany, N.Y., Oct. 27-29, 1925.

Chapter 7.
THE DEACONESS AUXILIARY AND VOLUNTEER SERVICES

1. EDS, *24th and 25th AR*, 1914, 27, 30.

2. EDS, *AA*, Article III, Membership; DA, Walser Family History, information from Loretta Schoenberg.

3. EDS, *24th and 25th AR*, 1914, 30; *19th AR*, 1907-1908, 18; *20th and 21st AR*, 1908-1909, 7.

4. *Evang. Wohltatigskeitfreund*, v. 2, n. 1, Jan. 1910; v. 6, n. 12, Dec., 1914; EDS, *24th and 25th AR*, 1914, 30; Dedication Bulletin, May 25, 1930.

5. EDS, *11th AR*, 1899, 17.

6. Ibid., 11, 18, 20; *12th AR*, 1900, 5.

7. *St. Louis Times*, Sept. 24, 1926, Part 2.

8. Ibid.; *St. Louis Star*, Sept. 24, 1926.

9. EDS, *40th AR*, 1929, 5; *41st AR*, 1930, 6; *47th AR*, 1936, 16.

10. EDS, *38th AR*, 1928, 6; *Ev. Benevolent Institutions*, v. 19, n. 10, Oct. 1927.

11. Ibid., June 1930.

12. EDS, *44th AR*, 1933, 3; *45th AR*, 1934, 3.

13. EDS, *47th AR*, 1936, 5, 7, 16.

14. EDS, *48th AR*, 1937, 7.

15. *St. Louis Post-Dispatch*, March 26, 1939.

16. Deaconess Auxiliary Minutes, January 30, 1941.

17. Ibid.

18. Ibid.

19. EDS, *41st AR*, 1930, 44; *52nd AR*, 1941, 2; Mrs. F. A. Keck, "Beginnings Reviewed by the First President," *Beginnings of the Evangelical Women's Union*, (St. Louis: Evangelical Women's Union, 1936),4; *Evangelical Year-Books*, Eden Archives.

20. Deaconess Auxiliary Minutes, March 25, 1941; *Deaconess Auxiliary Constitution* and Bylaws, October 28, 1986.

21. Deaconess Auxiliary Minutes, May 1941.

22. Ibid., Sept. 1941.

23. EDS, *52nd AR*, 1941, 6.

24. Deaconess Auxiliary Minutes, March 24, 1942.

25. Ibid., September 1942 and January 1943.

26. Ibid.,

27. Ibid., Oct. 1942.

28. EDS, *53rd AR*, 1942, 9.

29. EDS, *62nd AR*, 1951, 13.

30. EDS, *55th AR*, 1944-45, 20.

31. EDS, *60th AR*, 1949, 12; *63rd AR*, 1952, 8.

32. Deaconess Auxiliary, "Anniversary Banquet Program," 1953.

33. EDS, *65th AR*, 1954, 13; Deaconess Auxiliary, "20th Anniversary Dinner Program," 1961.

34. EDS, *65th AR*, 1954, 13.

35. Deaconess Auxiliary Minutes, October, 1956.

36. EDS, "Administrator's Report," *68th AR*, 1957, 6, 7.

37. EDS, "Administrator's Report," *70th AR*, 1959, 6.

38. Missouri Valley Synod of the E. and R. Church, *Voice of the Valley*, April, 1961.

39. EDS, *78th AR*, 1967, 3.

40. Deaconess Auxiliary, Record of Gifts, Auxiliary Files.

41. Deaconess Auxiliary Minutes, January 3, 1978; *Deaconess Auxiliary Constitution and Bylaws*, Revised 1978; Deaconess Auxiliary Membership Roster, 1989.

42. Deaconess Auxiliary, "95th Anniversary Program," 1984.

43. Jen Weber, Director, and Gertrude Miketta's retirement, 1981.

44. Deaconess Auxiliary, "President's Report to the Deaconess Society," 1980.

45. Deaconess Auxiliary, Program, 45th Anniversary Tea, 1986.

46. Deaconess Auxiliary, "President's Report to the Deaconess Society," 1988.

47. Deaconess Auxiliary, *The Diakonian*, v. 1, n. 1, 1988.

48. Deaconess Auxiliary, "Awards Luncheon Program," May, 1962, May, 1966, September, 1989; Volunteer Hours File, Office of the Director of Volunteer Services.

49. "Donor Profile: The Deaconess Auxiliary," *Deaconess Reports*, v. 3, n. 1, Spring, 1989, 24-25.

50. *The St. Louis Times*, Sept. 24, 1926, Part 2.

Chapter 8.
THE SPIRITUAL MINISTRY

1. *They Caught the Torch*, (Milwaukee: Will Ross, Inc., 1939), Quotation on title page; EDS, *52nd AR*, 1941, 3. Anna Sticker, *Friederike Fliedner*, (Germany: Neukirchener Verlag, 1961), 164.

2. Florence Nightingale, *The Institution of Kaiserswerth on the Rhine*, 19.

3. Bancroft, 83.

4. EDS, *AA*, Articles II-1 and VI-4, 1891.

5. *Deaconess Reports*, Spring, 1990, 14.

6. Bernie S. Siegel, M.D., *Love, Medicine & Miracles*, (New York: Harper & Row, 1986), 38.

7. EDS, 15th Anniversary Booklet, 1904, 9.

8. Ibid., 16; *Principles of Deaconess Work*, 47-72 and 8-17.

9. Ibid., 48-51; Author's interviews with older Deaconess Sisters including her aunt, Sister Clara Weltge.

10. DA, *Rules Governing the Evangelical Deaconess Home and Hospital*, 3.

11. *Evang. Diakonissenfreund*, v. 4, n. 6, Nov. 1896; EDS, Twenty-fifth Anniversary Booklet, 10.

12. Ibid., 3.

13. EDS, *11th AA*, 1899, 12.

14. Ibid.

15. Ibid., 12, 21.

16. EDS, *19th AR*, 1908, 21.

17. EDS, *20th and 21st AR*, 1909, 6.

18. Wheeler, 103-10

19. *Principles of Deaconess Work*, 82.

20. Ibid., 101.

21. Sister Adele E. Hosto, "Principles and Experiences in Parish Deaconess Work," *Der Evangelische Diakonissen-Herald*, v. 10, n. 2, Feb. 1916, 4.

22. Principles of Deaconess Work, 85.

23. Dr. J. H. Horstmann, *The First Twenty-five Years*, A Souvenir Booklet of Caroline Mission, 1913-1938 (St. Louis), 6, 12; *Evang. Wohltatigkeitfreund*, v. 7, n. 5, May 1915, 4; DA, Sister Anna Goetze's Notebook.

24. EDS, *41st AR*, 1930, 10.

25. EDS, *23rd AR*, 1921, 10, 11, 28; *38th AR*, 1928,26; *44th AR*, 1933, 16; and *46th AR* 1935, 16.

26. DA, Individual files for each of the Deaconess Sisters who served as missionaries.

27. "How a Medical Missionary Lives," *St. Louis Post-Dispatch*, August 7, 1951.

28. EDS, *41st AR*, 1930, 10. .

29. EDS *51st AR*, 1940, 23.

30. EDS, *58th AR*, 1947-48, 20-21.

31. EDS, *49th AR*, 1938, 11.

32. Horstmann, 15-17.

33. Scherzer, 229, 235-236.

34. EDS, *56th AR*, 1945, 30; *58th AR*, 10; American Hospital Association, 69th Annual Meeting, *Daily Bulletin*, Aug. 24, 1967, 3.

35. DA, Carl C. Rasche File.

36. EDS, *63rd AR*, 1952, 6.

37. EDS, *67th AR*, 1956, 3.

38. Ibid., 7.

39. EDS, *70th AR*, 1959, 6.

40. EDS, *71st AR*, 1960, 4.

41. DH, *Focus*, v. 1, n. 7, Sept./Oct., 1974, 2; Author's interview with Executive Chaplain Ernest Luehrman; Chaplaincy Program Records in Chaplain's office.

42. Ibid.; *The Tie*, Newsletter of the College of Chaplains, v, 26, n. 2, April, 1989, 7.

43. DA, Richard P. Ellerbrake File; *Eden Events*, v.4, n. 1, Fall, 1985, 3; *Focus*, April, 1989, 7.

44. *Tempo*, Spring, 1984, 4; *Focus*, Oct. 1985.

45. Author's interview with Executive Chaplain Luehrman.

46. *Principals of Deaconess Work*, 56.

47. Dan McCurry, Editor, "Preface," *Care Giver*, Journal of the College of Chaplains, v. 5, Sept. 1988, 11.

48. DHS, *Deaconess Reports*, Spring, 1990, 14.

Chapter 9.
THE CENTENNIAL

1. RPE, "Centennial Greetings," Rasche, *The Deaconess Sisters*, 1; DHSC, *Tradition with Vision*, Report to the Community, 1986, 1.

2. DHSC, *Deaconess Reports*, "Centennial, the Year in Pictures," v.3, n.2, Fall 1989, 14, 16.

3. DA, Executive Chaplain Ernest W. Luehrman's 100th anniversary sermon at Deaconess Chapel, March 19, 1989; EDS, *25th Annual Report*, 1914, 32.

4. *Focus*, June 1989, 4.

5. DF, Program, Deaconess Foundation Centennial Donor Recognition Gala, Oct. 6, 1989.

6. Ibid.; DHSC, *Deaconess Reports*, v.3, n.1, Spring 1989, 12.

7. Ibid., 10.

8. DHSC, *Deaconess Reports*, v.3, n.2, Fall 1989, 10.

9. DHSC, Program, Deaconess United Church of Christ, Centennial Family Celebration, October 29, 1989.

10. DA, Rev. Dr. Walter Brueggemann, "What the Church Has Always Known," 100th anniversary sermon given at Deaconess-UCC Centennial Family Celebration, Oct. 29, 1989; DHC, *Focus*, Nov. 1989, 4-5.

11. Program, Deaconess-UCC Centennial Family Celebration, 6.

12. DHSC, *Deaconess Reports*, v.3, n.2, Fall 1989, 14.

Index

St. Louis, City, 2, 61, 301
St. Louis City Hospital, 3
St. Louis College of Pharmacy, 38 48, 177
St. Louis Evang. Pastors' Assoc., 1, 3
St. Louis Globe-Democrat, 68
St. Louis League of Nursing, 38
St. Louis Medical College, 119
St. Louis Medical Society, 117, 122
St. Louis Star, 68-69
St. Louis Times, 68-69
St. Louis University Medical School, 148
St. Peter's Evangelical Church, 1, 2, 4, 9,119
Sanders, Susan, 302
Sauer, Dr. Dean, 146
Schaefer, Sister Elizabeth, 37-38, 132, 292
Schatzmann, Lois, 108, 301
Scheid, Sister Alvina,
  sister superior, 39, 72, 73, 249, 267
  Good Samaritan Home administration, 40
  parish work, 40, 280
  retirement, 44, 78
Schick, Sister Beata, 37, 210
  director of nurses, 72-73, 180, 216
  principal of the School, 211-212
  writer, 50th anniv. pageant, 41
Schmidt, Dr. Edwin H., 139
Schmitz, Homer H., 95
School for Deaconesses,
  admission requirements, 49, 209, 276
  apprentice-teaching, 201
  curriculum, 202-03, 205, 209-10. 212
  deaconesses educated, 49
  examinations, 203
  facilities, 77
  faculty, 37, 40, 210, 212
  first students (probationers) 15
  phased out, 47, 224-225
  primary training center, 208
  recreation, 211
  tuition, 204
School of Nursing, Deaconess, 216-17
  affiliations, 223
  alumnae, honors, 237, 238, 240
  Alumni and Friends, 237, 239
  curriculum, 217
  enrollment, 224, 228
  faculty, 217, 224, 225

faculty council, 232
first lay students, 45, 79
graduates, 219
homecoming, 237-239
male and married students, 227
prerequisites, 217
Sisters' Council and, 45
tuition, 217, 219, 224, 227
School of Radiologic Technology, 222
School of X-ray Technology, 80, 221
  curriculum, 221
  directors, 221
  phased out, 222
  tuition, 222
Scott, Dr. Henry, 136
Sherry, Rev. Dr. Paul, 305
Short History of the Deaconess Calling, 32, 60
Shomaker, Monte, 97
"Sister" title, 22
Sisters' Council, 45
Sisters' Home, 9, 28, 39, 43, 44, 77
Skinner, Dr. Caroline, 150
specialized services, 152, 179, 196, 197
spiritual ministry, and healing, 165, 276,
  277, 295
Sprick, Sister Marie, 41, 282
Standards for Chaplains, APHA, 287
state board exams, 34, 214
Stradal, Walter J., 84-85
  assistant administrator, 86
  campaign director, 84-85
  director of development, 93
  retirement, 98
Streib, Sister Katherine, 37, 173
structured nursing care, beginning, 25
Sudholt, Endowment Fund, 248
Summa, Dr. Henry, 5, 13, 119, 120
superintendent, of hospital,
  job description (1912) 62
superintendent of nurses, first, 177
surgery, 163, 173, 197
  one-day, 191
  recovery room, 188-189
Swaney, Larry A., 103, 106, 110

"teaching hospital," 132
teaching programs (1968), 228

340

The Author

Ruth W. Rasche is the Archivist and Historian in the Deaconess Archives, St. Louis, Missouri. A graduate of Washington University, she was elected to Phi Beta Kappa, taught in the university's Department of English and was Associate Law Librarian. Her research on the Deaconess Sisters as pioneer professional women has extended to many places over many years, and she is a past chairperson of the United Church of Christ Historical Council. Her husband is Deaconess President Emeritus Carl C. Rasche and they are the parents of three daughters.